Harnessing the Potential of Artificial Intelligence to Promote Environmental Sustainability

Harnessing the Potential of Artificial Intelligence to Promote Environmental Sustainability

EDITED BY

PARIJATA MAJUMDAR
Indian Institute of Information Technology, Agartala, India

ANIRUDDHA NAG
Techno India Group, India

AND

DIEGO ALBERTO OLIVA NAVARRO
University of Guadalajara, Mexico

emerald
PUBLISHING

United Kingdom – North America – Japan – India – Malaysia – China

Emerald Publishing Limited
Emerald Publishing, Floor 5, Northspring, 21-23 Wellington Street, Leeds LS1 4DL.

First edition 2026

Printed and bound by CPI Group (UK) Ltd, Croydon, CR0 4YY

British Library Cataloguing in Publication Data
A catalogue record for this book is available from the British Library

ISBN: 978-1-83662-997-9 (Print)
ISBN: 978-1-83662-996-2 (Online)
ISBN: 978-1-83662-998-6 (Epub)

Contents

About the Editors

Parijata Majumdar is an Assistant Professor at the Indian Institute of Information Technology, Agartala, a position she has held since August 2024. She earned her Bachelor of Engineering from the Tripura Institute of Technology, Narsingarh, and completed her PhD at the National Institute of Technology, Agartala. Her research areas include machine learning, optimization techniques, internet of things, precision agriculture, image processing, and blockchain technology. In recognition of her contributions, she received the EARG Award for Excellence in Research and Development in 2024.

Aniruddha Nag is an Associate Professor in TIG, Salt Lake. He has several years of industry and teaching experience. He has authored multiple research papers and is the author of several books, for example, *Linux*, *Networking*, *Internet for All*, and *Java*. He has co-authored books on *Comprehensive Research Methods: Frameworks, Techniques, and Real-world Applications.*

Diego Alberto Oliva Navarro is an Associate Professor at the University of Guadalajara, Mexico, with expertise in evolutionary computation and its applications in image processing, optimization, and artificial intelligence. He has served as a Visiting Professor at Tomsk Polytechnic University in Russia and as an Adjunct Professor at Tecnológico de Monterrey. With numerous peer-reviewed publications in prestigious journals such as *Expert Systems with Applications*, *Neurocomputing*, and *Computational Intelligence and Neuroscience*, he has made significant contributions to multi-level thresholding, bio-inspired algorithms, and medical image analysis. He has co-authored several books published by Springer and Alfaomega. He also serves as an Associate Editor for the *International Journal of Soft Computing and Software Engineering* and reviews for top journals, including Energy, Elsevier, and Hindawi Press. His academic work bridges theoretical innovation and real-world applications.

About the Contributors

Abhijit Bandyopadhyay is the Principal of Raniganj Institute of Computer and Information Science, India. He is pursuing his PhD in the Department of Computer and Information Science, Raiganj University, India. He has completed his BTech in Information Technology from Durgapur Institute of Advanced Technology and Management, West Bengal, India and MTech in Computer Science Engineering from Bengal College of Engineering and Technology, West Bengal, India under Maulana Abul Kalam Azad University of Technology formerly known as West Bengal University of Technology, India. He is doing his research work in Health Care Informatics. His areas of interest include Health Care Informatics, Social Informatics, Business Informatics, and so on.

Poulami Basu is a Research Scholar at the University of Engineering and Management, Kolkata. She is a young researcher pursuing her research in Management Studies, focusing on research in ethics. She has already published an article in a Scopus-indexed book of Springer Nature Singapore titled "Perceived Value of Prospect of AI-enabled Healthcare: View of Z Generation."

Aparajita Bhattacharya is a final-year student pursuing a Bachelor of Business Administration with a specialization in Marketing at the Institute of Engineering and Management, Kolkata, affiliated with the University of Engineering & Management Kolkata, India.

Indrajit Bhattacharya is an Assistant Professor at Kalyani Government Engineering College (KGEC) in West Bengal, India. He completed his PhD from Jadavpur University in West Bengal, India in 2014. He has obtained his Master's in Computer Science & Technology from the University of Calcutta, West Bengal. He has a teaching and research experience of more than 14 years in different institutes of repute. He is the Principal Investigator of the Project titled "DiSARM (Post-disaster Situation Analysis and Resource Management using Delay Tolerant Peer-to-Peer Opportunistic Networks)" at KGEC, funded by Information Technology Research Academy, Media Lab. Asia, Government of India. His research interests include delay-tolerant networks, wireless networks, sensor networks, and radio frequency identification. He has publications in Elsevier KBS, Springer Information Systems Frontier, IEEE CISS, Springer Wireless Networks, and Peer-to-Peer Networks.

Rabin Bhaumik is a Project Scholar in the Department of Computer Science and Engineering at Techno College of Engineering, Agartala. He is currently pursuing a PhD in Computer Science and Engineering at the National Institute of Technology Agartala. He holds a Master of Technology degree in Computer Science and Engineering from Tripura University. His research primarily focuses on medical image processing, deep learning, and air quality prediction using machine learning models. He is committed to advancing research in these fields, contributing to both academic and practical applications.

Aleksander Dimitriyevich Bragin is a Senior Lecturer of the Information Technology Department, National Research Tomsk Polytechnic University. His professional interests include machine learning in finance, applied sciences, mathematical modeling, and practical applications of machine learning. His work can be found in both local and international publications.

Darya Igorevna Dmitriychuk is a fourth-year graduate student of the Information Technology Department of the Engineering School of Information Technology Robotics of Tomsk Polytechnic University. Her research interests include artificial intelligence, the Internet of Things, blockchain, and distributed data storage systems. During her studies, she was actively engaged in research and software development. Her article "Development of a Blockchain Transaction Processing Class for Data Transmission in Smart Meter Networks Using Python" was awarded third place at the II All-Russian Scientific and Technical Conference "Intelligent Energy."

Shriya Chakraborty holds an MTech from Tripura University, Agartala, India. Her research focuses on machine learning, artificial intelligence (AI), and Internet of Things (IoT). She currently serves as an Assistant Professor in the Department of Computer Science at Techno College of Engineering. As an educator, she is dedicated to fostering an engaging and innovative learning environment, inspiring students to pursue meaningful advancements in the fields of AI and IoT.

Ritam Chatterjee is a Research Scholar in the Department of Computer and Information Science, Raiganj University, India. He is doing his research work in Computer and Information Science in the area of Digital Education. He has completed MPhil in Computer and Information Science, Department of Computer and Information Science, Raiganj University, India. He has completed Master of Computer Application from Maulana Abul Kalam Azad University of Technology, formerly known as West Bengal University of Technology, India. He did BSc in Computer Science (Hons.) from the University of Calcutta, West Bengal, India. He has research interests in cloud Computing, Big Data Analytics, Internet of Things, and so on. He has presented some of his research papers in different national and international events, conferences, and symposiums. Some of his works have been published as book chapters by various renowned publishers.

Tathagata Roy Chowdhury is an Assistant Professor in the Department of Computer Science and Engineering at Techno Engineering College, Banipur, India. He is currently pursuing a PhD in Medical Diagnosis using Machine Learning at the National Institute of Technology, Silchar. With over 10 years of teaching and research experience, his expertise includes machine learning, medical image processing, deep learning, and data hiding. He has authored multiple research papers in reputed journals such as Elsevier and IEEE and has co-authored books on anomaly detection and explainable artificial intelligence.

Nilanjan Das is an Assistant Professor in the Department of Computer Applications, Siliguri Institute of Technology, West Bengal, India. He has completed PhD in Computer and Information Science, Department of Computer and Information Science, Raiganj University, West Bengal, India. He has completed Master of Computer Application from Maulana Abul Kalam Azad University of Technology, formerly known as West Bengal University of Technology, West Bengal, India. He did Bachelor of Computer Applications from Vidya Sagar University, West Bengal, India. He has research interests in the areas of digitalization in smart cities, artificial intelligence, machine learning, deep learning, neural networks, and big data analytics. He has presented some of his research papers in different national and international events, conferences, and symposiums. Some of his works have been published as book chapters by various renowned publishers. He has around 40 publications in different journals and book chapters.

Sushanta Das is an Assistant Professor in the Department of Computer Science and Technology at Aryavart International University, North Tripura, India. He is currently pursuing a PhD in Computer Science and Engineering at the National Institute of Technology Agartala. He earned his Master of Information Technology degree from Tripura University, Agartala, India. His research primarily focuses on artificial Intelligence, machine learning, deep learning, natural language processing, and image processing. Through his dedication to academic excellence, he significantly contributes to the department's academic growth and research initiatives.

Sudakshina Dasgupta has done her MTech in Computer Science and Engineering in 2002 from the University of Calcutta, Kolkata, India, and PhD from Maulana Abul Kalam University of Technology, West Bengal, India in 2021. She is currently acting as Assistant Professor (Stage 3) in the Department of IT (Information Technology), the Government College of Engineering and Textile Technology, Serampore, India. She has more than 22 years of teaching and more than 15 years of research experience. Her research area includes wireless sensor network, machine learning, deep learning, and Internet of Things.

Alolika Datta is a final-year student pursuing a Bachelor of Business Administration with a specialization in Marketing at the Institute of Engineering and Management Kolkata, affiliated with the University of Engineering and Management Kolkata, India.

Anton Yuryevich Demin is Associate Professor of the Information Technology Department, Tomsk Polytechnic University (TPU) and Associate Professor of the Institute of Applied Mathematics and Computer Science, Tomsk State University. He graduated from TPU in 1995. He defended his dissertation "Design and evaluation of the quality of programs based on structural-graphical representations" in 1998. He was awarded the academic title of associate professor in 2006. His research area includes artificial intelligence, digital image processing, parallel computing, and simulation modeling of complex technical systems. In total, more than 100 works have been published in Russian and in English, including 3 monographs, 12 articles indexed in Scopus and Web of Science, 13 textbooks, and more than 20 publications were published jointly by him and his students. He has numerous awards. He was recognized as the best associate professor of TPU in 2015. He became the winner of the Golden Names of Higher Education in Russia in 2020.

Soumyadeep Dhol is a final-year student pursuing a Bachelor of Business Administration with a specialization in Marketing at the Institute of Engineering and Management (IEM) Kolkata, affiliated with the University of Engineering and Management Kolkata, India. During his undergraduate studies, he actively engaged in experiential learning opportunities. He participated in an entrepreneurship project under the guidance of the Wadhwani Foundation, demonstrating his entrepreneurial acumen. Furthermore, he conducted an academic research project investigating the "Effect of CSR Activities on Organizational Profitability," culminating in a significant achievement: he was awarded "Best Paper" at the 3rd International Student's Conference on Innovation, Entrepreneurship & Market Space (ISC IEM 2024) organized by the Department of Business Administration at IEM Kolkata.

Silambarasan Elkana Ebinazer is an Assistant Professor in the Department of Computer Science and Engineering – Cyber Security, Indian Institute of Information Technology Kottayam, Kerala, India. He received his BTech in Information Technology from Anna University, Chennai in 2009. He received his ME Computer Science and Engineering from Anna University, Chennai in 2012. He worked as an Assistant Professor at Anna University-affiliated colleges. His research interests include cloud security, malware analysis using artificial intelligence, and privacy-preserving healthcare data using federated learning.

Soumik Gangopadhyay, Professor at Institute of Engineering and Management, Kolkata, holds a PhD, MBA (Marketing and Health Systems), and Bachelor of Pharmacy. With 23+ years' experience in academia and industry, he has trained senior defense personnel and corporate executives (CESC, Eli Lilly, Indian Oil Corporation, Reserve Bank of India, etc.). He published in indexed journals (*Indian Journal of Marketing*, *Journal of Health Management*, etc.) and reviewed for journals like *Health Education*. He has authored and edited book chapters and an edited book on sustainable management. His awards include Excellence in Research (2022–2023) and ZYDUS CADILA Gold Medals.

Harsh Gupta is a final-year student in the Department of Computer Science and Engineering, Indian Institute of Information Technology Kottayam, Kerala, India.

Harish Vishwa S. M. is a final-year student in the Department of Computer Science and Engineering, Indian Institute of Information Technology Kottayam, Kerala, India.

Jabanesha S. received MCA degree from Anna University, Chennai, India in 2022. She is a Research scholar in Computer Applications at Anna University. Her current research interests include data mining, machine learning, and fuzzy systems.

Jeya Sutha M. received MCA degree from Mother Teresa Women's University, Kodaikanal, India in 2003. She has completed MPhil degree from Madurai Kamaraj University, India in 2005 and PhD degree from Bharathiyar University, Coimbatore, India in 2018. She has been in the teaching field since 2004. Her current research interests include stream mining, cloud computing, and fuzzy systems. She is a member of the IET.

Moupia Kundu is a final-year student pursuing a Bachelor of Business Administration with a specialization in Marketing at the Institute of Engineering and Management Kolkata, affiliated with the University of Engineering and Management Kolkata, India.

Likhitha S. is a final-year student in the Department of Computer Science and Engineering, Indian Institute of Information Technology Kottayam, Kerala, India.

Rabin Mazumder is a Professor and Head of the Business Administration Department at Institute of Engineering and Management, Kolkata. He holds PhD in Management and MBA in Marketing, he also holds an MSc in Economics. He is a prolific researcher, publishing in leading journals (*Journal of Retailing and Consumer Services*, etc.) on consumer behavior, marketing, and policy. He is a Series Editor for "Contemporary Management Practices" and has authored and edited multiple books. He has presented at national and international conferences and supervised industrial projects.

Archan Mitra, Assistant Professor at Nitte Institute of Communication, Nitte Deemed to be University, holds a PhD in Environmental Informatics from Visva-Bharati, Santiniketan. He is a certified Science Communicator and Corporate Trainer, with research expertise in environmental communication and disaster mitigation. He has worked on projects with the World Bank and ICSSR and launched the World Bank's first Green MBA MOOC. He has authored four books and published in leading journals such as Springer and Taylor & Francis. He developed the HECA model, transforming Noachar in West Bengal into an eco-village.

Tamal Mondal is currently working as an Assistant Professor at Symbiosis International (Deemed University) (Symbiosis Centre for Information Technology), Pune, Maharashtra, India. In 2021, he completed his PhD in the Department of Computer Science and Engineering, National Institute of Technology Durgapur, West Bengal, India. He was associated as a Researcher in two projects sponsored by the Government of India from 2015 to 2018 and from 2019 to 2021, respectively. He was ITRA Media Lab Fellow from 2015 to 2018, sponsored by the Government of India. His specialization lies in data mining, information retrieval, social media analytics, and disaster management. Right now, he has around 26 publications bagged in his name, including 8 SCI index journals, 3 book chapters, 1 Indian patent (submitted), and many publications in reputed conferences like ICDCN, CISS, ACM SigSpatial, and many more.

Amrita Mitra Mukherjee, Assistant Professor at Globsyn Business School, is a PhD scholar with numerous publications and over 19 years of expertise in media academics, business communication, and corporate training. An adept corporate trainer fluent across different languages, she holds degrees in Political Science from Presidency College, International Relations from Jadavpur University, and Law, with registration under the BAR Council of India. She has been associated with prestigious institutions like ISB&M, IIPM, and ILEAD, to name a few, contributing to both academia and corporate training with her vast experience and knowledge.

P. K. Paul holds prestigious and unique DSc in Information Science and Technology (IST) degree from Azteca University, Mexico, under DAYIPF Program. He also holds PhD in IST from IIEST Shibpur, Post-doctoral Fellow Certificate Program in Environmental Informatics. He holds degrees like MTech (by Research), MS (by Research) in addition to MSc (Double). He is working as Assistant Professor (IST) & Executive Director (MCIS Program) at Department of Computer & Information Sciences, and additionally Information Scientist Position at Raiganj University, West Bengal, India. Significantly, he also holds many national and international positions, viz. Honorary Professor, Logos University International, Louisiana, USA, Chief Advisor (Innovative Program & Research Planning), Srinivas University, Mangalore, India, credited over 35 books in diverse areas and 400+ research/review and policy papers, member in more than 150+ journals and 250+ international conference membership, organization, and holds more than a dozen of awards (https://orcid.org/0000-0003-1140-3369).

Tanmoy Paul received his BTech degree in Information Technology from Government College of Engineering and Textile Technology, Serampore, India in 2023. His research interests include machine learning, deep learning, and Internet of Things.

Doyel Mukherjee Prodhan is an Assistant Professor of Management and a doctoral research scholar with four years of teaching experience. She has published research papers on critical topics, such as sustainability and artificial intelligence, and authored two book chapters on sustainability. She has won two Best Paper Awards at international conferences, showcasing her contributions to contemporary management research, and her work has featured in ABDC-indexed journal. She has been affiliated with prominent B-schools and universities, bringing her expertise in sustainability and innovative practices to her teaching and research, which continue to inspire and shape future leaders in management.

Harsh Raj is a final-year student in the Department of Computer Science and Engineering, Indian Institute of Information Technology Kottayam, Kerala, India.

Ramesh Dhanaseelan F. received Post-graduate Degree in Computer Science from Bharathidasan University in 1992. In 1998, he received MTech degree in Computer Science and Engineering from Pondicherry University. He obtained PhD degree in Computer Science and Engineering from Alagappa University in 2009. He received MTech from M.S. University in 2011, specializing in Computer and Information Technology. He has been in the teaching profession for the past 30 years. His area of interest is data mining.

Mainak Saha is an Assistant Professor in the Department of Computer Science and Engineering at K L Deemed to be University, Hyderabad. He is currently pursuing a PhD in Computer Science and Engineering at the National Institute of Technology, Agartala, India. He earned his Master of Technology degree from Tripura University, Agartala, India. His research primarily focuses on artificial intelligence, machine learning, image processing, and pattern recognition. His commitment to academic excellence and his expertise in these domains significantly contributes to the department's academic and research endeavors.

Suhrit Tewary is a final-year student pursuing a Bachelor of Business Administration with a specialization in Marketing at the Institute of Engineering and Management Kolkata, affiliated with the University of Engineering and Management Kolkata, India.

Vladislav Aleksandrovich Zarubin is a fourth-year student at Tomsk Polytechnic University, specializing in Software Engineering. His primary research interests include backend development, artificial intelligence, Internet of Things, blockchain, and DevOps. During his studies, he has been actively engaged in research activities and software development. His article, "Developing a Blockchain Transaction Processing Class for Data Transmission in Smart Meter Networks Using Python," was awarded third place at the II All-Russian scientific and practical conference "Intelligent energy." He is also involved in project work, creating modern solutions to advance the implementation of innovative technologies in software engineering.

Preface

There has never been a greater need for creative, game-changing solutions to the growing environmental problems of rising global temperatures, declining biodiversity, contaminated oceans, and unsustainable resource usage. The question of whether the technology that is changing our world may also be used to save it must be asked as we stand at the intersection of ecological crisis and technological innovation.

That inquiry and a vision of possibilities are the inspiration behind this book, *Harnessing the Potential of Artificial Intelligence to Promote Environmental Sustainability*. It looks at how artificial intelligence (AI), with its ability to evaluate, forecast, optimize, and learn, can be a strong friend on our shared path to a more resilient and greener world.

This book, however, is more than just a celebration of technology; it is a critical analysis of the responsibilities that accompany it. AI implementation needs to be driven by moral principles, fairness, and a steadfast dedication to the welfare of both humans and the environment. Sustainability is a very human endeavor that calls for empathy, cooperation, and foresight; it is not only a scientific endeavor.

This volume's chapters each combine case studies, multidisciplinary ideas, and forward-looking viewpoints to help close the gap between environmental stewardship and AI. It seeks to give scientists, decision-makers, technologists, and environmentalists the information and motivation they need to use AI as a tool, not a goal, to create a sustainable future.

May this book serve as a reminder that although AI provides useful tools, how those tools impact our environment will ultimately depend on our collective aim, creativity, and conscience. For the sake of the planet and future generations, let this serve as a call to innovate with integrity, think creatively, and act quickly.

Dr Parijata Majumdar

Chapter 1

Designing an Application for Environmental Sustainability: Leveraging IoT and AI for Data Collection and Analysis

Anton Yuryevich Demin, Aleksander Dmitriyevich Bragin, Darya Igorevna Dmitriychuk and Vladislav Aleksandrovich Zarubin

Information Technology Department, Tomsk Polytechnic University, Russia

Abstract

This chapter explores the design and implementation of an application leveraging the Internet of Things (IoT) and artificial intelligence (AI) to promote environmental sustainability. By integrating IoT devices for automated data collection and AI for advanced analytics, the application offers personalized recommendations to users, helping them optimize resource consumption and reduce their environmental footprint. The paper delves into key technological aspects, including IoT architecture, data processing algorithms, and scalable, user-centric system designs. It emphasizes the synergy between IoT and AI as a driver for proactive environmental solutions, fostering awareness and sustainable behavior. Challenges like data security, scalability, and device efficiency are discussed alongside strategies for ethical and inclusive innovation. This work highlights the transformative potential of IoT and AI in achieving global sustainability goals.

Keywords: Internet of Things; Artificial intelligence ; environmental sustainability; resource optimization; data analytics; smart applications

Harnessing the Potential of Artificial Intelligence to Promote Environmental Sustainability, 1–12

doi:10.1108/978-1-83662-996-220251001

Introduction

Modern technologies open up new opportunities to solve environmental problems that are becoming more acute in the 21st century. Issues of sustainable energy consumption, waste minimization, and carbon footprint reduction require effective tools for monitoring, analysis, and recommendation development. The IoT and AI play a key role in this transformation, providing powerful tools for data collection and interpretation to support environmental sustainability.

Against the background of growing concern about the state of the environment, the role of technology is becoming increasingly important. Global challenges, such as climate change, depletion of natural resources, and pollution, require not only active actions from society but also new approaches to their solution. Modern innovations allow us to rethink traditional ways of human interaction with nature and contribute to the creation of an ecosystem where data becomes a central element in the development of environmental strategies. IoT provides opportunities for automatic data collection from a variety of sources, and AI allows the data to be turned into valuable insights, forming the basis for making informed decisions (Lin et al., 2019; Tan et al., 2022).

Of particular interest is the creation of applications that help users improve their environmental habits by providing personalized recommendations based on data analysis. Such applications can collect information from smart devices and sensors, such as water meters, electricity meters, or household appliances, to assess the level of resource consumption. With the help of AI, they analyze the collected data, identify inefficient usage patterns and propose specific actions to optimize them. This approach not only helps to raise users' awareness of the impact of their daily habits on the environment, but also helps them to consciously reduce resource consumption and their environmental footprint.

Designing such an application involves a number of technical and practical tasks. It requires the development of an IoT architecture for reliable data collection, secure transmission, and the integration of machine learning algorithms for analytics. Special attention needs to be paid to scalability, energy efficiency, and data privacy in order to make solutions accessible and ethically sound. In addition, successful implementation requires a user-friendly interface that effectively conveys analytical information and recommendations.

This chapter focuses on the design of an application that uses IoT and AI to collect and analyze data on users' environmental habits. It explores key aspects of development: from IoT architecture and data transfer protocols to analytics and decision support systems. Special emphasis is placed on the synergy of technologies, providing an adaptive and personalized approach to environmental sustainability. Examples of successful implementations that can serve as inspiration for further innovations are also considered.

In the context of rapid technological progress, such applications are becoming an important tool for the harmonious combination of individual actions and global sustainable development goals. Developing solutions that not only inform but also encourage people to behave in an environmentally responsible manner plays a key role toward a more sustainable future.

Literature Review

In recent years, many authors have focused their attention on the integration of the IoT and AI. At present, these are some of the most popular technologies which have proven themselves in many areas of our lives, from solving everyday tasks to application in the economy and industry. At the same time, many problems of our planet related to climate change, resource depletion, and various pollutants require the introduction of innovative approaches. Modern problems require modern solutions, and it is here that the IoT and AI can become key tools. These technologies already provide effective environmental monitoring, data collection, and analysis. This statement is supported by numerous scientific articles on the topic.

For example, the article "Sustainable Cities and the Internet of Things (IOT) Technology" examines how IoT can influence and interact with urban infrastructure (Drepaul, 2020).

The author highlights how IoT optimizes resource management, increases energy efficiency, and improves the quality of life of urban residents. This chapter emphasizes the potential of the IoT. This technology can significantly affect the solution of the environmental problems mentioned earlier.

AI is currently experiencing a period of remarkable development. AI is one of the main pillars of the IT industry and has proven itself effective in solving different tasks. Naturally, the scientific community pays close attention to this topic and examines it in detail in various academic works. For example, the work "Research of ecological environment monitoring based on artificial intelligence" examines the key role of AI in environmental monitoring (Li, 2023). The author examines how the use of AI can improve the quality of decisions made in environmental protection. According to this research, AI holds great potential in solving environmental problems. The application of this technology can significantly affect the strengthening of the environmental sustainability of our society.

It is also essential to mention the article "Integrating IoT and AI: Enhancing System Efficiency and User Experience," which examines in detail the aspects of interaction between the IoT and AI, demonstrating how the integration of these two technologies can be beneficial (Raja et al., 2022). The author considers both the advantages and the challenges of this integration. Despite the existing issues, the author considers their solutions, which may be useful in further scaling systems built on the connection of these two technologies. In addition, the chapter addresses the improvement of user experience, which is crucial when creating such a system that is focused on changing human behavior.

The literature demonstrates that the integration of AI and the IoT is a relevant field that can make a significant contribution to the development of the environmental sustainability of our planet. The application of these technologies already solves some problems and challenges related to the environment, and their combined use can solve even more.

Technology Overview

When designing such a system that combines work with the IoT and AI, modern trends should be taken into account not only in development, but also in user

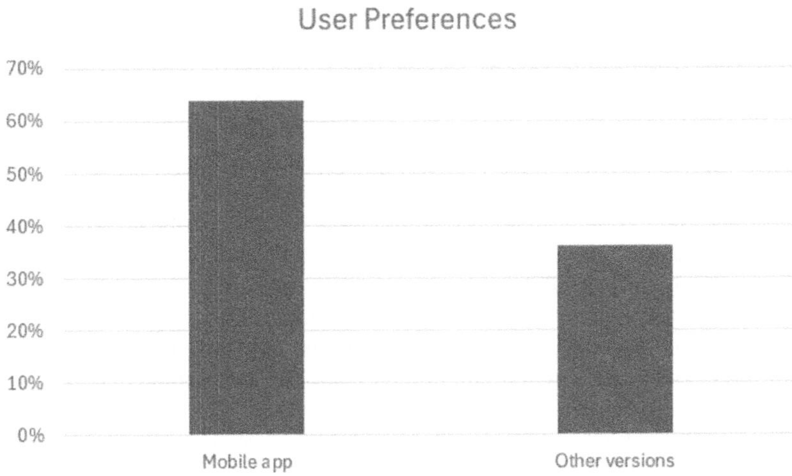

Fig. 1.1. User Preferences.

experience. Many surveys show that users usually prefer mobile applications over web versions, so the focus should be on developing a mobile version (Jenns, 2024). Mobile devices allow real-time monitoring because most users do not part with their smartphones. This is also relevant when working with IoT devices, which, in most cases, are controlled using mobile applications. Fig. 1.1 shows the user preferences.

At the design stage of such an application, it is critically necessary to choose the right development tools that will allow you to create a scalable, high-performance system with the integration of mobile devices, AI models, and the IoT. This chapter will provide an overview and selection of key development tools.

At the heart of any system that works with the IoT is the IoT framework. There are a large number of different frameworks for working with IoT, each having its advantages and disadvantages. For example, in the open-source segment, one of the good solutions is the ThingsBoard framework (TheTips4You, n.d.). ThingsBoard features a powerful data visualization system and management of IoT devices. The framework itself is a horizontally scalable platform that does not have a single point of failure. ThingsBoard works with cloud technologies, ensuring high performance. Devices are connected using the standard Internet of Things (IoT) protocols: Message Queuing Telemetry Transport (MQTT), Constrained Application Protocol (CoAP), and Hypertext Transfer Protocol (HTTP).

ThingsBoard has a strong competitor, which is no longer in the open-source segment. This is Amazon's AWS (Amazon Web Services) IoT Core. This framework provides unmatched scalability and integration with Amazon cloud services, including machine learning analytical tools. AWS IoT Core exchanges information using the previously mentioned MQTT and the more secure HTTPS protocol compared to HTTP. The fact that this framework is being developed by one of the largest IT companies in the world ensures its rapid development. However, its proprietary nature is also a significant disadvantage, as it makes the user dependent on Amazon. Both frameworks have their pros and cons, but the proprietary nature of AWS IoT Core forces us to make a choice in favor of ThingsBoard.

The choice of programming language is also crucial when designing such a large-scale application, as it affects the overall efficiency of the system, scalability, speed of development, and ease of integration. Python is often preferred for its wide range of libraries for working with IoT and its simplicity of syntax. The existence of frameworks such as Flask, Django, and FastAPI can make it an excellent language for implementing the backend and providing interaction with analytical models. However, the language is not without problems related to the Global Interpreter Lock (GIL), dynamic typing, and low speed. An alternative to Python is C++, which has proven itself in creating highly loaded, scalable systems. This language provides incredible performance due to its strict typing, the fact that it is compiled, and well-established memory management. Despite these advantages, choosing C++ makes the development process more complicated and slower, plunging the project into production hell. A middle ground between these approaches can be the Golang language, which combines the high performance of C++ with the relative simplicity of Python syntax. Golang provides fast compilation, excellent concurrency, scalability, and features strong typing. Golang is also known as a language for writing microservices. The use of microservice architecture may be crucial in the system under consideration.

We must not forget about effective data storage, which is of paramount importance when working with analyzing data. InfluxDB, a time-series database (TSDB) developed by InfluxData, has been gaining increasing popularity in recent months. It has become a reference tool for developers and engineers who want to implement real-time monitoring in their infrastructure. TSDBs, based on the name, are database systems specifically designed to process time-related information. That is why InfluxDB can be an excellent solution for the system in question (Oswald, n.d.). On the other hand, there are NoSQL databases. For example, MongoDB can also be an excellent solution for managing unstructured or semi-structured data.

Considering data warehouses, it is impossible not to mention relational databases. Although they provide extensive capabilities, their demanding nature may limit their use in telemetry. Therefore, the combination of the NoSQL database MongoDB and InfluxDB can be an excellent solution in this situation. MongoDB can be used to manage user profiles, while InfluxDB can handle data collected from smart devices.

Since the development of a mobile application is being considered, we must not forget about the language for mobile development. It is impossible not to mention the native development languages – Kotlin and Swift. These languages are the most popular and are used everywhere, but their most significant disadvantage is that both are designed only for their platforms – Android and iOS, respectively. A great alternative is the Flutter framework. It has proven itself to be a reliable cross-platform development framework. Using the compiled Dart language provides applications written in this framework with high performance. Flutter also offers a large number of widgets, simplifying the process of developing user interfaces and making them intuitive.

To summarize, the design of a system that interacts with AI models and the IoT requires the use of the most modern technologies specialized in solving specific tasks of the system, and does not depend on any corporation. Using ThingsBoard for IoT development, Golang for backend, Flutter for mobile development, and InfluxDB and MongoDB for data storage, it is possible to achieve high performance and scalability.

Architecture

The architecture of the system under consideration is based on a microservice approach. In a microservice architecture, an application is divided into a number of independently deployable services that interact using Application Programming Interfaces (APIs). Thanks to this approach, each individual service can be deployed and scaled independently of the others. As a result, teams can deliver voluminous and complex applications faster and more frequently. Unlike monolithic applications, microservice architecture enables teams to implement new features and make changes faster, without rewriting large portions of the existing code (Harris, n.d.; Oswald, n.d.).

The central component of the system is the data collection layer, which is represented by analytical models forming the core of the project. This core collects device data, analyzes it, and presents a recommendation based on the analysis. Additionally, there is an API layer that provides interactions with IoT devices through lightweight protocols such as MQTT and HTTP. Data are transmitted from IoT devices in JavaScript Object Notation (JSON) format through the central Apache Kafka message broker. The received data are stored in InfluxDB and MongoDB. This ensures reliable routing of data in the system.

If we talk in more detail about the core itself, then it consists of many microservices that are wrappers over analytical models. Each microservice is responsible for processing data from a specific type of device. For example, an energy consumption microservice analyzes electricity usage, identifies anomalies, and provides users with recommendations for optimizing the performance of their smart devices. The model performs analysis and transmits data to users of the system via the API to mobile devices. Each microservice is encapsulated in an isolated Docker container.

The Golang language is used to develop the API. The API is the key link between the core and mobile devices. Through the API gateway built with GraphQL, users receive analytical data on the operation of their smart devices. Based on the data and recommendations provided by the core, users can adjust the operation of devices to improve efficiency and ecological sustainability. Golang also provides user authentication and authorization logic, which is designed as a separate microservice.

Such a large system implies the presence of monitoring and diagnostic systems. Tools such as Prometheus, Grafana, Sentry, and Jaeger are used for this purpose. Prometheus is used for monitoring and alerting. It collects metrics that are visualized using Grafana, which simplifies the interpretation of large log streams. The next tool in line is Jaeger. Jaeger tracks distributed request routes and provides insight into which requests are passing through the system from users. This tool is extremely useful for detecting bottlenecks. And the last maintenance tool worth mentioning is Sentry. This system allows you to track errors in the work of the frontend and backend.

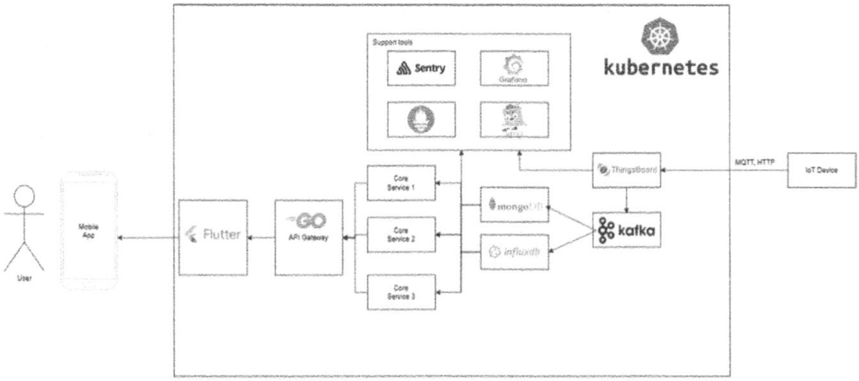

Fig. 1.2. Architecture Using IoT Devices.

As mentioned earlier, services are deployed in containers, which in turn become Kubernetes pods. Kubernetes cluster provides a high degree of automation in container orchestration, as well as scalability and fault tolerance due to the availability of resources such as ReplicaSet and load balancer. Development tools such as Kafka, MongoDB, Grafana, or Redis are also deployed in the Kubernetes cluster. We can also mention the use of the GitOps approach, which will allow automatic uploading of data from the version control system to the Kubernetes cluster using a tool, such as Flux. Fig. 1.2 shows the architecture using IoT devices.

The described architecture will ensure high performance, scalability, and user-friendliness of the system. The microservice architecture will make it easy to add new types of devices, as well as modify existing services, adapting the system to changing market requirements. For example, sensors can be integrated to monitor the state of the soil or solar panels, which will expand the application's capabilities in the field of environmental sustainability, which goes beyond mass-scale user IoT devices. This approach makes the system a universal and reliable platform for working with big data and managing smart devices, which is especially important in today's rapidly growing IoT industry.

Algorithms and Methods of Data Analysis

Applications for tracking and analyzing environmental data arrays using IoT devices as data sources often require the introduction of data analysis algorithms that allow not only the efficient extraction of significant parameters from a huge stream of heterogeneous information, but also their processing and the provision of recommendations to users for updating their environmental habits. The development of systems at this level involves the use of AI, machine learning, and deep learning methods for the most accurate analysis of various types of information, as well as providing personalized user characteristics. To study environmental data, an integrated approach is needed, including the following steps: purification, standardization, integration, and the construction of prediction models.

These data processing points are interconnected, so their gradual implementation will allow the development of personalized recommendations and the building of long-term sustainable development strategies.

Due to the peculiarities of the data collected from IoT devices, their nature is rather heterogeneous, arrays of information are subject to noise and missing values. This is easily explained by the diversity of data sources, ranging from smart meters to satellite monitoring systems. Therefore, the initial stage of data research is preprocessing. This process consists of cleaning the data, for example, by filtering algorithms, filling in missing values, removing duplicates, and standardizing parameters. For example, when training a model on a set of air quality data from the University of California, Irvine Air Quality set, it is important to unify the formats of pollutant concentrations and meteorological parameters. This is necessary, first, to simplify their processing, and second, to minimize errors. An important aspect is the combination of data from different sources; for example, water consumption data from household meters can be combined with information on weather conditions to account for the influence of temperature on resource consumption. All these data sources (sensor readings, satellite images, and statistical reports) are necessary for tracking a complete picture of a user's environmental habits. Of course, the key step in this process is identifying the most significant characteristics whose impact on the current environmental phenomenon is maximal. The selection of such parameters (CO_2 level, power consumption, water consumption, etc.) helps to narrow the entire analysis to the most critical features.

Analytical models are built on the basis of preprocessed data, and machine learning is a fundamental tool for implementing analytical solutions. Forecasting is obviously an important task in machine learning. In environmental applications, it is often associated with the analysis of time series, such as the dynamics of CO_2 emissions, temperature changes, or seasonal fluctuations in energy consumption. For example, time-series forecasting using models such as Long Short-Term Memory (LSTM) networks or Prophet helps predict energy consumption levels or changes in pollutant concentrations. These methods are particularly relevant in the context of urban resource management and environmental risk assessment. Alternatively, forecasting models, including linear regressions and recurrent neural networks, allow the prediction of changes and the taking of preventive action before adverse or dangerous situations occur. For example, forecasting air pollution levels based on historical data and current weather conditions enables warnings to users about unfavorable conditions. The next important step is data clustering. This process helps identify similarities and patterns between objects. One way to use these algorithms is to identify groups of houses with similar electricity consumption when analyzing household energy usage and propose strategies to increase their energy efficiency or identify groups with the greatest potential for energy-saving technologies. In this way, hidden dependencies are revealed at first glance. The main methods include *k*-means and DBSCAN, adapted for processing big data. On the other hand, data classification using machine learning algorithms is used to identify characteristics and assess risks. The main methods include random forests and gradient boosting models.

As mentioned earlier, the system for accounting for the user's environmental habits contains input data of various types, including images and audio files. Deep learning methods are necessary for analyzing these types of complex and unstructured information. Convolutional neural networks, such as ResNet, are used to process satellite images, enabling the tracking of changes in forests or the state of water resources, or U-Net to separate pollution zones. This method of information research is used in the context of Amazon Forest Dataset data analysis, providing detailed forecasts about the degree of deforestation. In an urban environment, WaveNet technologies are used to study sound data, such as noise pollution levels, to identify sources of noise pollution.

A small digression regarding the implementation stack of these algorithms: data analysis technologies rely on powerful tools and frameworks that provide high performance and flexibility. Frameworks such as TensorFlow and PyTorch are widely used. These tools allow for the development of algorithms to analyze data on air quality, energy consumption or ecosystem states. Libraries such as pandas and NumPy provide tools for working with environmental data, including cleaning, processing, and statistical analysis. Integration with databases such as MongoDB and PostgreSQL enables the effective management of large volumes of data from various IoT devices and sensors. In environmental sustainability tasks, the choice of metrics for evaluating models depends on the specific goal. For example, when predicting air pollution levels, the mean square error (MSE) may be an important metric because it evaluates the accuracy of quantitative forecasts. For classification tasks such as determining the risk of environmental disasters, it is useful to use the F1-score to balance accuracy and completeness. For example, SHapley Additive exPlanations (SHAP) can be used to analyze the effects of emissions and weather factors on air quality. This tool allows the identification of parameters, such as PM2.5 concentration or temperature, that most strongly influence the predictions of the model, providing transparent explanations for informed decisions.

In the context of applications aimed at human environmental sustainability, personalized recommendations and adaptation to the individual needs of specific users are of particular value. A collaborative filtering algorithm based on neural networks can be applied here, for example, neural collaborative filtering (NCF), which allows users to analyze interactions and find patterns of behavior to predict the most effective user actions based on data on the behavior of other users with similar habits. An equally important aspect of the system is data visualization, which will make the perception of information understandable, native, and intuitive. Graphs, interactive dashboards, and reporting systems simplify the understanding of environmental issues. Users can monitor in real-time how their actions affect overall resource consumption. Integrative elements, such as a carbon footprint calculator, can help users track the impact of their actions, motivating them to maintain and expand their environmentally friendly habits. Ensuring security and confidentiality is the final stage of data analysis. The collection and processing of large amounts of personal data require compliance with ethical standards and legal regulations. Adhering to the algorithms of explicable artificial intelligence (Explicable AI) will enhance model transparency, which is especially important for applications that influence users' daily habits.

Thus, modern data analysis methods, combining the capabilities of IoT and machine learning, form the foundation for creating and implementing innovative solutions in the field of environmental sustainability. All current life processes are becoming not only more understandable and open, but also manageable. Everyone can take measures that contribute to long-term improvements in the management of natural resources.

Development Prospects

In the section on algorithms and methods for analyzing data coming from IoT devices, the most pleasant aspects of the system, its advantages and value, were mentioned, but like any technology, this area has its own areas where it is possible and necessary to become better. Specifically, in this system, the issue of scalability, as well as further expansion of functionality, becomes a priority. Information flows from a huge number, about a million, IoT devices, a priori require a decentralized infrastructure capable of not only stably working with huge amounts of data, but also withstanding critical peak loads. The use of technologies such as Apache Kafka and Spark allows for high-speed data processing in real time.

The area of development of the system is also an increase in overall energy efficiency. On the one hand, since IoT systems often work on devices with limited resources, it is essential to develop algorithms that minimize energy consumption. On the other hand, creating energy-efficient and autonomous sensors powered by renewable energy sources is equally important. For example, sensors powered by small solar panels, or devices with the ability to recover energy from the environment. This will create more autonomous and sustainable monitoring networks. Ideally, both of these factors are implemented simultaneously. Even now, however, devices are becoming more compact, which greatly simplifies their implementation into the daily lives of ordinary users.

Ensuring the security and privacy of users' personal data has always been, and will remain a critically important aspect of the entire system. It is impossible not to take into account that in modern realities there is a rapid growth of connected IoT devices (by 15% annually) and, accordingly, the volume of information collected. Therefore, the development of more reliable data protection protocols is becoming a priority. At the same time, research is underway in the field of explicable AI, which will increase user confidence in systems and minimize the risks of misinterpretation of the analysis results.

From the perspective of global environmental initiatives, such an application could serve as a valuable tool for achieving international sustainable development goals. Large-scale user participation in environmental monitoring will be an important step. The development of user applications, where data comes not only from IoT devices but also from people themselves, who can report local environmental problems (e.g., illegal deforestation or water pollution), will enhance the value of platforms.

Obviously, for the successful implementation of technology, it is important to take into account the cultural and social aspects of different segments of the population. This includes adapting interfaces and recommendations to the specifics of a particular ethnic, social, and demographic group, such as language preferences, levels of technical literacy, climatic conditions, mentality, and the influence of traditions on lifestyle, and much more.

Conclusion

The technologies of the IoT and AI in the modern world open up new opportunities for solving environmental problems, which are becoming increasingly important in the context of global climate change, depletion of natural resources, and deterioration of environmental quality. These technologies not only facilitate the collection of data on the state of ecosystems but also provide tools for their analysis, forecasting, and management, making them one of the key elements of a sustainable development strategy.

The use of IoT and AI enables the creation of systems that can adapt to changing conditions and user needs. Innovative solutions developed based on these technologies can optimize the use of energy, water, and other resources, while increasing people's awareness of the consequences of their daily actions for the environment in general and their surroundings in particular. Such approaches are already being applied in smart buildings, urban infrastructures, agriculture, and industrial systems, where their impact on sustainability is becoming increasingly evident.

Of particular value is the synergy of IoT and AI, which makes it possible to transition from traditional responses to environmental problems to proactive, predictive behaviors. AI algorithms can analyze large amounts of data, identify hidden patterns, and propose solutions that address not only current problems but also potential long-term risks. This approach minimizes the impact of human activity on nature and contributes to the formation of conscious consumption at the individual level.

However, the adoption of these technologies is associated with a number of difficulties that require special attention. These include issues of data privacy, system scalability, device energy efficiency, and equitable access to innovation. Solving these problems requires the efforts of not only developers and researchers but also politicians, regulators, and the public, who must unite to create a regulatory framework that stimulates the development of environmentally friendly technologies. Transparency and openness in the operation of IoT and AI systems, along with the ethical principles governing their use, are essential for achieving trust from users and broad public support.

In conclusion, it can be noted that IoT and AI are becoming the most important tools on the way to a sustainable future. Their impact extends beyond technology, forming a new attitude toward nature and interaction with the environment. The use of these technologies gives hope that humanity will be able to cope with global challenges, maintaining that delicate balance between progress and the preservation of the planet for future generations. It requires a combination of efforts, foresight and a constant drive for improvement, but the reward for this work – a cleaner, safer and more harmonious world – is undoubtedly worth it.

References

Drepaul, N. (2020). Sustainable cities and the Internet of Things (IoT) technology: IoT technology improves the development of smart cities' infrastructures and reduces over-population stresses. *Consilience, 22*, 39–47. https://doi.org/10.7916/consilience.vi22.6742

Harris, C. (n.d.). *Microservices architecture*. Atlassian. https://www.atlassian.com/ru/microservices/microservices-architecture

Jenns, C. (2024, May 2). *Survey reveals customers prefer mobile apps to mobile websites*. Yahoo Finance. https://finance.yahoo.com/news/survey-reveals-customers-prefer-mobile-092144971.html

Li, N. (2023). Research of ecological environment monitoring based on artificial intelligence. *Proceedings of the 2023 International Conference on Environmental Geoscience and Earth Ecology*, *7*, 110–115. https://doi.org/10.54254/2753-8818/7/20230120

Lin, Y.-W., Lin, Y.-B., & Liu, C.-Y. (2019). AItalk: A tutorial to implement AI as IoT devices. *IET Networks*, *8*(3), 195–202. https://doi.org/10.1049/iet-net.2018.5182

Oswald, K. (n.d.). *Знакомство с InfluxDB и базами данных временных рядов*. Tproger. https://tproger.ru/translations/influxdb-guide

Raja, P., Kumar, S., Yadav, D. S., & Singh, T. (2022). Integrating IoT and AI: Enhancing system efficiency and user experience. *International Journal of Information Technology and Computer Engineering*, *2*(6), 39–50. https://doi.org/10.55529/ijitc.26.39.50

Tan, J., Sha, X., Lu, T., & Dai, B. (2022). A short survey on future research of AI and IoT technologies. In *Proceedings of the 2022 International Wireless Communications and Mobile Computing (IWCMC)* (pp. 190–195). IEEE. https://ieeexplore.ieee.org/document/9825425

TheTips4You. (n.d.). *Top 10 open source IoT platforms*. http://www.thetips4you.com/open-source-iot-platform-top-10-open-source-iot-platform/

Chapter 2

Applications and Challenges of Real-time Data Analysis in the Field of Disaster Prevention, Reduction, and Relief

Jeya Sutha M., Ramesh Dhanaseelan F. and Jabanesha S.

Department of Computer Applications, St. Xavier's Catholic College of Engineering, Tamil Nadu, India

Abstract

Disaster management is now highly significant due to the increasing frequency and intensity of natural and man-made disasters. Real-time analysis means acquiring, storing, and analyzing data in near real-time from various sources, which include satellite imagery, IoT devices, and social media, which are vital analyses whose results are important in decision-making during disasters. This chapter will review works concerned with the real-time data usage for disaster prevention, reduction, and relief. Real-time data analysis is crucial in noticing problems early and developing a response to problems before they occur, in deciding where resources should be dedicated in an emergency, and in evaluating the aftermath of a disaster situation. There are several challenges that slow down the use of real-time data analysis, including data quality and data reliability, data privacy, and data compatibility across the various sources. In response to these challenges, this chapter advocates for the development of both technology and infrastructure, a set of rules on data exchange, improved education of members, and engaged communities. Overcoming these challenges and enhancing the management of real-time data would dramatically enhance the ability of communities to respond to disasters. The chapter finally concludes that real-time data analysis is an indispensable component for improving disaster management practices and that there is still much

Harnessing the Potential of Artificial Intelligence to Promote Environmental Sustainability, 13–33

doi:10.1108/978-1-83662-996-220251002

research needed and continuous progress to be made toward creating a better future.

Keywords: Data analyses; disaster prevention; early warning systems; crisis mapping; business intelligence; real-time data

1. Introduction

Real-time data analysis is one of the most significant information resources in disaster management that helps governments, organizations, and communities to be ready to face disasters, react to them, and recover after the disasters (Linardos et al., 2022). This need has grown more important due to the rise of natural disasters like hurricanes, earthquakes, and wildfires, as well as their intensity (Oktari et al., 2020). Real-time data covers information that is gathered from sources such as satellites, networks, interfaces, social networking services (SNS), and geographic information systems (GIS). This information is analyzed and released in a short time, and as a result, it makes appropriate decisions aimed at improving the operation of disaster management techniques.

Disaster and crisis information that can be timely and appropriate can be crucial during catastrophes (Akhyar et al., 2024). The transmission of identification and risk assessment of hazards involves the provision of real-time information for early warning systems (EWS) (Xu & Xue, 2024). In disaster response, real-time data is useful in evaluating the status of a disaster, determining the appropriate resources to allocate, and how exactly to deploy them. It's in this phase that real-time data feeds inform about the extent of damage, the progress of the recovery process, and which reconstruction steps to undertake next. The implementation of real-time data in disaster management procedures improves the assessment of disasters and provides an opportunity for preventive measures execution.

The focus of this chapter will be to understand how real-time data analysis can be applied and used, as well as its limitations when applied to disaster prevention, reduction, and relief. It will explore the uses of "real-time" data in disasters, such as in warning systems, mapping of disasters, use in disaster resource mobilization, and disaster relief efforts. Also, the challenges of real-time data analysis to the absence of data quality, privacy issues, and technological impediments will be discussed in the chapter. Therefore, this chapter focuses on case studies and future research avenues that aim to shed light on how real-time data can be effectively adopted for enhancing disaster management strategies.

2. The Role of Real-time Data in Disaster Management

EWSs are vital instruments in the disaster risk reduction processes. These systems, which include hazard identification and alerting to at-risk communities, operate using real-time data. EWS incorporates data from stations ranging from meteorological, seismological, and even satellite data (Khan et al., 2023). For instance, tsunami warning systems use real-time oceanography to identify undersea earthquakes and to determine the warning if they are tsunami-capable. These alerts afford the communities an opportunity to prevent the loss of lives and property through measures such as evacuation (Krichen et al., 2024).

Thus, real-time analysis of the data is particularly important during disaster situations to enrich the activities of decision-makers. Some of the possible uses of real-time information by emergency management agencies are to be able to determine the areas to be attended to and to establish their priorities. For instance, drone and remote sensing information can be used to assess the extent of infrastructure loss, population shelterlessness, and accessible routes (Cicek & Kantarci, 2023). Combining real-time data with GIS enables responders to see the effects of disasters and distribute resources where they would be most effective.

Real-time analysis of the data is critical once a disaster has occurred to determine the extent of the losses and how to proceed. Aerial imagery, together with satellite photographs, can help to give a rapid appraisal of the extent of damage and assist in the early earmarking of the priorities of a community (Kondraganti et al., 2024). Recovery can also be monitored in real-time to allow decision-makers to make necessary changes to the strategies with regard to the progress obtained. For instance, the United Nations Organization has been using real-time data analysis to help with disaster relief efforts in different global nations (Treiblmaier & Rejeb, 2023).

As we can see, real-time data analysis has numerous advantages; however, there are several issues that are still questionable. Specifically, data quality and data accuracy are also important factors, since wrong or old information may negatively influence decisions during disasters (Moghadas et al., 2023). It also means that more data privacy and security questions should be answered, especially when the concern is on the use of personal data during disastrous events. Problems such as integration and system interface are not a walk in the park since various agencies and organizations work with disparate systems. The development of future technologies in disaster management can be attributed to new technologies that include artificial intelligence and machine learning to span the different elements of real-time data analysis capabilities.

3. Uses of Real-time Business Analytics

Especially for EWS, real-time analysis represents a key contributing factor. Such systems apply numerous inputs to issue timely alarms in regard to diverse types of risk, including meteorological turmoil, tsunami, and earthquake. For example, the National Oceanic and Atmospheric Administration (NOAA) applies numerical weather prediction models and current data from geostationary satellites and Doppler radar to forecast and mitigate severe weather conditions (Conboy et al., 2020). The implementation of machine learning algorithms to EWS makes it possible for improved forecasting and therefore better timing of the alerts that are issued.

3.1. Meteorological Data Analysis

Meteorological data has the essence or purpose of furnishing data in near-real time to avoid lessening and responding to disasters, such as forecasting, warning, and prevention. The data used in this field are satellites, radar, weather stations, and IoT sensors. These insights are useful in hindcasting and preventing natural disasters, including hurricanes, floods, heat waves, droughts, and storms. Weather data processing remains one of the most important aspects of EWS. Data from the ground-based stations, and satellites, as well as radar systems underlying weather information, is processed in real-time to determine developing weather and partage risks. For example, the global precipitation measurement (GPM) mission gives information about precipitation rates global information and allows flood regions to issue timely warnings (Samani et al., 2023). The aspect of processing meteorological data in real-time increases the reliability of the probabilities for predicting negative conditions for settlements.

Information on weather conditions can be applied to develop specific risk mapping that separates places that are prone to natural disasters based on historical data, climate, and even real-time data. For instance, regions that are vulnerable to hurricanes or floods can be used, and predicting models assist in outlining how they will affect the built environment and the people. Extreme weather conditions cause mishaps that affect our daily lives, and by comparing long-term meteorological records, experts can deduce ways in which climate change might worsen the resulting occurrences (Turk et al., 2023). This is useful when subsequent disasters occur and strategies for their prevention are needed. The meteorological data, as it is received, is important when responding to disasters. It enables the placing of food stocks, establishment of relief camps, and rigging up of rescue squads in view of areas mainly at risk from storms or floods. This analysis should also hold up well after the disaster. For instance, tracking post-storm precipitation or wind velocities determines whether the situation is enhancing or deteriorating, hence determining the further course of recovery.

Temperature, relative humidity, and wind speed are also important in order to accompany satellite data for the early detection of wildfires. This way, it is possible to know the areas or regions where conditions that may lead to infernos are obtained, hence alerts can be developed early enough to avoid large losses. Wind and humidity data, in particular, can subsequently be used to predict how the fire will spread and assist the firefighters in responding appropriately. These sources involved are satellite data, synoptic station data, Doppler radar data, and other various data acquisition devices (Nova, 2023). Such data sources differ in format, size, and resolution, and indeed can only be merged with a lot of difficulty into an encompassing analytical framework. One key problem is maintaining the integration of the data into a consistent format. Numerical data, satellite images, radar data, etc., cannot be assimilated in the same way, and therefore, the assimilation of these data types can be a significant challenge.

Using real-time meteorological data requires the evaluation of huge data volumes in very limited time frames. Even in the present circumstances, meteorological models have evolved greatly, but apprehending the behavior of systems such as tropical storms or tornadoes is not easy. Fluctuations in forecast results are also vulnerable to tiny variations in the input data, and this characteristic tends to worsen as the forecast horizon extends. Weather predicting is by its nature probabilistic and this means that many of the predictions that are made entail a level of risk. This is a problem for disaster decision-making as the authorities are confronted with the probability of raising an alarm call when there is no catastrophe only to be faced with time wastage when a disaster strikes they are hesitant.

At times when meteorological data is to be believed numerical models can be a useful tool to forecast the disaster, but the problem arises when the relevant information is available the core issue of disseminating the warnings and response mechanisms to a community afflicted by the disaster is the real issue. The advantage of forecast accuracy is reduced when there is a communication failure or early warnings of its implementation. There might also be false alarms or ambiguous warnings that eventually weaken people's response to actual warning signals. The application of machine learning and artificial intelligence in determining meteorological data has drawn hopes of making the prediction tool better and faster. Successful use of artificial intelligence models can help process a large amount of data and detect patterns that traditional approaches can hardly recognize, which contributes to early warnings. It is being applied in practice to such activities as image recognition in satellite imagery and fine-tuning numerical forecast models. IoT devices are being commonly implemented for weather forecasting, as there are more such devices available that generate large amounts of hyper-local data. This assists in materials and conditions monitoring of the atmosphere at a regional scale in real time to enhance local disaster readiness. When it comes to big data processing, cloud computing is the best option for meteorological agencies to store and analyze big volumes of data. The cloud-enabled platforms help in the sharing of information among global weather agencies, as well as help in real-time analysis, which is critical in disaster risk forecasting.

3.2. Tsunami and Earthquake Monitoring

Seismic and tsunami observance procedures are used to forecast, identify, and alert the public about an impending earthquake or tsunami in order to reduce the effects and the extent of the damage. These systems envelop sundry kinds of sensors, technologies, and communication networks to furnish actual time data and prior notices to authorities as well as the general populace. Systems based on real-time consist of the detection of seismic activity and the potential occurrence of the respective tsunamis. The Pacific Tsunami Warning Center (PTWC) receives information from seismic networks and ocean buoys on undersea earthquakes and proceeds to issue warnings on tsunamis (Zhou et al., 2024). Earthquake monitoring systems are based on seismological networks by means of various types of sensors and stations installed in seismically active areas. In the case of an earthquake, prediction enables early evacuation and minimization of loss in case of a tsunami based on the area. Similarly, earthquake EWS, including ShakeAlert in California, alert people a few seconds before they start shaking (Papatheodorou et al., 2023). Earthquakes and tsunamis in Alaska monitoring needs international cooperation since earthquakes and tsunamis impact upon countries' territories. Inter-governmental agencies like the United Nations Education, Scientific and Cultural Organization (UNESCO), the Inter-governmental Oceanographic Commission, and the Global Seismic Network integrate directly in the process of standardizing monitoring, reporting, and response patterns.

3.3. Crisis Mapping and Situational Awareness

Crisis mapping is one of the most important uses of real-time big data in disaster response. It entails the use of data visualization so that the consequences of a disaster can be observed at a glance and the response formulated. Some of these are Social Media and Baseline Mapping (BM) reports, which are collected and displayed in tools like Ushahidi and Arc GIS (Tomaszewski, 2020). In disasters, these technologies support the assessment of the environment by enabling responders to identify the areas that require their assistance, monitor the availability of resources, and disseminate information to persons within the affected region.

The information sources that are utilized in crisis mapping to study the data in real-time are several tools and technologies. GIS offer strong spatial analysis tools, which enable the responder to view data in context. After combining different territorial maps among which there are population density, the degree of damaged infrastructures, and access to them, operational decisions on the use of resources will be proper (Kamil et al., 2021). Furthermore, the analysis of social networks can identify key sentiments and discuss shifts in clients' needs that occurred after a disaster. The utility of crisis mapping can be explained by presenting different examples. In January 2010 in the Haiti earthquake, social media were used to display the effects of the strike and how the process of disaster response could be initiated. It showed that social media posts, satellite images, and reports from the ground were collected by volunteers and helped responders demonstrate a more effective interaction (Ausat, 2023). Likewise, crisis mapping applications facilitated the observation of the intensity of the flood in certain locations and the areas that require response during the calamity like Hurricane Harvey in 2017 (Tzavella et al., 2024). Real-time has proved to be very effective in making response to disasters more efficient in terms of resource utilization. Population density, extent of infrastructure destruction, and available access ways help in identifying regions that should be the priority for relief agencies. GIS gives the responder the ability to look at the information in terms of space and make decisions on where to take the response such as medical teams, food, water, and shelter.

Spatial analysis requires the use of GIS to be effective in disaster management. In particular, the mobile application allows for receiving actual data on the distribution of people and the extent of the destruction to promptly allocate resources. For instance, GIS was employed in response to the Hurricane Sandy disaster in 2012 to locate vulnerable regions for attending to escaping services (Harper et al., 2023). The spatial data presentation increases awareness of the distribution of relief and makes the coordination of relief more efficient because the focus is given to areas that need resources. Contemporaneous information from different sources can be incorporated into the resource management systems in order to meet pertinent supply and manpower requirements. For instance, information from mobile apps and social sites can be employed to monitor requests for help and establish sections bearing an inadequate workforce (Cicek & Kantarci, 2023). Such an approach to managing disaster relief not only optimizes the supply, delivery, and distribution but also increases accountability and "show cause" for the distribution of funds.

In the recovery phase of a disaster, real-time data analysis is as critical as during the disaster event. Satellite images, drones, aerial photography, and aerial photographs help governments to carry out evaluations of assets within the first hours of a disaster and therefore determine the extent of destruction (Damaševičius et al., 2023). Such data is essential for the deployment of recovery measures, allocation of resources, and the identification of the steps required for the reconstruction of societies. There are several approaches that can be used to evaluate the losses in the wake of a disaster in order to determine the extent of loss in real-time. Satellite images offer flexibility that can be used to map areas that have been destroyed and the number of people who have been rendered homeless (Ijaz et al., 2023). Furthermore, the use of specially fitted cameras and sensor-mounted aerial platforms to reach and document the disaster-affected before and after areas and gain insights on losses and disruptions caused. The real-time information provided helps decision-makers decide where and when to focus recovery actions because some risks are more critical than others.

3.4. Monitoring Recovery Efforts

Another objective of real-time analysis of data is to track recovery work and assess the impact of interventions. Demographic information regarding shifted populations, the condition of structures, and the roles people are expected to play in the recovery process allow for evaluating the program's accomplishments and adjusting the course of action if needed (Galera-Zarco & Floros, 2024). For instance, the World Bank uses time series data to track the progress on the reconstruction in the disaster-prone areas which makes the intervention more innovative in reaching out to the communities. From this, agencies can combine past data with present time data so as to see areas that are at risk and the potential risk (Cao et al., 2023). Such knowledge is useful for designing measures that will help reduce disaster impacts, including upgrading structures, better planning, and organizing information dissemination (Guo et al., 2025).

Business intelligence refers to the use of real-time data to evaluate potential disaster events together with their risks (Rakhonde et al., 2024). Because agencies can use past events data and feed current information into the system, they can discern trends that are likely to pose a threat in the future. For example, in the mining of diseased patients' photographs, health care can use machine learning to examine meteorological data results that will help communities avoid such effects. This active strategy in risk evaluation contributes to the improvement of the community's stability and minimizes susceptibility to disasters. Real-time data analysis also aids in fashioning community resilience strategies. To this end, interventions from the agencies aimed at strengthening community resilience for people with developmental disabilities can be based on the determination of vulnerable groups as well as their needs assessment. Public information and sensitization through the use of data that is being collected in real-time can foster change and ensure people are ready to prevent future disasters (Guerrero Granados et al., 2024). Moreover, robust real-time data can help in land use planning and infrastructure development so that communities' coping capacity for future disasters is enhanced.

4. Issues on the Use of Real-time Data Analysis

Data quality and accuracy are mainly due to the need to check on the kind of data being fed into the real-time data analysis process in disaster management. Thus, the provision of inaccurate or the use of outdated information results in the wrong decisions and inefficient action (Sathianarayanan et al., 2024). For example, if weather predictions rely on inaccurate information, the populations will not receive timely alerts, resulting in many deaths in disasters. In order to meet this challenge, it is necessary to develop effective mechanisms for data acquisition and verification to guarantee that data obtained in real-time can be used effectively.

All these make data privacy and security big issues that need to be considered, especially when implementing real-time data for disaster responses. The sampling of personal data from social media and mobile applications is therefore an issue of ethics, especially privacy and consent (Tarei et al., 2024). Furthermore, threat in cyberspace also brings vulnerability to data systems that are employed within disaster management (Bania et al., 2024). Any real-time data should be collected, stored, and processed with proper security measures and, at the same time, paying due regard to each person's privacy rights is critical to the sustainable, effective, and acceptable use of real-time applications.

Disaster management also has severe issues with data system interconnection and compatibility. A number of agencies and organizations may have different platforms and technologies that are not linked, and thus, data cannot flow from one system to another freely; hence, effective data analysis becomes a challenge. Ideally, agencies within and across sectors should have standardized procedures to maximize information exchange (Dash & Dixit, 2024). Further, staff development and capacity awareness of all people operating in disaster management can enhance the use of real-time data. Challenges like infrastructure and technology limit the use of real-time data analysis in disaster management. Despite particular challenges in this sphere being seen in many regions and developing countries in particular, poor technological covering often puts constraints on the possibilities of getting vital real-time information and, thus, enhances the effectiveness of the response measures (Pognon et al., 2024). To overcome all these barriers, enhanced investments in technology and infrastructure are mandatory. This involves enhancing the internet infrastructure, increasing access to data collection instruments, and strengthening the ability of indigenous groups to use real-time information in disaster response.

Real-time data application in disaster management requires further investigation of human factors such as cognitive biases and decision-making. Leaders tend to use bounded rationality and heuristics in the decision-making process, rather than adopt extensive rationality and take real-time data into consideration (Conges et al., 2023). In order to address this challenge, training programs designed to improve decision-making and support senior decision-makers in organizations and stakeholders involved in disaster management and recovery should be designed. Also, enhancing the relationship between those who produce the data and the ones who use them can enhance the implementation of such data into operation at the same time.

5. Case Studies

5.1. Case Study 1: The 2010 Haiti Earthquake

The case study relating to the use of real-time data for and in response to the 2010 Haiti earthquake provides a useful example. The 2010 Haiti earthquake was considered one of the most devastating disasters that have occurred in contemporary history, claiming the lives of more than three million people and hundreds of thousands of homes. Such a disaster taught not only people about the potential consequences of an earthquake but also showed the importance of real-time data as well as crisis maps in improving the existing crisis management activities. The earthquake also led to a flood of changes in social media usage, volunteering crisis mapping, and real-time data, the utilization of which enhanced the observation of the situation and management of the aid. After the earthquake, social media and crisis mapping applications were immediately used as tools to represent the effects of the disaster and response activities. People voluntarily furnished information on social media, satellite images, and radio through smartphones and tablets, which helped the responders (Shani-Kadmiel et al., 2021). Real-time data proved worthwhile in enhancing the application of resources when realizing the job, as well as enabling the realization of situation awareness during the response phase.

This was evidenced by the quick launching of crisis mapping tools after the Haiti earthquake to show how timely analysis of real data fed into improved disaster management (ten Brink et al., 2020). A powerful lesson was learned in the utilization of real-time data in disaster relief, using local and international organizations, agencies, and volunteers, and the impact that can be made by working together. These experiences from the Haiti earthquake suggest that better mechanisms of data gathering and integration are required in disaster response. To increase the effectiveness of real-time data analysis in future disasters, connections between organizations and technological investments must improve (Deane, 2023). Furthermore, the experience underscored the necessity of training personnel on the factors considered in selected data analysis tools and techniques in decision-making in disaster response.

5.1.1. Real-time Data and Crisis Mapping Applications

Many real-time data applications could be employed post-earthquake in response, relief management, and monitoring systems. For both survivors and the responders, social media, which included Twitter and Facebook, played a vital role in communication. Persons on the ground reported live about the conditions in camps, missing people, and areas requiring some assistance, while other persons who were not in Haiti helped compile and disseminate such information to humanitarian organizations. Social tools such as Ushahidi this crisis-mapping application proved very helpful in displaying this information and enhancing situation awareness.

Real-time data response is also comprised of the use of satellite imagery. Google and other such providers offered satellite MAPS within hours of the earthquake hitting the region. These high-definition pictures were relied on to determine the level of devastation and guide on which parts had been irreparably lost or weakened in terms of structures. Incorporating crowdsourced data on top of these images allowed responders to attain a greater knowledge of the disaster which enhanced the speed and accuracy of the response to the event.

5.1.2. Social Media as a Communication Tool

Besides crisis mapping, it was evident that text-based SNSs played a critical real-time communication function during the Haiti earthquake. People who were in the affected areas used less formal means such as social media, via Twitter, Facebook, and MT messaging to inform the public where they were, that they were stranded, and the current situation in their respective areas. This led responders to access needy people who were stuck or in need of immediate medical attention. Many non-governmental organizations, governments, and International organizations also employ social media to disseminate important information, give status of events, and safety information, and mobilize volunteers. People from all over the world also contributed to the effort, which brought together people from all four corners of the globe to share the needed information. Those who were not physically in Haiti but wanted to assist did so through the use of social media to translate messages, pull together data, and coordinate fundraising efforts. This high involvement of volunteers, added to technology, signaled a new approach toward the possibility of international coordination of disaster response.

5.1.3. Optimizing Resource Allocation and Situation Awareness

Real-time processing of data during the Haiti earthquake provided major insights into resource optimization and awareness in the event situation. It also speaks about emergency responders who were struggling with numerous unpredictable changes at night, and thus, having received updates on the situation, they could get a clearer picture of what kind of demands might be urgent at certain times. For example, when food and water were delivered in the form of airdrops, the data received from crisis maps were useful for identifying the areas that required those deliveries most urgently. The coordinators could monitor regions where the previous shipment had been delivered, and target areas that had not been accessed before for the new shipment. Also, the information received from social networks and crisis maps allowed us to orient on the location of the collapsed buildings, blocked streets, and places where people could be under the debris. With such statistics and data in place, governments, the United Nations, and major aid agencies were able to synchronize relief measures and strategies; no two agencies would be repeating what the other was doing, and efforts were focused on the troubled parts of the world. This was especially important in this type of disaster, where different organizations were working at the same time.

5.1.4. Lessons Learned from the Haiti Earthquake

One of the valuable lessons learned from the Haiti Earthquake was that the integration of local knowledge, volunteers, and high-tech technologies can boost the rate and efficiency of disaster response. Separate agencies were operating with their data, and there were cases where information flows were inadequate or more than one agency had kept duplicating the same information. This also brought out the issue and the general lack of a more efficient way of collecting, incorporating, and disseminating real-time information to multiple organizations in the event of a disaster. Another important lesson that was learned from the Haiti earthquake was the lack of training that was provided for members of the emergency team on how to use real-time data tools. However, for some of the responders, satellite imagery and Ushahidi were not familiar tools, and the procedures of how to use the information received and how to further process it were unknown.

The response of local responders was supplemented by individuals and organizations from all over the world, many of whom supplied real-time information and expertise. Better connections between Intergovernmental Organizations (IGOs), national and local governments, agencies, and communities will be crucial for post-disaster coordination in the future. Challenges realized in Haiti meant living up to enhancing technologies that could quicken and enhance the efficiency of real-time data analysis during disasters. National governments and international organizations must therefore continue to fund and support technologies such as active crisis mapping platforms, satellite imagery analysis, machine learning, and decision support systems that have the potential to predict the extent and form of disaster impacts and facilitate effective response. After the year 2010, many countries, along with different organizations, have developed the idea of collecting data, analyzing, and making new integrated systems for large-scale disasters. Satellite monitoring, mobile applications, and crowdsourcing platforms have evolved, and responders can access the needed information frequently. Today, organizations have come to understand the need for and practice public participation in data collection and the use of social media and crowdsourcing platforms in engaging with locals during a crisis. It has been applied later in subsequent disasters, such as the Nepal earthquake of 2015 and the COVID-19 pandemic in 2020. But it was not without exposing the dexterity of data integration, training, and technology, which should be of great concern in future disaster management planning.

5.2. Case Study 2: Hurricane Katrina

Another important example of the use of real-time data analysis for management can be traced back to Hurricane Katrina in 2005. Instead, the disaster identified inefficiencies in the flow of timely information within the United States, including the Federal Emergency Management Agency (FEMA). This became a disaster, and they learned how bad it was to do things the old way, not have collaboration between departments, and have slow decision-making. This incident demonstrated that the Katrina response brought lots of issues in data gathering, collaboration, and utilization of assets (Margus, 2023). While analyzing FEMA, its slow response and poor application of timely data collected throughout the disaster was criticized. The coordination experience of Hurricane Katrina demonstrated the gap in data sharing between agencies (Gershon et al., 2021). The absence of a data centralization system hampered an evaluation of the situation and the proper distribution of resources in time. Furthermore, the deployment of old technologies and practices also explains the sluggishness evident during the response. After Hurricane Katrina, a series of indispensable novelties of real-time data applications appeared (Smith & Vila, 2020). The use of GIS and other mapping techniques grew in popularity for use in disaster response in order that the impact of disasters can be more accurately gauged. The experiences from Katrina remain relevant for disaster response and preparedness and underscore the value of real-time data integration into emergency activities.

Unable to collect and analyze information properly during Hurricane Katrina was one of the main problems. A dysfunctional communication structure was apparent within and across multiple governmental agencies, including FEMA, since they failed to effectively estimate the level of damage and thus gather the required resources as soon as could have been possible. Local, state, and federal agencies gathered information, yet there was no one point where all the information was located, so emergency responders did not have a clear picture of what was going on. Thus, without some systems operating in accordance with rationalized sets of rules for the exchange and processing of data, organizational resources could not be optimally deployed. The lack of a centralized data management system that runs in real-time also posed the additional challenge of coordination between the agencies. This absence of interoperability was a significant barrier when identifying locations requiring intervention, as it inhibited integrative awareness of the situation across agencies. For instance, most of the emergency shelters received a lot of traffic because the information concerning the shelters' whereabouts and available capacity was either scarce or moved around slowly.

5.2.1. FEMA's Slow Response and Outdated Technologies

FEMA was most criticized, especially for acting slowly. One of the main reasons that were identified in the course of the analysis of the presented case was the unsuitability of the technologies that were employed by the agency to collect and analyze the data, and the focus of the agency on the application of traditional approaches to responses. This was evidenced by FEMA, after Katrina, where all the agency practices showed that many of the methods of data collection were manually put in forms, and then had to be reported, often after considerable delay. Some of the causes for the slow response include: communications hardware, maps, and other resources were outdated. It takes only one minute to respond, yet FEMA could not process and give an adequate response to the real-time data collected. Furthermore, the application of such practices as paper-based reporting, slow satellite feeds, and minimal use of the mobile data solution intensified the problem of responding to the dynamic.

5.2.2. Real-time Data Applications After Katrina

Some of the achievements that were made in response to disaster management after Hurricane Katrina include; the use of real-time data applications. The greatest change of all was the ready acceptance of GIS and other forms of mapping. These tools offered an improved way of comprehending the extent of loss and illustrating this to the emergency responders in real-time. GIS evolved into a tool for much more than simply determining flood areas to finding out which communities were most affected. Real-time data analysis tools also evolved rapidly for use by emergency management teams when assessing quickly changing factors such as water levels and human migrations. These tools enhanced the ways of determining where resources were to be assigned, where capable emergency staff was located, and where assistance was required to reach the people who were most in need of help. Katrina also found that there has been a creation of a more integrated system that enables the distribution of data among the various agencies.

5.2.3. Analysis of Hurricane Katrina

Disaster management proved that real-time data was vital in the aftermath of Hurricane Katrina. Lack of proper communication, inadequate data dissemination, and improper use of technologies in response highlighted during the disaster forced agencies and responders to reconsider their strategies. In particular, the use of a single platform for disseminating data collected by agencies is vital because all responders must work with the same up-to-date data. The use of sophisticated software analysis, GIS mapping, and automated monitoring is critical in enhancing the rate at which response is delivered and decisions are made. Stakeholder cooperation ensures cooperation between different governmental and non-governmental organizations in the organization of large-scale disaster response and management. In general, such lessons remain authoritative at present as they focus on the significance of the effective use of systematic data while dealing with natural disasters such as Hurricane Katrina. The process of data processing in emergencies and the further development of methods to counteract natural disasters are now viewed as the fundamental elements of emergency preparedness.

5.3. Case Study 3: The Australian Bushfires of 2019–2020

An example of the practical application of real-time data analysis on the contemporary level is the 2019/2020 fire in Australia. Australian Bushfires of 2019–2020 are also known as the "Black Summer fires" and remain one of the worst environmental crises in the 21st century, which resulted in the burning of around 46 million acres of land, thousands of homes, and affected nearly 3 billion animals, either by killing them or forcing them out of their natural habitats. This was a clear revelation of how live data feed is essential for the organization when it comes to handling big calamities of natural origin. Mature technologies were used by the government, emergency services, and responders to gather, analyze, and share data to instantly improve fire management and response. In this period actual time data was collected from satellite imagery and meteorological sources to observe fire behavior and risks, and to co-ordinate the fight against fires (Ahmed & Ledger, 2023). Data analysis in real-time incurred a central part in formulating response strategies in the bushfires. The agencies handling emergencies were able to manage the fire incidences by using real-time data aimed at providing the right intensity and rate (Mellish et al., 2024). Further, there was active surveillance of social media sites to capture the sentiments of the people and also to provide updates on the status of the disaster, including likely paths of destruction as well as safety measures for those likely to be affected.

In the case of the Australian Bushfires, some of the data sources include satellite imagery, Meteorological data, drone videos, ground sensors for real-time imagery of fire behavior, and strategies that will be applicable. This data offered constant dynamics of the fires, their progression, and area, to allow the response teams to determine where resources should be taken and the kind of firefighting tactics to use. The involvement of real-time data analytics during the Australian bushfires enabled quick evaluation of impact and recovery. Sometimes satellite imagery offered the first glimpses of the impact of the disaster and helped to determine how and when they would reconstruct. The knowledge acquired notably during the bushfires helps governments to underline the necessity of stemming money and capital in the development of technology and structures that can improve the effectiveness of real-time data processing in disaster management.

5.3.1. Satellite Imagery and Meteorological Data

Satellite images as a method of receiving real-time data were one of the most effective sources in terms of sharing information about the spread and magnitude of the fires. High orbit cameras, including Himawari-8 and National Satellite (NS) Commercial and scientific satellite imagery, and NASA's moderate resolution imaging spectroradiometer (MODIS) were used to track the fire occurrence in real-time. These satellite systems produced images in infrared and thermal and assisted in discovering hot spots, fire start points, and patterns of active fire fronts over large distances. It was then employed to draw fire perimeters to make calculated forecasts of the areas that are most threatened. Meteorological data from the Australian Bureau of Meteorology, as fresh weather information, was relayed to the firefighters to predict changes in the fires' behavior. For instance, behavior like a sudden change in wind direction exposes areas that were not affected by the fire risk. This data was needed for developing fire spread models, which predict the behavior of the fire and help direct residents to evacuate and plan resources where the next fire would likely occur.

5.3.2. Real-time Surveillance and Social Media Monitoring

Besides using satellite and meteorological data real-time surveillance techniques were also used on the ground to collect the information. The fires in regions that were too risky or inaccessible for people to approach were observed using drones that come with thermal imaging cameras. Their specific uses include surveillance of fire, as well as monitoring of the effectiveness of the suppression process through mapping of heat signature. Fixed or portable sensors and cameras stationed in important locations also supplied the fire situation data in real-time. Impulses from the bushfire response also revealed somewhat a surprising level of significance of social networking sites. Feed from popular social media platforms including Twitter, Facebook, and Instagram were followed to get social feelings on affected communities in addition to zonal and official announcements of evacuation and road closure or provision of safety measures. Twitter, Facebook, and other similar sites emerged as good sources of information where people came forward with their accounts and experiences, real-time updates regarding fire incidence and situations prevailing in a particular region were observed, and other details. Civil contingencies also employed the Facebook platform to pass information directly to the public about the areas that are under evacuation zones, the hotspots prone to fire, and the available shelters. This one-way communication enabled the emergency services to provide feedback on the areas that required help from the public and the public received feedback from the emergency services on how to protect themselves from the disaster.

5.3.3. Impact on Response and Recovery

A large number of people and companies have to be coordinated in efforts to put the fire out and safeguard the areas that the fire has reached. With the help of real-time data fire agencies like the New South Wales Rural Fire Service (NSW RFS) and the Country Fire Authority (CFA) were able to identify where fires were likely to intensify and where more resources had to be deployed. For instance, real-time fire models helped to evacuate aircraft, crews, and water in a timely manner to the regions that faced high risk. But it also significantly contributed to the post-disaster relief processes as well, due to utilizing data. Aerial photographs were employed in evaluating the effects of the fires meaning that for the first time, visual signs pointing to the losses experienced in some regions were noticed. Such images were useful to relevant ministries and search and rescue operations to determine where to provide aid and rebuild. As a result of identifying which areas were most affected, they were in a position to dual address certain needs, such as food, water, medical needs, and shelter, to the areas that required the most of it.

5.3.4. Lessons Learned and Technological Advancements

Some of the lessons learned in using real-time data during the Australian bushfires include the following. Response to disasters can be very effective and much more efficient, especially given that decision-making in disasters has to be made in real-time. The capability to detect conditions while they progress enables predetermining the migration of natural disasters and distributing assets in the most appropriate ways. It is, therefore, important that departments and responders involved in disaster management share up-to-date information. Preliminary data collected by satellite agencies, meteorological services, fire departments, and emergency relief organizations were pooled together and fed into a system that created a unified point of contact. An added focus of this new investment was the necessity to constantly update technology systems following the increased importance of real-time data during the bushfires. Governments and agencies are now more aware of the necessity to provide funding for such satellites for the future, and unmanned aerial systems, and also enhancing the machine learning algorithms and other artificial intelligence-based models that help in future disaster response. Using the control of the social media sources, it was found that real-time data is not necessarily only technical data. The process of active listening, involving the concerns of the public together with the use of the social media platform, helped agencies to enhance their ability to get information to the relevant people. This also pointed out a problem of giving the public adequate and timely information to avoid unnecessary scares and also make people or the public undertake adequate precautions to ensure that they are not affected.

New and lasting demands for real-time analyses are driving governments and organizations involved in the management of emergencies to develop various machine learning solutions, new satellite observation systems, and communication tools. With climate change making natural disasters more frequent and severe, the efficacy of real-time data collection, analysis, and usage is set to become even more important in the future, as it will help reduce death tolls and prevent losses and damage. It was evident, especially in the Australian bushfires, that technology and data are weapons of mass destruction in a battle against disasters, but there is still much to learn and adapt, even as the nation seeks the best way of fighting calamities.

6. Future Directions and Innovations

Based on the growth in technological innovation, several innovations are likely to improve the indication of real-time data in disaster management. Some of these technologies are artificial intelligence, machine learning, the Internet of Things (IoT), and blockchain. Real-time analysis of data in disaster management can very much benefit from artificial intelligence and machine learning. Aspects such as historical data and information derived from real-time can be used by the machine learning algorithms to distinguish between actual disasters and those that are Inevitable. For instance, it can predict severe weather conditions by analyzing meteorological data provided, so preventive steps can be taken. Additionally, resource allocation can be improved by using machine learning and factoring previous response efforts in order to find better solutions.

The IoT allows data to be gathered from different sources in real-time, that are very useful to disaster management systems. In its active form, IoT devices can measure environmental conditions, accountability of resources, and examine the integrity of infrastructure in real-time. Real-time data processing can be increased by edge computing, which provides data processing at the data source rather than at every out-of-network information center. It makes it possible to make decisions much faster during incidents and enhance response efforts. Disaster management can benefit from blockchain technology in increasing the efficiency of managing data security. Blockchain can also make real-time data accurate and reliable since it offers maximum decentralization and minimal possibility of alteration to data transactions. Altogether, this technology can be especially useful when dealing with data from different sources, improving the integration of related agencies and organizations. In the same way, using blockchain can help increase transparency in the distribution of resources and enhance the efficiency and accountability of disaster response agencies.

Based on the research findings, the following policy recommendations can be made with regard to the use of real-time data for disaster management. These include:

1. *Investing in technology and infrastructure*: Authorities and organizations should direct their resources to technology and the improvement of infrastructure to improve the capabilities of real-time data analysis. This is achieved through labeling, evaluation, and enhancement of data collection structures, internet connectivity, and local organizations, respectively.
2. *Establishing standardized protocols*: Better practice, and increased use of standardized protocols during data collection, data sharing, and analysis have benefits for increased agency and organizational cooperation. Effective disaster response efforts will be boosted by frameworks for the integration of data.
3. *Enhancing training and capacity building*: It is recommended that various training programs should be conducted with the view of improving the personnel who handle the disaster management processes. This entails orientation on the use of data analysis tools, decision-making tools, and related policies and precautions of data security and privacy.
4. *Promoting community engagement*: People can also be used in disaster preparedness and response to improve the use of "real-time" data. Consciousness-raising efforts in the community can influence the extent to which data is used to advance proactive disaster risk measures.
5. *Fostering research and innovation*: Promoting Research and Technological Development (RTD) in real-time data analysis can make different stakeholders produce new and efficient tools and technologies to strengthen the field of disaster management. Increased synergy between college and academia, government, and private organizations may lead to better developments in this area.

7. Conclusion

Living in times when disasters are not only more frequent, but if we decide to consider the integration of real-time data analysis into frameworks of disaster management as beneficial, then we must say it is an essential step. In this chapter, the reader has witnessed the far-reaching possibilities of real-time data integration for EWS, resource management, and post-disaster recovery. With the help of data acquired from different sources, including satellite images, sensors, social media, and IoT devices, it is possible for stakeholders to get a better view of disaster behavior and improve their responses. Time-sensitive information is said to be crucial; it forms the bedrock of any decision-making process that emergency responders are likely to undertake. That is, such knowledge as the identification of hazardous meteorological phenomena with the help of processing enables timely evacuation and the use of protective measures, and prevents many casualties and losses. In addition, real-time data analysis helps to automate the assessments of situational awareness, which can help the disaster management agencies better allocate their assets in a crisis. Nevertheless, the transition toward rendering real-time data analysis optimally can be a challenging path. Concerns about data quality, ownership, and sharing remain and should be resolved in order to optimize conditions for the use of data in decision processes. Thirdly, the ethical practices regarding the collection and analysis of data, especially personal data posted on social media and other platforms, require more attention and elaborate policies to support them. In order to address these issues, there is a need to work together with other stakeholders, especially the government, non-profit organizations, and business organizations. Standard operating procedures for sharing data must be set, and technical platforms should be improved to support the improved organization of work and better handling of catastrophes. Other capacity-building activities that will be required will include developing training programs that provide knowledge to disaster management personnel on the various data analysis methodologies. Thus, real-time data processing and analysis provide important benefits for improving disaster prevention, occurring rate reduction, and disaster relief. If communities and organizations are to develop and enhance their coping capacity for an unpredictable future involving climate change and more frequent disasters, then understanding and incorporating technology used in data analysis will be critical. Further studies with a focus on the subject, as well as ambitious policy-making and effective community involvement, can help design a future that is more flexible and adaptive in disaster management. Finally, though, the efficient use of real-time information enables not only one's efficient response to disasters but also the gradual rebuilding of societies and supportive environments in the long run.

References

Ahmed, I., & Ledger, K. (2023). Lessons from the 2019/2020 'Black Summer Bushfires' in Australia. *International Journal of Disaster Risk Reduction*, *96*, 103947.

Akhyar, A., Zulkifley, M. A., Lee, J., Song, T., Han, J., Cho, C., Hyun, S., Son, Y., & Hong, B. W. (2024). Deep artificial intelligence applications for natural disaster management systems: A methodological review. *Ecological Indicators*, *163*, 112067.

Ausat, A. M. A. (2023). The role of social media in shaping public opinion and its influence on economic decisions. *Technology and Society Perspectives (TACIT)*, *1*(1), 35–44.

Bania, A., Iatrellis, O., Samaras, N., & Panagiotakopoulos, T. (2024). FiReS: A semantic model for advanced querying and prediction analysis for first responders in post-disaster response plans. *International Journal of Disaster Risk Reduction*, *109*, 104592.

Cao, Y., Xu, C., Aziz, N. M., & Kamaruzzaman, S. N. (2023). BIM–GIS integrated utilization in urban disaster management: The contributions, challenges, and future directions. *Remote Sensing*, *15*(5), 1331.

Cicek, D., & Kantarci, B. (2023). Use of mobile crowdsensing in disaster management: A systematic review, challenges, and open issues. *Sensors*, *23*(3), 1699.

Conboy, K., Mikalef, P., Dennehy, D., & Krogstie, J. (2020). Using business analytics to enhance dynamic capabilities in operations research: A case analysis and research agenda. *European Journal of Operational Research*, *281*(3), 656–672.

Conges, A., Breard, L., Patruno, W., Ouro-Sao, A., Salatge, N., Fertier, A., Lauras, M., Graham, J., & Benaben, F. (2023). Situational awareness and decision-making in a crisis situation: A crisis management cell in virtual reality. *International Journal of Disaster Risk Reduction*, *97*, 104002.

Damaševičius, R., Bacanin, N., & Misra, S. (2023). From sensors to safety: Internet of emergency services (IoES) for emergency response and disaster management. *Journal of Sensor and Actuator Networks*, *12*(3), 41.

Dash, B. P., & Dixit, V. (2024). Disaster supply chain with information and digital technology integrated in its institutional framework. *International Journal of Production Research*, *62*(8), 3003–3022.

Deane, V. L. (2023). A five-year case study analysis of USAID local governance programming and public investment spending in post-earthquake Haiti. *World Development Perspectives*, *32*, 100546.

Galera-Zarco, C., & Floros, G. (2024). A deep learning approach to improve built asset operations and disaster management in critical events: An integrative simulation model for quicker decision making. *Annals of Operations Research*, *339*(1), 573–612.

Gershon, R. R., Muska, M. A., Zhi, Q., & Kraus, L. E. (2021). Are local offices of emergency management prepared for people with disabilities? Results from the FEMA Region 9 Survey. *Journal of Emergency Management*, *19*(1), 7–20.

Guerrero Granados, B., Quintero M. C. G., & Núñez, C. V. (2024). Improved genetic algorithm approach for coordinating decision-making in technological disaster management. *Neural Computing and Applications*, *36*(9), 4503–4521.

Guo, Y., Song, Y., & Zhang, M. (2025). Value realization of intelligent emergency management: Research framework from technology enabling to value creation. *Data Science and Management*, *8*(1), 11–22.

Harper, A., Mustafee, N., & Pitt, M. (2023). Increasing situation awareness in healthcare through real-time simulation. *Journal of the Operational Research Society*, *74*(11), 2339–2349.

Ijaz, H., Ahmad, R., Ahmed, R., Ahmed, W., Kai, Y., & Jun, W. (2023). A UAV-assisted edge framework for real-time disaster management. *IEEE Transactions on Geoscience and Remote Sensing*, *61*, 1–13.

Kamil, N. M. F. N. M., Razak, K. A., Yatim, F. M., & Hidzir, A. H. (2021, February). GIS-based crisis response system for electric distribution utility: A case study of COVID-19 pandemic in Malaysia. *IOP Conference Series: Materials Science and Engineering*, *1051*(1), 012046.

Khan, S. M., Shafi, I., Butt, W. H., Diez, I. D. L. T., Flores, M. A. L., Galán, J. C., & Ashraf, I. (2023). A systematic review of disaster management systems: Approaches, challenges, and future directions. *Land*, *12*(8), 1514.

Kondraganti, A., Narayanamurthy, G., & Sharifi, H. (2024). A systematic literature review on the use of big data analytics in humanitarian and disaster operations. *Annals of Operations Research*, *335*(3), 1015–1052.

Krichen, M., Abdalzaher, M. S., Elwekeil, M., & Fouda, M. M. (2024). Managing natural disasters: An analysis of technological advancements, opportunities, and challenges. *Internet of Things and Cyber-Physical Systems*, *4*, 99–109.

Linardos, V., Drakaki, M., Tzionas, P., & Karnavas, Y. L. (2022). Machine learning in disaster management: Recent developments in methods and applications. *Machine Learning and Knowledge Extraction*, *4*(2), 446–473.

Margus, C., Hertelendy, A., Tao, Y., Coltey, E., Chen, S. C., Luis, S., Shyu, M. L., & Ciottone, G. R. (2023). United States Federal Emergency Management Agency regional clustering by disaster exposure: A new paradigm for disaster response. *Natural Hazards*, *116*(3), 3427–3445.

Mellish, S., Ryan, J. C., & Litchfield, C. A. (2024). Short-term psychological outcomes of Australia's 2019/20 bushfire season. *Psychological Trauma: Theory, Research, Practice, and Policy*, *16*(2), 292.

Moghadas, M., Fekete, A., Rajabifard, A., & Kötter, T. (2023). The wisdom of crowds for improved disaster resilience: A near-real-time analysis of crowdsourced social media data on the 2021 flood in Germany. *GeoJournal*, *88*(4), 4215–4241.

Nova, K. (2023). AI-enabled water management systems: An analysis of system components and interdependencies for water conservation. *Eigenpub Review of Science and Technology*, *7*(1), 105–124.

Oktari, R. S., Munadi, K., Idroes, R., & Sofyan, H. (2020). Knowledge management practices in disaster management: Systematic review. *International Journal of Disaster Risk Reduction*, *51*, 101881.

Papatheodorou, K., Theodoulidis, N., Klimis, N., Zulfikar, C., Vintila, D., Cardanet, V., Kirtas, E., Toma-Danila, D., Margaris, B., Fahjan, Y., & Panagopoulos, G. (2023). Rapid earthquake damage assessment and education to improve earthquake response efficiency and community resilience. *Sustainability*, *15*(24), 16603.

Pognon, M. C., Quintero, A., & Pierre, S. (2024). *Adaptive priority scheduling of Internet of things data for disaster management in smart cities*. IEEE Access.

Rakhonde, G. Y., Ahale, S., Reddy, N. K., Purushotham, P., & Deshkar, A. (2024). Big data analytics for improved weather forecasting and disaster management. In K. Pandey, N. L. Kushwaha, C. B. Pande, K. G. Singh (Eds.), *Artificial intelligence and smart agriculture: Technology and applications* (pp. 175–192). Springer Nature Singapore.

Samani, S., Vadiati, M., Nejatijahromi, Z., Etebari, B., & Kisi, O. (2023). Groundwater level response identification by hybrid wavelet–machine learning conjunction models using meteorological data. *Environmental Science and Pollution Research*, *30*(9), 22863–22884.

Sathianarayanan, M., Hsu, P. H., & Chang, C. C. (2024). Extracting disaster location identification from social media images using deep learning. *International Journal of Disaster Risk Reduction*, *104*, 104352.

Shani-Kadmiel, S., Averbuch, G., Smets, P., Assink, J., & Evers, L. (2021). The 2010 Haiti earthquake revisited: An acoustic intensity map from remote atmospheric infrasound observations. *Earth and Planetary Science Letters*, *560*, 116795.

Smith, G., & Vila, O. (2020). A national evaluation of state and territory roles in hazard mitigation: Building local capacity to implement FEMA hazard mitigation assistance grants. *Sustainability*, *12*(23), 10013.

Tarei, P. K., Gumte, K. M., Patnaik, J., & Oktari, R. S. (2024). Analysing barriers to humanitarian logistics for distributing relief aid in pre- and post-disaster situations. *International Journal of Disaster Risk Reduction*, *104*, 104388.

ten Brink, U., Wei, Y., Fan, W., Granja-Bruña, J. L., & Miller, N. (2020). Mysterious tsunami in the Caribbean Sea following the 2010 Haiti earthquake possibly generated by dynamically triggered early aftershocks. *Earth and Planetary Science Letters*, *540*, 116269.

Tomaszewski, B. (2020). *Geographic information systems (GIS) for disaster management*. Routledge.

Treiblmaier, H., & Rejeb, A. (2023). Exploring blockchain for disaster prevention and relief: A comprehensive framework based on industry case studies. *Journal of Business Logistics*, *44*(4), 550–582.

Turk, F. J., Rohaly, G. D., Hawkins, J. E. F. F., Smith, E. A., Marzano, F. S., Mugnai, A., & Levizzani, V. (2023). Meteorological applications of precipitation estimation from combined SSM/I, TRMM and infrared geostationary satellite data. In P. Pampaloni & S. Paloscia (Eds.), *Microwave radiometry and remote sensing of the Earth's surface and atmosphere* (pp. 353–363). CRC Press.

Tzavella, K., Skopeliti, A., & Fekete, A. (2024). Volunteered geographic information use in crisis, emergency and disaster management: A scoping review and a web atlas. *Geo-Spatial Information Science*, *27*(2), 423–454.

Xu, C., & Xue, Z. (2024). Applications and challenges of artificial intelligence in the field of disaster prevention, reduction, and relief. *Natural Hazards Research* *4*(1), 169–172.

Zhou, B., Zhang, X., Wan, X., Liu, T., Liu, Y., Huang, H., & Chen, J. (2024). Development and application of a novel tsunami monitoring system based on submerged mooring. *Sensors*, *24*(18), 6048.

Chapter 3

Providing an Intelligent Sustainable Solution for Electricity Management

Sudakshina Dasgupta[a], Tamal Mondal[b], Indrajit Bhattacharya[c] and Tanmoy Paul[d]

[a]*Department of IT, Government College of Engineering and Textile Technology Serampore, Maulana Abul Kalam Azad University of Technology, West Bengal, India*
[b]*Symbiosis Centre for Information Technology, Symbiosis International (Deemed University), Pune, India*
[c]*Department of Computer Applications, Kalyani Government Engineering College, Maulana Abul Kalam Azad University of Technology, West Bengal, India*
[d]*Department of IT, Government College of Engineering and Textile Technology, Maulana Abul Kalam Azad University of Technology, West Bengal, India*

Abstract

The climbing in population displacement in urban sectors has accelerated the adaptation of smart city policies across developing regions. Utilization of clean and sustainable energy is of utmost importance such as the demands of the entities can be met without any resource constraints. The management of energy in terms of electricity is therefore crucial to human livelihood. However, the present management process has flaws, leads to inefficiencies, and fraudulent activities, which further result in economic loss and resource wastage. To address such issues, this chapter proposes an intelligent Internet of Things (IoT) framework that uses tools like microcontrollers and sensors to minimize the need for human involvement, enhancing the system's transparency and reliability. With such a consumer-friendly and secure system, live meter readings, automatic power cuts, and the detection of power theft, accidental situations can be performed effectively. The absence of wiring not only reduces installation costs but also minimizes the likelihood of faults. The integration of technologies such as IoT and artificial intelligence (AI) further improves reliability and

Harnessing the Potential of Artificial Intelligence to Promote Environmental Sustainability, 35–53

doi:10.1108/978-1-83662-996-220251003

consumer service. This proposed system can be a real game-changer that minimizes the involvement of intermediaries, promoting transparency and streamlining electricity management.

Keywords: Internet of Things; wireless meter reading; track malpractice; short-circuit prevention; artificial intelligence; machine learning

1. Introduction

Electricity has become an indispensable aspect of human existence, permeating every facet of modern life, from household gadgets to industrial machinery. There have been researches which are going on to effectively utilize the energy consumptions for improving energy efficacy and reducing the loss which takes place due to several malpractices like electricity theft, unwillingness to pay bills within deadlines, and many more (Aloul et al., 2012). The service provider incurs huge losses due to such activities which further creates a lot of challenges regarding the survival of company. Through literature, it is evident that there are two types of losses that the company would incur, that is, technical and nontechnical loss (Parvin et al., 2020). Technical loss takes place while transmitting energy from generator to the consumers and nontechnical losses include: false meter reading, theft, wrong billing, and many more. In this digital age, manual billing systems are also a riddled with such risk of malpractice (Al-Ali et al., 2017; Aloul et al., 2012; Hasan et al., 2022; Parvin et al., 2020). Several researchers in recent past have tried to address these nontechnical challenges and also proposed solutions using cutting edge tools and technologies (discussed in detail in Section 3). Most of them have proposed the solutions like recognizing consumption patterns of spurious consumers (Aloul et al., 2012), automatic feature extraction models for fraud consumer detection (Dangar & Joshi, 2014; Jain et al., 2016), introducing smart meter readings to enhance remote monitoring (Sardar & Sanaullah, 2015), and incentive awards (Tarannu et al., 2017). Although, the design of an end-to-end architecture providing solutions for minimizing losses and maximizing efficient energy utilization still be an issue. For addressing such gap, this chapter proposes a smart wireless electricity management system using IoT (Al-Ali et al., 2017; Tastan et al., 2019) and machine learning (ML) (Areekkara et al., 2021; Roesch et al., 2020). The system is designed to automate meter reading procedures by wirelessly collecting power consumption data from residential households. The broad objective of this chapter is to provide a robust and secure solution to eradicate the risk of malpractice, while also offering a secure payment method that allows subscribers to pay their bills anytime, anywhere by simply recognizing their face via any mobile device with a camera. By employing a centralized server (Sulthana et al., 2020), live power readings of every subscriber can be monitored and displayed, enabling the power supply center and subscribers to track the consumption. This chapter aims to create an entirely automated system that reduces human interaction (Kirmani et al., 2022) to a bare minimum. In case of delayed payments, the system can promptly terminate or establish the power supply, without any human intervention, thus ensuring swift action and accountability. Moreover, the system is designed to prevent electricity theft and detect hazards such as short circuits, ensuring both physical and digital safety (Smith, 2004). Further, to address consumer queries, the system will feature an all-time chatbot accessible via the official website, maintaining the same features as a regular electric meter and billing system, while also offering advanced features.

Moreover, the motivation behind the work is to make a paradigm shift from the conventional manual system (Chandrasekar & Sangeetha, 2014; Islam & Bhuiyan, 2017), which is fraught with numerous drawbacks, including economic losses, wastage of paper, and more, to an online smart billing system. The online smart system boasts of several unique features that set it apart from the manual system. For instance, subscribers can view live power supply on the meter box (Newell & Duffy, 2019), ensuring accurate payment and clear payment details for both the subscriber and the supply center. The wireless system (Nguyen et al., 2010) eliminates wiring costs, and subscribers can monitor live readings in real-time (Othman & Zakaria, 2020). The system can manage all aspects of billing, including adding new subscribers and storing the database on the server. The prime contributions of this chapter are the following:

- Tracking of live meter reading and corresponding bill amount using a mobile application, anytime and anywhere.
- Partial bill payment is possible.
- Crystal-clear evidence of meter reading, payable amount, and payment details are provided to both the user and the supplier.
- Automatic power cut in case of an emergency like fire, theft, or nonpayment of bills.
- Interact with customer service using a 24×7 chatbot.
- Secure payment using two-factor authentication using an ML-based face recognition system.

2. Sustainability in Energy Management and Proposed Approach

The rapid escalation of urbanization process and population in 20th century have given rise to the reconsideration of urban plans and policies for enhancement of modernization of cities in such a way that it should be resilient and sustainable for years to come. Such significant increase in population and their displacement into urban sectors would result in imbalanced energy consumption. It is evident from studies (Ahmed et al., 2023; Abu-Rayash & Dincer, 2021) that around 47% of global energy are being consumed by residential buildings and sectors. Besides, the rapid urbanization demands huge energies which is also an utmost concern (Abu-Rayash & Dincer, 2021). Hence, the development of new tools and technologies are becoming the interest points for energy saving. As a significant bit of "Smart City," "Smart Home" has become the new trend of residential sectors where the

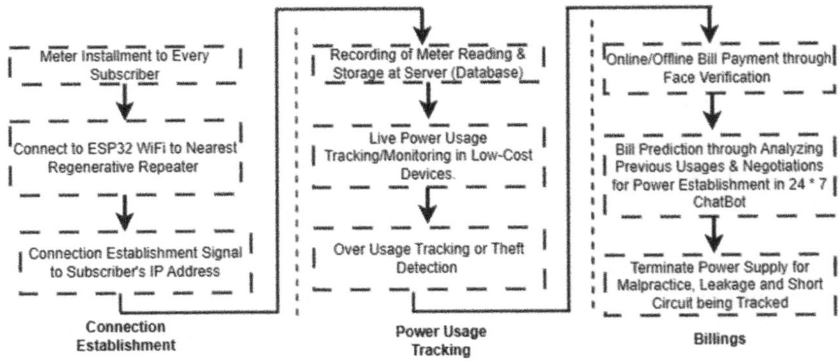

Fig. 3.1. Workflow of the Proposed System.

home appliances are integrated through industry 4.0 technologies like Information and communications technology (ICT), IoT, and AI (Abu-Rayash & Dincer, 2021). Utilization of such technologies into products, that is, appliances, load monitoring reduced wastage of energy resources like power and electricity and augmented the need for a sustainable energy utilization and management (Fig. 3.1).

In the proposed work, we have tried to contribute to this sustainable development through introducing a smart electricity management application for residential sectors that would be beneficial for both subscribers and service providers. The objective of the proposed system is to provide a cost-effective, compact, secure, and sustainable smart electricity management system that eliminates intermediaries, prevents malpractice, and ensures authenticity. The system includes key features such as live meter reading, automated power cuts for non-payment, excessive power consumption, or short circuits, and online and offline billing and meter reading for both consumers' and subscribers' convenience. With AI- and ML-based face recognition and sensor-based IoT systems, the system aims to ensure maximum security at every step, including subscriber registration and online payment. The 24×7 chatbot customer service and reporting feature allows subscribers to request reconnection of the power supply from a remote server without physical visits. By providing crystal clear evidence of meter reading and transaction records, the system enhances transparency and reduces corruption, which further ensures minimum resource loss and reduces inefficient power utilization. Thus, the ultimate objective of the proposed system is to make electricity management more accessible, secure, and hassle-free for all, even for people with busy schedules or no technical knowledge.

3. Literature Study and Current Approach

In this section, the state-of-the-art technologies developed for effective energy management in terms of electricity are discussed along with the challenges associated to them. Most of these contemporary techniques have utilized the IoT hardware devices like Arduino, Raspberry Pi, etc., application protocol stacks like Blynk and many more, communication protocols like internet, Global System for Mobile Communications (GSM), etc., storage or cloud and data mining and AI tools to implement smart electricity management services. The authors in Othman and Zakaria (2020) conducted extensive research on wireless monitoring systems using the Blynk application, which allows access to the ESP32 microcontroller via the internet. The authors have also highlighted the advantages of this system, including the ability to measure power consumption from anywhere using a mobile device through the Blynk application. This results in more efficient energy monitoring. However, the system functioning should be cross-platform, means that the meter readings should be detected through low-cost devices like Personal Computers (PCs), laptops or smartphones. Besides, the poor internet connectivity might not be able to provide accurate meter readings. The authors in Maity and Das (2011) conducted research on online billing system and presented a software solution. The advantage of this research is that the system is designed for three-phase measurement, enabling the measurement of values from all three phases simultaneously. However, proper authentication process should be there to avoid any intrusion. The authors in Cahyono et al. (2019) proposed a digitized solution for improving customer service in the electricity sector. The advantage of this research is the implementation of AI for enhancing customer service. However, smart detection of electricity theft and incorporating advanced sensor-based safety protocols for electricity transmission are also of utmost importance. A microcontroller-based system that enables control of home appliances using Arduino and IoT devices has been designed in Deny et al. (2021). However, the implementation safety features would be required to prevent any short circuit or leakage which is essential for ensuring safety. The authors in Choi et al. (2018) propose a system that eliminates the need for man power by automating meter readings and bill generation, thereby reducing the flaws that contribute to energy-related corruption. The system sends data to the Blynk cloud for further processing and storage, allowing consumers to access real-time monitoring and record-keeping from anywhere in the world through the user-friendly Blynk app. Storing the data in a cloud server ensures greater security. One of the future works proposed was to monitor power theft and meter tampering, which can be easily accomplished through real-time notifications. Personal load monitoring can enhance transparency between the electricity board and the consumer, reducing corruption. Additionally, more detection systems, such as those for leakage, current, low voltage, and high voltage, can be added to the system for safety purposes. The main objective is to achieve efficient power management by automating home appliances through IoT using the internet, and to provide system security by utilizing sensors such as Passive Infrared (PIR), gas sensor, temperature sensors, and a camera module. The android application serves as the user interface through which devices can be monitored and controlled anytime and anywhere, and a separate username and password are provided for log into ensure security. However, the security system proposed in the chapter has limitations and may not be completely reliable. Therefore, further development is required to enhance the security system and ensure fool-proof protection of the system (Alahakoon & Yu, 2015) proposed various techniques for implementing smart electric meter technology in a smart grid-based management system are proposed. The authors also present potential solutions for measuring power transfer from diverse sources such as photovoltaic (PV) panels, batteries, wind and solar, and plug-in hybrid electric vehicles (PHEVs). However, advanced data authenticity features and practical implementations such as employing specific types of highly accurate sensors are required to specific applications. The authors in Mishra et al. (2018) introduced an IoT powered smart energy management system (EMS) which implements Arduino and Raspberry Pi to transfer the analog meter data to the webpage and smart meter app using the ThingSpeak Application Programming Interface (API) to estimate power consumption in small office or houses. However, the requirement for two microcontrollers or microprocessors (Arduino and Raspberry Pi) to measure the wattage value, which makes it expensive for widespread use. Additionally, the lack of two-factor authentication, which leaves the data vulnerable to prospective cyberattacks in the event that the ThingSpeak server is compromised. Nelson et al. (2021) proposed an IoT-based smart energy meter system that utilizes ML to accurately measure energy consumption. The system also automates the bill data entry process, reducing the need for manual effort. However, there are potential security concerns associated with the use of IoT-based devices, such as smart energy meters, as they are connected to the internet and could be vulnerable to cyberattacks. Hadi et al. (2022) proposed a ML-based bill prediction system that utilizes a smart energy metering system for efficient utility management. The system allows users to monitor their energy consumption and make decisions based on energy conservation measures by providing bill predictions. However, the use of IoT-based devices and software platforms like If This Then That (IFTTT; Xianghang et al., 2017) could pose security risks, and the accuracy of the system could be affected by external factors such as power outages or system faults.

3.1. Toward a Sustainable Solution

So far it can be observed from above studies that most of the researchers have utilized ICT-based services, IoT devices, AI, and data mining techniques for automating the functionalities of electricity management. However, in terms of meeting the requirements of a sustainable solution, the technologies proposed should invite the features, that is, safety, security, accuracy, and ease of access. Most of the techniques discussed above, provides some of those sustainability measures (e.g., Cahyono et al., 2019; Hadi et al., 2022; Maity & Das, 2011), the solutions handle the features, that is, automatic reading on mobile devices and online billing but the factors like security, authenticity, and cross platform access still not addressed. Besides (Choi et al., 2018; Mishra et al., 2018; Xianghang et al., 2017), in the factors like detection of theft or over usage, cyberattacks, system faults were nonexistent. Note, an intelligent solution to become sustainable, one should incorporate all such factors as a whole to foster the efficient utilization of energy resource, that is, electricity and minimize the loss to further augment toward the resource reservation. Hence, along with the incorporation of advanced tools and technologies, one should also consider the sustainability in the solutions proposed. Now, the proposed smart electricity management system offers a wide range of unique characteristics such as live meter reading capability, providing real-time updates on electricity consumption, allowing users to monitor their usage and plan accordingly. Besides, with the wireless communication, the system eliminates the need for cumbersome wiring, making it easy to install and use that further minimizes cost. In addition, it also incorporates over current detection mechanisms to track malpractice and prevent short-circuits, ensuring digital safety. The system is also designed to be user-friendly, offering online and offline billing and meter reading, making it accessible to everyone, including those with no technical knowledge. The chatbot customer service and reporting feature enables seamless communication between users and the provider. Overall, this system provides a comprehensive and advanced solution that addresses the challenges of present electricity management system, offering an innovative and reliable way to manage electricity consumption while ensuring transparency and security.

4. Proposed Solution for Electricity Management

The workflow of the proposed solution has been depicted in Fig. 3.1. The first step is to install a meter for each consumer, which will be connected to a regenerative Wi-Fi repeater. This repeater will transmit the data from each meter to the server via a series of repeaters connected together. The meter reading for each second is stored in database server for every consumer. Through such a storage, the customers will be notified about their bills via online or offline methods. If payment is not received within due date, power supply will be automatically terminated until the bill is paid. To establish the power termination, the signal can be sent from the database server through the regenerative repeater. Through such kind of setup, any issues or malpractices such as electricity theft, short-circuit prevention, automatic power supply, or termination for gas leakage and fire smoke detection on the customer's side can be implemented through different sensors, which are discussed later in detail in this section. Besides, consumers can pay bills online or offline at any time within the month and must register through a face verification. They can also track their live meter reading at any time with mobile devices like smartphones, tabs, etc. The system also includes a display that shows live power consumption to increase authenticity, and consumers can contact the supply center via 24×7 chatbot, offline or online for any enquiries, or negotiations regarding bill payment.

4.1. Hardware and Connection

In this system, the ESP32 microcontroller is used, which is from the NodeMCU open-source platform, manufactured by Espressif Systems. This microcontroller has a large number of analog-to-digital converter (ADC) pins, making it ideal for the proposed application. The ESP32-WROOM-32 variant is chosen for its affordability and suitability for the system. To measure the wattage value, the microcontroller is interfaced with voltage and current sensors. The ZMPT-101B voltage sensor is used to measure voltage, and the SCT-013-0303 current sensor is used to measure current. Both sensors are designed to operate with an AC supply only and have an accuracy rate of over 95%. The ZMPT-101B voltage sensor uses a small-sized voltage transformer to transform voltage from 0 to 1,000 V in the primary winding, which is connected to the main supply measuring terminals. In the secondary winding, there is a burden resistance that reduces the voltage correspondingly. By calculating the analog data, the voltage can be measured. This sensor needs to be connected to any of the ADC pins of the ESP32 and requires a 5 V power supply from the ESP32. The SCT-013-030 current sensor, also known as a split core transformer, can measure up to 30 amps of current. To interface with this sensor, a wire needs to be passed through it, and the generated magnetic flux from the wire induces a corresponding voltage in the split core of the transformer. An inbuilt burden resistance is integrated, and to interface with the ESP32, a voltage divider circuit of 10–400 kΩ needs to be connected to the ADC pin of the microcontroller. To establish and terminate the power supply, a 5V relay module is connected in series with the power supply. This module operates at 3.75–6 V DC, which can be provided by the ESP32 and controlled by General Purpose Input/Output (GPIO) pins. The operating voltage is 250 V AC, and the current usage can range from 10 to 100 amps. A16 row 2 column I2C digital display with driver (PCF8574 IC) is interfaced with the Serial Clock Line (SCL) and Serial Data Line (SDA) pin of the ESP32 to display live meter readings in the meter box. Finally, an MQ2 gas sensor is used to detect excess CO_2, fire, or leakage of Liquefied Petroleum Gas (LPG) (butane), and it is interfaced with an ADC pin of the ESP32 for data acquisition. To power up the ESP32 microcontroller, a 5 V power supply from an Switched-Mode Power Supply (SMPS) is used. The ESP32 has a 5-V output supply. The ZMPT-101B voltage sensor has four terminals, one for Vcc, another for an analog output, and two grounds. We provide 5 V from ESP32 to the Vcc and ground terminals, and the analog output pin is connected to the GPIO34 pin of ESP32.To interface the SCT-013 current sensor, we have to connect it with a voltage divider circuit. Two 17 kΩ resistors are connected in parallel with the 5 V and ground terminals of the ESP32. The SCT current sensor has two terminals and an integrated burden resistance inside it. One terminal of the current sensor is connected to the combined point of two resistances, and the other terminal is connected to GPIO36, which is an ADC terminal of ESP32. The relay also got 5 V and ground from ESP32 and the SMPS, and the operational terminal is connected to the GPIO2 pin of ESP32. The digital display needs to be connected to 5 V and ground of the microcontroller, and to provide I2C communication, we have to connect the SCL and SDA pin with GPIO22 and GPIO21, respectively. The measuring wire should pass through the split core of the SCT current sensor, and the ZMPT voltage sensor input terminals should be connected in parallel with the measuring wires. The relay is connected in series with the total load, which power supply is given from ESP32. A detailed diagram of the connection of sensors and microcontroller is shown in Fig. 3.2.

4.2. Workflow of the Solution

In Fig. 3.3, the current sensor and voltage sensors are utilized to gather raw current and voltage readings, which are then transformed into corresponding

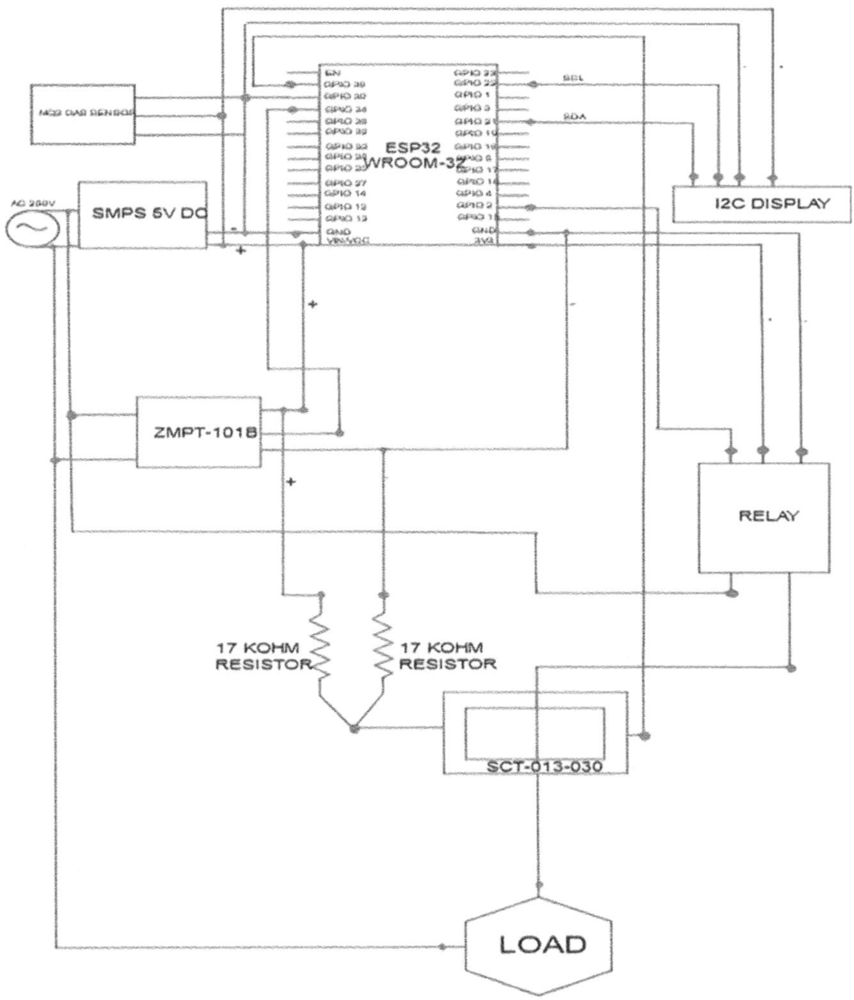

Fig. 3.2. Schematic representation of sensor–microcontroller interfacing.

analog values by the sensors and transmitted to the ESP32 microcontroller. In order to send this data to the server, the ESP32 is connected through a regenerative repeater, which must be installed every 100 m to ensure the vicinity of subscriber's meter. The ESP32 is responsible for multiplying the voltage and current values and sending the resultant string to the server via these repeaters. For identifying instances of over-usage or short-circuits, a predefined wattage value is registered for each subscriber upon their registration to the server. If the microcontroller detects the current value beyond this limit, it will cut off the connection by turning off the relay (Fig. 3.3), which can be reconnected by contacting customer support or manually from the meter (in the case of a short circuit). In the event of a gas leak, the MQ2 gas sensor will detect it and prompt

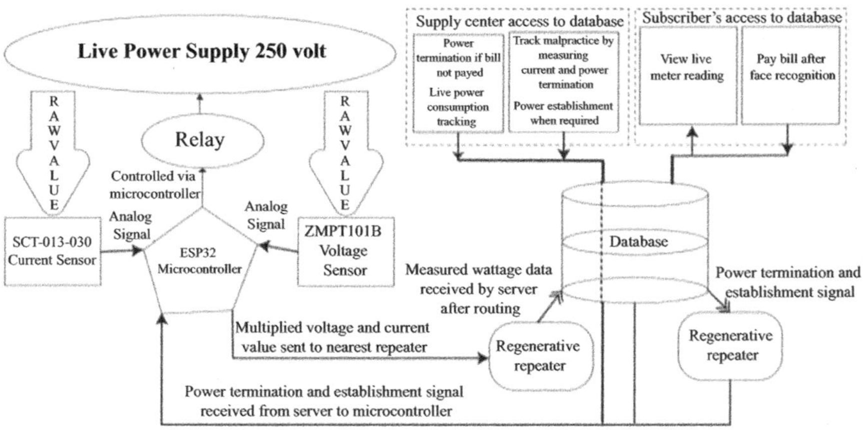

Fig. 3.3. Connection Diagram of Proposed Solution.

the microcontroller to turn-off the relay, preventing any potential fire damage. The relay will remain off until the gas sensor's detection falls below the predefined threshold value.

4.3. Other Application Protocols and Usage

Storing the wattage value for each subscriber every second, an Oracle 6-based database server is used. A script is executed continuously for each subscriber to store the value, which is obtained using the socket library to extract the string value from the microcontroller. A web page has been developed, hosted on a Flask server, where subscribers can log in using their user ID and password to view their bills and real-time meter readings. To display the live meter reading, the electric consumption is added and shown on the web page. This system offers subscribers the flexibility to pay their electricity bills at any time of the month, providing them with a sense of independence and control over their finances. In the event that a subscriber opts to pay their bill in the middle of the month, the system will generate the next bill only after the previous one has been settled. Moreover, in order to ensure optimal security measures, the system requires facial recognition verification during the registration process. The intricate workings of the face verification or recognition systems are explained later in Section 4.6. Further enhancing the customer experience, a 24×7 Natural Language Processing Toolkit (NLTK)-based chatbot has been implemented to assist subscribers with a range of services (Section 4.5). Notably, the chatbot can predict future bills by analyzing previous electricity usage records, thereby allowing customers to plan and budget accordingly. This feature is also detailed further in this section. For addressing the issue of electricity theft and malpractice, each power supply transformer is equipped with a microcontroller-based smart meter in every subscriber's household. The sum of the readings from each individual meter must be equal to the reading from the smart meter installed in the transformer. Any discrepancy between these values may indicate an instance of electricity theft or fraudulent activity, and the necessary measures can be taken accordingly. The server also allows for meter readings to be monitored, and power termination and establishment can be executed from the supply center, enabling swift action to be taken in response to any detected malpractice.

4.4. Connection Protocol

Each smart meter is equipped with two unique IP addresses: one for transmitting the wattage value to the server, and the other for controlling the relay that governs the power supply, both from the server and the customer's end. Through the web interface hosted on Flask, customers can remotely turn their household's power supply on and off by sending the relay turn-on and turn-off signal to the specific IP address associated with their meter. If a customer fails to pay their bill within the specified time frame, they will receive a notification, and if the situation persists, the server can send a signal to the meter's IP address to disconnect the power supply. The power supply can also be restored by sending an on signal to the specific IP address of the meter. This entire smart meter system operates on a decentralized network, where all IP addresses are assigned independently from the mainstream internet. This enables the network to accommodate a vast number of IPv4 addresses, which are individually tracked by the server. By establishing a connection to the internet, the server can monitor all meter readings to regulate power supply anywhere and anytime.

4.5. Utilization of Multilingual Interactive Chatbot

The proposed system is an innovative solution for managing electricity bills and usage. It utilizes a chatbot, which is built using natural language processing (NLP) techniques. The chatbot is designed to interact with subscribers and provide them with information related to their electricity bills and usage. To use the chatbot, subscribers must log in with their ID and password or through face recognition (discussed later). The system reads previous usage data and provides a corresponding prediction to users. Here, periodic electric usage data is stored in a server to predict future bills. Although here we have used simple averaging of past usage values to provide an estimate of the future bill, this method is a simple and effective way to predict future bills, and is commonly used by utilities to provide customers with estimated bills. The proposed chatbot is multilingual and works in three languages, that is, English, Bengali, and Hindi, and stores the user's language preference for future usage. The chatbot is hosted on a webpage that is further hosted on a server and uses the NLTK API for generating randomized results to user queries. Various other features, such as live meter reading and bill payments, can also be performed by utilizing the chatbot. This chatbot feature also makes the system a useful tool for tasks such as retrieving account information, providing billing details, and usage data.

4.6. Facial Recognition for Authentication

The system has adopted a two-factor authentication process. First, the user is required to input their unique user ID and password combination for swift authentication. This initial step provides a basic level of security; however, the system also employs a second factor of authentication to eliminate the risk of unauthorized access and ensure that only authorized users are granted access to the system. This factor of authentication facial detection and matching techniques to authenticate the user's identity. When a customer attempts to log in to the system, they are redirected to anew webpage where the user would be asked for facial verification. Then the current picture showing in device's camera will be matched with one provided during the registration process. After the successful verification of the user's face, the user is redirected to the payment webpage where they can proceed to check usage, pay their bills, and provide queries to the chatbot. This results robust security measures to ensure that only authorized users can access the system, providing an additional layer of security and minimizing the risk of unauthorized access to sensitive user data. This face recognition model has been deployed on the server side, and integrated on the client side to provide a web-based user experience. The captured image is sent to the server using an HTTP request, and the server responds with the predicted identity of the user's face. The facial recognition component of the system utilizes state-of-the-art Deep Face technology (Taigman et al., 2014; Wang & Deng, 2021). Deep Face is a facial recognition system developed by Facebook's AI research (FAIR) team. It was introduced in 2014 and gained attention for its high accuracy in face recognition, outperforming many existing methods such as FaceNet, VGGFace, and OpenFace. Here we have performed a comparative analysis between two techniques, that is, FaceNet and DeepFace API which are crucial for practical applications, especially in the proposed system. Both APIs are already trained with predefined datasets – FaceNet using VGGFace2 and DeepFace using Facebook's internal dataset. To conduct the analysis, 100 images were used. Here, initially, the face detection precision of both APIs was compared. FaceNet performs significantly better than DeepFace in terms of execution time, as shown in Fig. 3.4(a). To plot the results, the average of every 10-image detection time was taken, resulting in a total of 10 results for each model. It is evident that FaceNet's precision for face detection is much better than DeepFace, hence the time taken by FaceNet is much less than that of DeepFace. Next, the accuracy was evaluated by taking one face image and comparing it with another face image. Criteria such as different resolutions, different individuals, and eyeglasses (transparent) were considered since face detection needed to be done remotely from any device with varying individual appearances and camera resolutions. For performing the analysis, 20 face images with glasses and the same person, 20 face images with different people, and transparent glasses, 20 face images with the same person but without glasses, and 40 face images of the same person under different lighting positions and angles were used. Here, all images were tested at varying resolutions, ranging from a minimum of 640 pixels width and 480 pixels height to a maximum of 5,152 pixels width and 3,864 pixels height. As shown in Fig. 3.4(b), DeepFace has better accuracy than FaceNet for face verification between two images. Fig. 3.4(b) also reveals that DeepFace is more accurate than FaceNet, with DeepFace accurately verifying 36 out of 40 images, while FaceNet can only verify 31 images

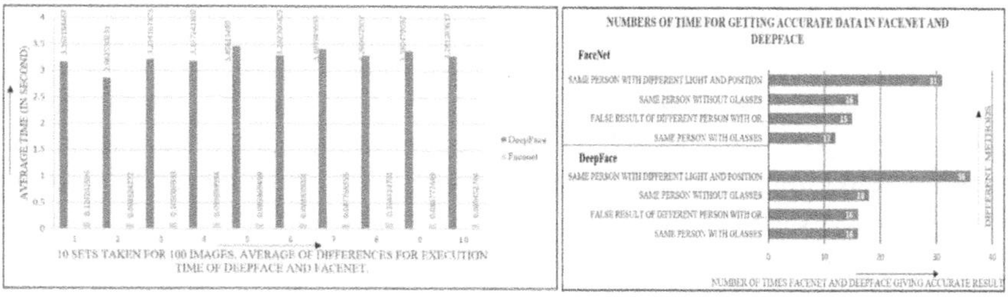

(a) (b)

Fig. 3.4. (a) Comparison of Execution Time for DeepFace and FaceNet. (b) Accuracy of DeepFace and FaceNet Models.

accurately. These results are consistent with the other cases considered, where DeepFace exhibits a superior ability to recognize images under various conditions. For instance, in the second case, DeepFace can accurately recognize 18 out of 20 images of the same person without glasses, while FaceNet can only verify 16 images accurately. Besides, DeepFace performs better than FaceNet in recognizing different persons with or without glasses, as FaceNet has false records of 15 out of 20, while DeepFace has 16 out of 20 false records. Finally, in the last case, when using transparent glasses, DeepFace is also more accurate than FaceNet, as DeepFace verifies 16 out of 20 images accurately, whereas FaceNet can only verify 12 images accurately. However, as depicted in Fig. 3.4(a), the average time taken for every 10 images is approximately 3 s more for DeepFace than that of FaceNet. This suggests that using FaceNet for face verification would result in a significantly shorter verification time, with less processing power required to complete all verification tasks. Here, we have given the importance to the accuracy for our particular application, which involves face recognition as a part of two-factor authentication. Therefore, security is of paramount importance, and any compromise could result in serious consequences. Therefore, in our application, accuracy takes priority over computational cost or time consumption, and we have chosen the DeepFace API, which provides the highest accuracy for our specific needs.

4.7. Data Storage and Analysis

In order to maintain a comprehensive database of user information, the proposed system has opted to use Oracle as the database management system for efficient storage and retrieval of personal data. Additionally, for ensuring secure access to the system, the database involves storing individual face data for the facial verification. Such images are stored in the server repository along with the subscriber's unique ID. Hence, data storage and structure are highly comprehensive, easily accessible and allowing for effective retrieval of user information at times. It's also preventing Oracle injection attacks which is an intricate task that requires various techniques to secure an application's database.

4.7.1. Over Usage Tracking and Power Termination

Whenever the electrical load is applied, the corresponding power usage is recorded with a timestamp. For instance, in the sample graph shown in Fig. 3.5, an electric heater with a power of 600 W has been used for testing, and there is an almost constant power draw of 600 W during the first 10 s (shown in Fig. 3.5). Following that, an inductive load in form of a 1,200-W motor has been started in addition to the heater. As is typical with induction motors, the motor drew more power while it starts, leading to a spike in the power usage. However, once it achieved inertia, it drew a consistent amount of power. The electrical meter continuously records the total power usage and stores it in the server for future analysis. The recorded data can be further used to optimize the energy usage and reduce overall energy costs. For ensuring the restriction on over usage by subscribers, a power limit is set in the system. If the limit is exceeded, the power supply will automatically shut down. This feature is demonstrated in Fig. 3.6. The power usage limit in this case is set to 1 KW for testing. The system is designed to provide a warning and notification before the power supply is turned down in practice. During the testing phase, the heating element of 600 W was used for the first 10 s, and the power supply was established during this time. When the 1,200-W inductive motor was started, the power usage exceeded the limit, causing the relay to turn-off and the power supply to be terminated. The reestablish time of the power supply is set to approximately 5 s. Once the power supply is reestablished, the heating element was turned on and drew 600 W of power (Fig. 3.6). Since this was within the allowed power limit, the power supply continued without interruption. This feature is essential for ensuring the reduction of the over-usage rate.

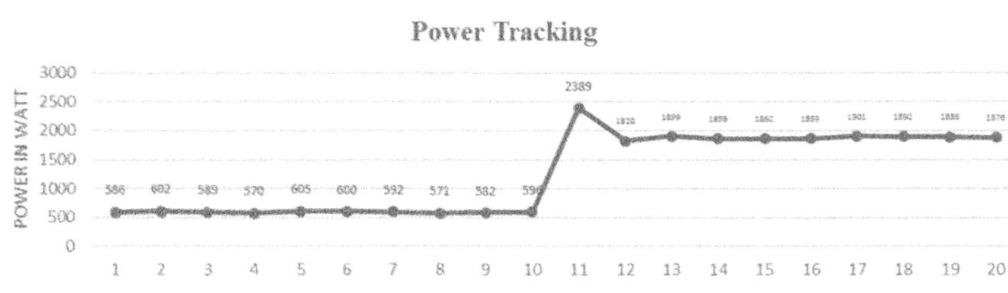

Fig. 3.5. Tracked Power Value in Watt.

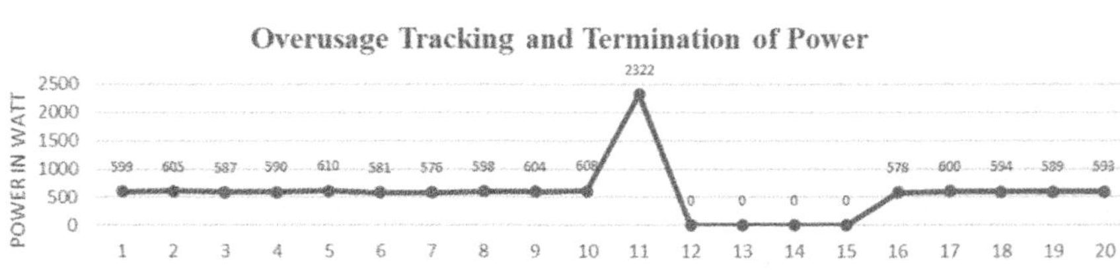

Fig. 3.6. Over-usage Detection with Tracking.

4.7.2. Power Theft Detection and Accuracy

For the detection of power theft, another meter is used alongside the current meter, and a load, that is, a light bulb, has been connected to it. In the initial phase of the testing, the heating element of 600 W is turned on, and both meters measure the same amount of power usage, as shown in Fig. 3.7. After 10 s, the 100-W bulb is turned on, and the first meter measures the value of the heating element, that is, 600 W, whereas the second meter, considered for installation in the transformer, measures the value of both loads. By subtracting these values, the theft power usage can be calculated and tracked down. By comparing the readings taken by the pre-calibrated meter with the readings of the smart meter, it is possible to determine the accuracy. It should be noted that the accuracy of both the voltage and current sensors used in the smart meter is approximately 99%, which is quite impressive. Fig. 3.8 illustrates the comparison between the readings taken from the pre-calibrated meter and the smart meter. For testing, a heating element of 600 W was used for about 10 s. It can be observed that for most of the readings, the accuracy of the smart meter is around 99%. These findings highlight the effectiveness and reliability of the smart meter in accurately measuring power usage.

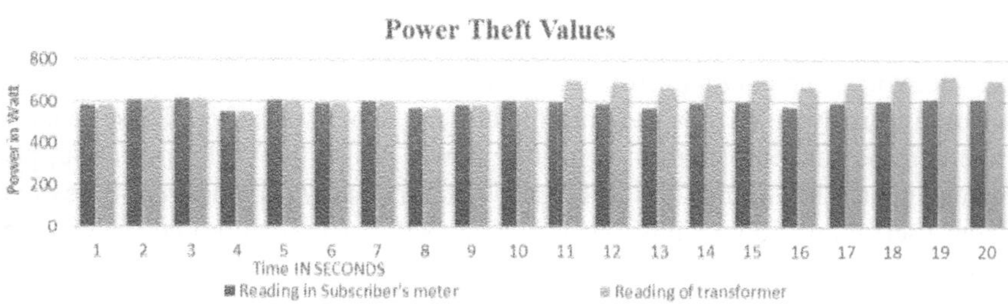

Fig. 3.7. Power Theft Detection.

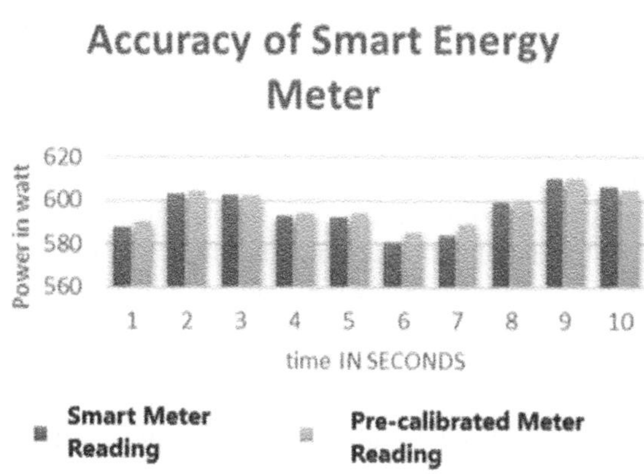

Fig. 3.8. Accuracy of the Meter Reading.

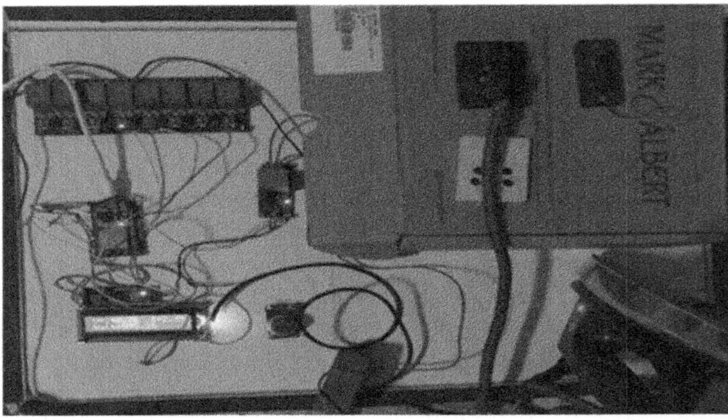

Fig. 3.9. Experimental Setup and Snapshot of the Proposed Architecture.

4.8. System Prototype and Discussion

Fig. 3.9 depicts the various hardware components required for the system, as well as the interface between the microcontroller and the sensors. For testing purposes, these sensors were mounted on a cardboard and all the joints were soldered by hand. However, in real time, these components would be integrated into a compact meter box for each subscriber. Besides, a dedicated network would be implemented solely for meter reading purposes, presently which is tested on a local network. The microcontroller, receives data through voltage sensor, current sensor, and relay and sends the data to the server for processing. These sensors provide important information regarding power usage, theft, and power supply management. The Liquid Crystal Display (LCD) display provides real-time data to the user about power consumption. The use of a pre-calibrated meter with better precision allows for accurate measurement of power consumption and provides a way to compare the readings taken by the smart meter for accuracy. Note, the design and assembly of the hardware were carefully considered to ensure the proper functioning of the system, and the use of a cardboard model allowed for testing and modification before final implementation. The subscriber can access the information regarding meter readings current bill (if any) and predicted bills through a webpage. Besides, an automatic power termination has also been developed. For preventing unauthorized access, every subscriber is required to log in using their unique user ID and password before making payments. Upon successful login, the subscriber is prompted to verify their identity by providing a facial recognition scan. Once the authentication gets completed, the consumer will be directed to the payment webpage where they can securely pay their bill.

5. Solution Design, Results, and Sustainability

In this technologically advanced world, finding innovative and sustainable solutions to complex problems is of paramount importance. The development of a smart system to manage electricity usage and billing addresses the issues of high requirements of manpower, inaccurate billing, malpractices, and irregular payments, which further augments the wastage of resources. It can be observed that the system prototype proposed here provides solutions to these aforementioned problems succinctly through introducing modern tools and technologies for building sustainability in terms of optimizing energy usage. Moreover, the high future scope of the system ensures its relevance and effectiveness in the years to come. The incorporation of advanced features such as face recognition, conversational agents, along with the use of a dedicated network for meter reading, highlights the commitment to innovation and constant improvement. This system serves as a testament to the importance of investing in technological advancements to achieve greater efficiency and accuracy in our daily lives. Although it might have required a significant financial investment at the initial stage, the benefits of increased efficiency and accuracy make it a worthwhile investment in the long run in terms of a sustainable solution. The features of this system, such as reduced human interaction, decreased opportunities for theft, easy payment methods, fault-free database management, excellent customer service, and reduced manpower requirements, make it a top priority solution for meeting the criteria of SDG 7 in 2030, that is, expanding and improving technology for improving energy productivity. Besides, the incorporation of such features can also be effective in building resilient urban spaces due to increasing community migration toward urbanization (SDG 11).

References

Abu-Rayash, A., & Dincer, I. (2021). Development of integrated sustainability performance indicators for better management of smart cities. *Sustainable Cities and Society*, *67*, 102704.

Ahmed, A. A., Belrzaeg, M., Nassar, Y., El-Khozondar, H. J., Khaleel, M., & Alsharif, A. (2023). A comprehensive review towards smart homes and cities considering sustainability developments, concepts, and future trends. *World Journal of Advanced Research and Reviews*, *19*(1), 1482–1489.

Alahakoon, D., & Yu, X. (2015). Smart electricity meter data intelligence for future energy systems: A survey. *IEEE Transactions on Industrial Informatics*, *12*(1), 425–436.

Al-Ali, A. R., Zualkernan, I. A., Rashid, M., Gupta, R., & AliKarar, M. (2017). A smart home energy management system using IoT and big data analytics approach. *IEEE Transactions on Consumer Electronics*, *63*(4), 426–434.

Aloul, F., Al-Ali, A. R., Al-Dalky, R., Al-Mardini, M., & El-Hajj, W. (2012). Smart grid security: Threats, vulnerabilities and solutions. *International Journal of Smart Grid and Clean Energy*, *1*(1), 1–6.

Areekkara, S., Kumar, R., & Bansal, R. C. (2021). An intelligent multi agent-based approach for autonomous energy management in a microgrid. *Electric Power Components and Systems*, *49*(1–2), 18–31.

Cahyono, W., Atmaja, W. H. K., & Karyuniati, A. P. (2019). Digitalization solution on customer services to leverage the ease of getting electricity. In *2019 international conference on technologies and policies in electric power & energy* (pp. 1–6). IEEE.

Chandrasekar, P., & Sangeetha, T. (2014). Smart shopping cart with automatic billing system through Fid and Zigbee. In *International conference on information communication and embedded systems (ICICES2014)* (pp. 1–4). IEEE.

Choi, K. W., Aziz, A. A., Setiawan, D., Tran, N. M., Ginting, L., & Kim, D. I. (2018). Distributed wireless power transfer system for Internet of Things devices. *IEEE Internet of Things Journal*, *5*(4), 2657–2671.

Dangar, D., & Joshi, S. K. (2014). Electricity theft detection techniques for distribution system in GUVNL. *International Journal Research and Analytical Reviews*, *7*, 513–524.

Deny, J., Narasimha, A. B., Reddy, R. G. V., & Sathish, S. (2021). Electricity monitoring and auto bill generation using IoT. In *2021 3rd international conference on signal processing and communication (ICPSC)* (pp. 695–698). IEEE.

Hadi, W. N. H. W. A., Rashid, R. A., Sarijari, M. A., Hamid, S. Z. A., & Muhammad, N. A. (2022). Machine learning bill prediction for IoT-based utility management system. In *2022 IEEE 6th international symposium on telecommunication technologies (ISTT)* (pp. 74–78). IEEE.

Hasan, M. K., Alkhalifah, A., Islam, S., Babiker, N. B. M., Ahasan Habib, A. K. M., Aman, A. H. M., & Hossain, M. A. (2022). Blockchain technology on smart grid, energy trading, and big data: Security issues, challenges, and recommendations. *Wireless Communications and Mobile Computing*, *1*, 9065768.

Islam, M. S., & Bhuiyan, M. S. R. (2017). Design and implementation of remotely located energy meter monitoring with load control and mobile billing system through GSM. In *2017 International conference on electrical, computer and communication engineering (ECCE)* (pp. 158–163). IEEE.

Jain, S. M., & Karandiakr, A. M. (2016). A survey on power theft detection. *International Journal of Innovative Research in Computer and Communication Engineering*, *4*(1), 509–511.

Kirmani, S., Mazid, A., Khan, I. A., & Abid, M. U. (2022). A survey on IoT enabled smart grids: Technologies, architectures, applications, and challenges. *Sustainability*, *15*(1), 717.

Maity, T., & Das, P. S. (2011). A novel three phase energy meter model with wireless data reading and online billing solution. In *2011 IEEE symposium on computers & informatics* (pp. 74–77). IEEE.

Mishra, J. K., Goyal, S., Tikkiwal, V. A., & Kumar, A. (2018). An IoT based smart energy management system. In *2018 4th international conference on computing communication and automation (ICCCA)* (pp. 1–3). IEEE.

Nelson, I., Annadurai, C., Ramya, E., Shavian, R., & Mathusathana, V. (2021). IoT based smart energy meter system using machine learning. *Smart Intelligent Computing and Communication Technology*, *38*, 358.

Newell, D., & Duffy, M. (2019). Review of power conversion and energy management for low-power, low-voltage energy harvesting powered wireless sensors. *IEEE Transactions on Power Electronics*, *34*(10), 9794–9805.

Nguyen, N.-H., Tran, Q.-T., Leger, J.-M., & Vuong, T.-P. (2010). A real-time control using wireless sensor network for intelligent energy management system in buildings. In *2010 IEEE workshop on environmental energy and structural monitoring systems* (pp. 87–92). IEEE.

Othman, A., & Zakaria, N. H. (2020). Energy meter based wireless monitoring system using Blynk application via smartphone. In *2020 IEEE 2nd international conference on artificial intelligence in engineering and technology (IICAIET)* (pp. 1–5). IEEE.

Parvin, K., Hafiz, W. M., Abdullah, M. A., Hannan, M. A., & Salam, M. A. (2020). Estimation of building energy management toward minimizing energy consumption and carbon emission. *Journal of Advanced Manufacturing Technology (JAMT)*, *14*(2), 247–258.

Roesch, M., Linder, C., Zimmermann, R., Rudolf, A., Hohmann, A., & Reinhart, G. (2020). Smart grid for industry using multi-agent reinforcement learning. *Applied Sciences*, *10*(19), 6900.

Sardar, S., & Sanaullah, A. (2015). Detecting and minimizing electricity theft: A review. *Journal of Emerging Trends in Engineering*.

Smith, T. B. (2004). Electricity theft: A comparative analysis. *Energy Policy*, *32*(18), 2067–2076.

Sulthana, N., Rashmi, N., Prakyathi, N. Y., Bhavana, S., & Shiva Kumar, K. B. (2020). Smart energy meter and monitoring system using IoT. *International Journal of Engineering Research &Technology*, *8*(14), 50–53.

Taigman, Y., Yang, M., Ranzato, M., & Wolf, L. (2014). DeepFace: Closing the gap to human-level performance in face verification. In *Proceedings of the IEEE conference on computer vision and pattern recognition* (pp. 1701–1708). IEEE.

Tarannu, M., Sharma, D., & Singh, D. (2017). Electricity theft in India: Its measure and solution. *International Journal of Advance Research, Ideas and Innovations in Technology*, *3*(5), 406–409.

Tastan, M. (2019). Internet of Things based smart energy management for smart home. *KSII Transactions on Internet and Information Systems (TIIS)*, *13*(6), 2781–2798.

Wang, M., & Deng, W. (2021). Deep face recognition: A survey. *Neurocomputing*, *429*, 21–244.

Xianghang, M., Feng, Q., Ying, Z., & XiaoFeng, W. (2017). An empirical characterization of IFTTT: Ecosystem, usage, and performance. In S. Uhlig & O. Maennel (Eds.), *Proceedings of the 2017 internet measurement conference* (pp. 398–404). Association for Computing Machinery.

Chapter 4

Ethical Perspectives of Artificial Intelligence: A Bibliometric Analysis

Soumik Gangopadhyay[a,b], *Rabin Mazumder*[b,c], *Poulami Basu*[c], *Soumyadeep Dhol*[b,c], *Alolika Datta*[b,c], *Moupia Kundu*[b,c], *Suhrit Tewary*[a] *and Aparajita Bhattacharya*[a]

[a]*Institute of Engineering & Management, Kolkata, India*
[b]*School of University of Engineering and Management, Kolkata, India*
[c]*Department of Bachelor of Business Administration, Institute of Engineering & Management, Kolkata, India*

Abstract

AI has a very important implication on almost all fields of our industry across nations. Different research has proved that AI has a profound role in the healthcare sector. After careful investigations, different researchers have undergone constructive research in the field of the importance of AI in healthcare, but its justification from an ethical point of view is yet to be addressed, managed, and explored. Although modern technology and techniques are equally important in healthcare, they should not divulge the value of ethical practices and their importance in the field of healthcare tools. Under such circumstances, this study has concentrated on the gap that persists after careful investigation of research articles published in the last five years and available on the Scopus platform. These articles have been screened further with the help of an open-source software named Vos viewer, and the screening has revealed that AI has not yet touched the connection between healthcare use of artificial intelligence (AI), and informed consent. Under such a backdrop, this study has carefully investigated the published research work done by several countries in recent years and has identified a new area of research that can be undertaken.

Keywords: AI; ethics; informed consent; governance; healthcare

Harnessing the Potential of Artificial Intelligence to Promote Environmental Sustainability Sustainability, 55–69

doi:10.1108/978-1-83662-996-220251004

1. Introduction

AI in marketing has completely transformed how companies tend to communicate with their customers by providing more tailored experiences and increased engagement. It has innovated the consumer interactions by providing more individualized experiences and increased engagement. But as AI becomes more prevalent in many areas, ethical issues become critical. AI-driven marketing in the healthcare industry needs to put patient privacy and informed consent first. Application of chatbots with AI capabilities should be transparent about their artificial origin and intent to collect data. Additionally, personalized treatment advice powered by AI also needs to guarantee accountability and openness. Even AI-driven marketing technologies in the workplace should not be biased or discriminatory to provide all employees with equal chances. Transparency and accountability are key factors that AI-driven marketing in the business world needs to emphasize. Several studies explored an integrated perspective on AI research in psychology, consumer research, and marketing (Mariani et al., 2022). The transformational potential of AI in personalizing marketing techniques explores how AI can be used to create relevant and targeted marketing experiences as well as the theoretical foundations of consumer engagement (Babatunde & Odejide, 2024). Influencer marketing driven by AI, for instance, ought to make sponsored content more evident. Moreover, AI-powered chabot for customer support ought to facilitate the smooth transfer of cases to human agents as needed.

Concerns over the ethical and regulatory implications have tempered the exciting, rapid surge in interest in AI in the marketing domain (Rana, 2024). The ethics of AI is a problem that needs to be continuously addressed by both corporations and studies (Sara & Mandour, 2022). A model-based study has emphasized many factors, including risk, acceptance, trust, and attitudes regarding the use of AI in marketing, outlining the moral and ethical dilemmas related to AI's acceptability (Gangopadhyay et al., 2024). It addresses many AI techniques used in market research and draws attention to some of the downsides of AI, including the requirement for diverse and unbiased data and the need for monitoring and evaluating results (Lukaszewski & Stone, 2024). Despite developments like the general data protection regulation (GDPR) aimed at protecting personal data, research underscored the difficulties authorities confront in differentiating between the use of AI that is ethical and that is not ethical (Goncalves et al., 2023; Nazer et al., 2023; Saéz Ortuño et al., 2023). Studies have recommended how AI in marketing might be used to advance societal and environmental well-being in order to address some of these conflicts and explain the AI-for-social-good viewpoint (Hermann, 2022). AI's have a revolutionary impact on advertising, that is, targeting, personalization, content creation, and Ad optimization (Gao et al., 2023).

Differential privacy is emphasized as a crucial technique for maintaining patient confidentiality in AI-driven healthcare systems in this organized investigation of these problems (Williamson & Prybutok, 2024). Some examined the effects of data breaches and customer vulnerability, as well as methods to reduce perceived vulnerability through privacy protections (Deslée & Cloarec, 2024). Previous studies have also emphasized how ethical AI might be integrated into sustainable e-commerce, emphasizing concepts like algorithmic bias, data privacy, and AI–human interaction (Andrieux et al., 2024). The way AI is incorporated into E-commerce is changing it more and more, thus it's important to strike a balance between technology development and consumer privacy (Kuchipudi et al., 2024). It also brings up moral concerns around the gathering, use, and privacy of data (Jones, 2018). Predictive analytics, chatbots, content personalization, and the difficulties and uses of AI in several marketing domains influence marketing (Hicham et al., 2023). But there are also significant ethical questions raised by this growing reliance on AI, especially in chatbot-driven industries.

AI and robotics systems are already beginning to have an impact on our daily lives. Research on the ethical implications of AI and robotics in the hospitality and tourism industries, however, yet to be explored. This is a field of study and application that needs special attention because of the significance of creating technologies that transcend national boundaries and since the tourism and hospitality sectors are essentially based on intercultural exchanges (Ivanov & Umbrello, 2021). Further, ChatGPT driven by AI allows users to communicate with machines; changing the way humans engage with AI technology by making use of machine learning and natural language processing techniques, however there are leery of generative AI due to ethical concerns (Rivas & Zhao, 2023). Several corporate enterprises, academic institutions, and government agencies have released ethical AI concepts and guidelines. EU regulation has credibility to tackle the long-term concerns to consumer autonomy associated with the use of AI in markets (Fassiaux, 2023). Though it seems that everyone agrees that AI should be "ethical," there is disagreement on what "ethical AI" is and what ethical standards, best practices, and technical prerequisites are necessary to make it a reality (Jobin et al., 2019). Based on the literature social scientists have analyzed on the government's duty to protect moral values, including citizens' privacy, that validate the privacy dilemma (Schmid et al., 2022). It is expected to fundamentally alter the advertising and marketing landscape possibly in a positive way before widespread adoption is encouraged (Arango & Singaraju, 2023). AI biases, ethical design, consumer privacy, cybersecurity, individual autonomy and well-being, and unemployment are a few of the major ethical challenges that the Chapter highlights (Du & Xie, 2021). By embracing ethical AI use in marketing, business can build trust with customers and stakeholders, avoid reputational damage and legal issues, foster a culture of responsibility and innovation and drive sustainable growth and success. To ensure responsible application, however, substantial ethical considerations must be addressed along with the advances (Gangopadhyay et al., 2024). There are growing significance of incorporating ethical issues into the development of AI systems and introduces a special emphasis on AI ethics, highlighting the necessity for ethical AI practices in order to uphold human rights and foster trust, and it poses important considerations regarding the ethical, societal, and legal ramifications of AI decision-making (Dignum, 2018). By addressing the ethical and legal issues surrounding AI in marketing and offering workable answers, this manuscript seeks to identify this gap. By doing this, companies can fully utilize AI's potential while upholding the highest moral standards, which will ultimately be advantageous to both enterprises and customers.

This chapter is a literature review and bibliometric analysis of the published research available in the SCOPUS database. The primary objective of this study is to explore subjective and objective perspectives of AI in marketing in great detail and present unbiased ways to allay them.

2. Literature Review

AI is reshaping health and medicine, especially through its potential to address health disparities in low and middle-income countries (Zhui et al., 2024). The value of AI in health care and its ability to address healthcare delivery issues has been a subject of discussion within the scientific community for several years (Romagnoli et al., 2024). Patient safety in intensive care units (ICUs) has improved, and AI is emerging as a disruptive technology with new prospects (Barea Mendoza et al., 2024). AI is rapidly becoming a valuable tool in healthcare, providing clinicians with a new AI lens perspective for patient care, diagnosis, and treatment, exploring the potential applications, benefits, and challenges of AI chatbots in clinical settings, with a particular emphasis on ChatGPT 4.0, even in the field of allergy and immunology (Goktas et al., 2023). Ethical and governance issues regarding digital innovations developments like AI have attracted abundant debate and research in the area of healthcare (Salgado-Criado et al., 2024). With the accelerating prevalence of AI and other digital technologies in healthcare, the ethical debate surrounding their adoption is becoming more prominent (Pruski, 2024). Examining sociotechnical imaginaries is important for emerging technologies in high-stakes contexts such as the case of emotion AI to address mental health care (Karizat et al., 2024). There is a gap in the area of research on the best practices for using AI in the healthcare sector. As most of the institutions do not have formal guidelines for AI use, leading to confusion among the stake holders (Song, 2024). Additionally, wide range of research from disciplines outside of infectiology, epidemiology, and immunology has been spurred by the COVID-19 pandemic. These studies can offer a framework for interdisciplinary dialogue and develop a roadmap for the use of digital COVID-19 diagnosis, considering all disciplinary stakeholders (Bartenschlager et al., 2024). These shed light on systemic issues plaguing care (nursing) homes, from staff shortages to substandard healthcare; AI technologies, including robots and chatbots, have been proposed as solutions to such issues (Neves et al., 2024). The integration of AI into healthcare holds immense potential for transforming diagnostic, prognostic, and therapeutic approaches and explores the opportunities and risks associated with implementing AI technologies in Romanian healthcare (Fitzek, 2024). Increasing integration of AI in healthcare presents a host of ethical, legal, social, and political challenges involving various stakeholders (Bouhouita-Guermech & Haidar, 2024). With recent development of AI technology, ChatGPT – a new AI practice has enormous potential in a variety of fields. It seeks to provide users with essential information, enabling informed decision-making, skillfully managing any difficulties that may arise when using ChatGPT, and keeping up with the quickly changing field of this technology (Hua et al., 2024). Examining the moral and ethical concerns related to AI and its application is another option (Zebec &

Indihar Štemberger, 2024). Human-like programs will become more and more prevalent as AI algorithms advance. If these algorithms are sentient – a possibility we may never fully understand – then this attribute is essential to morality-related ethical deliberations (Hansen, 2023).

The policy agenda currently being established for AI is a domain marked by complex and sweeping implications for economic transformation, tempered by concerns about social and ethical risks (Schiff, 2023). Highlighting key themes in these policies, including ethics, transparency, the balance between innovation and regulation, and data privacy, it also identifies areas for improvement, such as the need for specific guidelines on mitigating biases in AI systems and navigating data privacy issues (Pierson & Hildt, 2023). It aims to fill this gap by establishing ethical guidelines: marketing professionals need to develop ethical rules for the creation and implementation of AI-powered marketing strategies (Kumar & Suthar, 2024). The challenges and limitations of AI technology, such as ethical concerns, data privacy and security issues, technical expertise and knowledge, and high implementation costs, are also a matter of concern (Gurjar et al., 2024). In financial services, there is a broad spectrum of potential ethical issues, from data usage to customer vulnerabilities, scrutinizing the impact of morality and where accountability resides in the use of AI service robots in financial services (Tóth & Blut, 2024). Historically, studies emphasize how important it is for libraries to actively participate in these regulations as well as adapt to them, helping to create more thorough and efficient AI governance (Lo, 2023b). Ethical perspectives from the viewpoint of consumers have been described in Fig. 4.1. Key ethical considerations across sectors are: (a) privacy such as unauthorized access, data vulnerability and surveillance anxiety: protect consumer data and maintain confidentiality (Williams et al., 2023); (b) transparency such as obscure AI processes

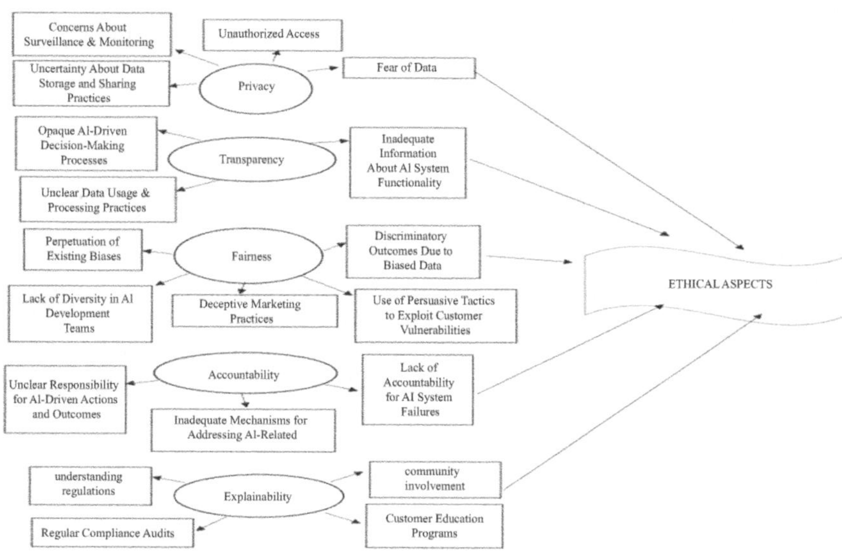

Fig. 4.1. Ethical Aspects of AI. *Source*: Author's analysis.

and data usage, unexplainable AI (NEXAI): clearly disclose AI's role in marketing efforts (Saéz Ortuño et al., 2023); (c) fairness such as AI bias amplification, algorithmic discrimination, diversity deficit, deceptive persuasion, chatbot deception, and human-AI ambiguity: avoid bias and discrimination in AI-driven marketing practices (Mitov, 2021); (d) accountability such as Vague oversight, unaccountable AI, ineffective issue escalation: ensure human oversight and responsibility for AI-driven decisions (Hermann, 2022); (e) explainability such as legal adherence, periodic evaluations, educational outreach, social engagement: ensure AI-driven decisions are understandable and justifiable (Mariani et al., 2022).

3. Research Methodology

We have initially identified and classified the 629 screened articles based on a keywords-based search from the SCOPUS database. Keywords were AI, generative AI, ethical perspectives, and marketing ethics. Search was further screened based on selective search from 2010 to 2024, social science, management, and economics research, and journal articles. Finally, 20 articles were examined according to the mentioned specific inclusion and exclusion criteria, according to the alignment with the theme of our research. VOSVIEWER is an open-source tool designed for visualizing and analyzing scientific literature, which has been used for categorizing research outputs into clusters based on shared keywords and thematic relevance.

Among the 29 articles, a distinct split between objective and subjective themes were observed. Nine articles emphasized objective factors, addressing broader, policy-related topics that guide national administration decisions across different countries. These articles contribute to standardized insights that inform policymakers and highlight implications of AI. In contrast, we have observed 21 subjective themes, focusing on individual and social perceived value of AI and its ethical impact among the consumers. The studies illustrate dual focus of AI research on both regulatory standards and personalized viewpoints.

4. Analysis and Findings

About 22 publications have emphasized country-specific contributions, indicating the global diversity in AI research. This geographical distribution highlights the universal relevance of AI, with studies spanning multiple regions to capture various national approaches. Also, the temporal breakdown shows a surge in research from 2023 to 2024, with 6 articles from 2023 and 23 from 2024. This sharp increase in the latest publications reflects the increasing focus on AI as technological advancements prompt more nuanced exploration of its ethical and practical dimensions.

AI, as a general term, appeared in 23 articles, underscoring its centrality in this research. This keyword encompasses fundamental AI technologies and applications that impact various sectors and guide the ongoing development of ethical guidelines (Table 4.1). Ethics was a prominent word, appearing in 20 articles. This frequent mention signifies the high concern surrounding ethical issues, especially

Table 4.1. Overview of Recent Literature on Ethical, Legal, and Governance Aspects of AI Across Diverse Sectors.

Authors	Article	Journal	Keywords
Salgado-Criado et al. (2024)	How should we govern digital innovation? A venture capital perspective	*Technological Forecasting and Social Change*	Artificial intelligence; ethics; global health; low- and middle-income countries
Yu and Zhai (2025)	Use of artificial intelligence to address health disparities in low- and middle-income countries: a thematic analysis of ethical issues	*Public Health*	AI ethics; AI governance; digital governance; digital innovation; ESG
Bouhouita-Guermech and Haidar (2024)	Scoping review shows the dynamics and complexities inherent to the notion of "responsibility" in artificial intelligence within the health care context	*Asian Bioethics Review*	AI ethics; artificial intelligence; healthcare; responsibility
Bartenschlager et al. (2024)	The AI ethics of digital COVID-19 diagnosis and their legal, medical, technological, and operational managerial implications	*Artificial Intelligence in Medicine*	AI ethics; digital diagnosis of COVID-19; interdisciplinary stakeholders
Bar-Gil et al. (2024)	AI for the people? Embedding AI ethics in HR and people analytics projects	*Technology in Society*	AI ethics; ethical deliberation; HR analytics; people analytics
Romagnoli et al. (2024)	Healthcare systems and artificial intelligence: focus on challenges and the international regulatory framework	*Pharmaceutical Research*	AI, artificial intelligence; healthcare; therapeutic treatment regulatory framework
Kumar and Suthar (2024)	Ethical and legal challenges of AI in marketing: an exploration of solutions'	*Journal of Information, Communication and Ethics in Society*	AI in marketing; artificial intelligence; ethical challenges; legal implications; marketing; solution proposals

(*Continued*)

Table 4.1. (*Continued*)

Authors	Article	Journal	Keywords
Tóth and Blut (2024)	Ethical compass: The need for corporate digital responsibility in the use of artificial intelligence in financial services	*Organizational Dynamics*	Accountability; artificial intelligence; business ethics; corporate digital responsibility; locus of morality; moral intensity
Drage et al. (2024)	Engineers on responsibility: feminist approaches to who's responsible for ethical AI	*Ethics and Information Technology*	AI ethics; artificial intelligence; ethics; feminism; responsibility
Gurjar et al. (2024)	An analytical review on the impact of artificial intelligence on the business industry: applications, trends, and challenges	*IEEE Engineering Management Review*	AI and healthcare; AI and marketing; artificial intelligence (AI); business
Karizat et al. (2024)	Patent applications as glimpses into the socio-technical imaginary: ethical enabled human resource management	*Proceedings of the ACM on Human–Computer Interaction*	AI ethics; data subjects; emotion AI; emotion artificial intelligence; emotion recognition; ethical speculation; healthcare; human resource management (HRM)
Hansen (2023)	On the existence of robot zombies and our ethical obligations to AI systems	*Journal of Social Computing*	Artificial intelligence; ethics; sentience
Lo (2023b)	An initial interpretation of the U.S. Department of Education's AI report: implications and recommendations for academic libraries	*Journal of Academic Librarianship*	Academic libraries; AI guidelines; AI implementation; AI literacy; artificial intelligence; US Department of Education
Pruski (2024)	AI-enhanced healthcare: not a new paradigm for informed consent	*Journal of Bioethical Inquiry*	Artificial intelligence; clinical informatics; GDPR; health informatics; patient consent

Lo (2023a)	From principles to practice: comparative analysis of European and United States ethical AI frameworks for assessment and methodological application	*Proceedings of the Association for Information Science and Technology*	AI ethics; artificial intelligence; international information issues; legislation and regulation; value-sensitive AI design
Fitzek (2024)	Ethical challenges and transformative potential: examining the impact of artificial intelligence on patient care, data security, and the healthcare workforce in Romania	*Journal of Community Positive Practices*	Artificial intelligence; data privacy; ethical implications; patient quality of life; Romanian healthcare; workforce transformation
Mouta et al. (2024)	Comprehensive professional learning for teacher agency in addressing ethical challenges of AIED: insights from educational design research	*Education and Information Technologies*	Agency; artificial intelligence in education; continuing professional development; ethics; teachers; training
Barea Mendoza et al. (2024)	Current perspectives on the use of Artificial Intelligence in critical patient safety	*Medicina Intensiva*	Adverse events; algorithms; artificial intelligence; critical care; machine learning; patients safety; prediction; risk assessment
Goktas et al. (2023)	Artificial Intelligence chatbots in allergy and immunology practice: where have we been and where are we going?	*Journal of Allergy and Clinical Immunology: In Practice*	AI chatbots; allergy; artificial intelligence; ChatGPT; ethical considerations; generative pretrained transformer; healthcare; natural language processing
Pierson and Hildt (2023)	AI policies across the globe: implications and recommendations for libraries	*IFLA Journal*	AI governance; AI policies; artificial intelligence; comparative analysis; data privacy; ethics

as AI capabilities evolve. Further, 13 articles linked AI to healthcare, illustrating how AI technologies are increasingly used in medical applications. Safety and security, noted in five articles, reflect concerns regarding AI's potential risks, particularly in safeguarding and preventing misuse. Five articles have emphasized generative AI by highlighting its transformative potential and the ethical challenges associated with its use in content creation, media, and data manipulation. Several other domains were also identified, such as feminism, education, human resources, digitalization, governess, legal, analytics, emotion, and technology, weakly associated with ethical value. Feminism brings a unique point of view on AI's social implications, focusing on gender bias and representation within AI systems. Four articles discussed AI in education, examining its role in personalized learning, administrative support, and digital literacy. Human resources indicates ethical interest in how AI affects hiring, employee management, and workforce analytics. Four articles have covered ethical aspects of AI in HR, as digitalization and governance reflect AI's role in the digitizing process and ensuring ethical governance frameworks. Three and five articles covered digitalization and governance, respectively. Finally, the keywords, legal, analytics, emotion, and technology, applications in legal analytics, emotional AI, and technological advancements were less frequently mentioned but are still significant.

Firstly, a network visualization analysis has been conducted. This technique helps us understand the relationships and connections between different topics within the field of AI ethics. In this case, "artificial intelligence" is placed at the center as the core theme. The closer a topic is to the center, the more it is connected to AI research. Interestingly, it has been observed, as mentioned in image 1, that while topics like "technology" and "sustainability" are closely linked to AI, there's a noticeable gap in research done between "AI ethics" and "informed consent." This suggests that while there's significant research on the technical aspects of AI, its ethical implications and ensuring informed consent in AI applications seem to be less explored areas of research.

Secondly, an overlay visualization technique has been employed. This visualization helps identify overlapping areas of research. By overlaying different topics, we can see where they intersect. In our case, the overlap between "artificial intelligence," "AI ethics," and "informed consent" is minimal. This further reinforces the finding from the network visualization that there's a dearth of research at the intersection of these three crucial areas.

Finally, density visualization has been utilized. This technique provides a more granular view of the research landscape. It highlights areas with high research density, indicating where more research has been conducted. In our case, the density visualization clearly shows that the area surrounding "artificial intelligence," "AI ethics," and "informed consent" is relatively less dense compared to other areas. This provides us with definitive evidence that there's a significant research gap in the particular area.

The proposed model provides a comprehensive overview of the ethical aspects regarding AI, and all are interconnected and essential for the ethical development and deployment of AI. It balances a wide range of issues, from privacy and transparency to fairness and accountability. The outlined challenges in this chart, by nature, are not static. As AI technology continues to evolve, further new ethical challenges will emerge. It is important to remain observant and adapt our approaches accordingly.

Overall, this chart is an insightful tool for understanding the ethical implications of AI. It provides a transparent and concise overview of the issues and can help inform discussions regarding how to develop and use AI in a responsible and ethical manner. We can conclude that customers' privacy is related to transparency, as a lack of transparency can lead to privacy breaches. Similarly, transparency is related to fairness as transparency helps to identify and address biases in AI systems. Further, fairness is related to accountability as it is necessary to hold accountable those who are responsible for creating and situating biased AI systems. Thus, accountability is related to explainability as explainable AI systems can help in identifying and rectifying errors or biases. Finally, explainability is related to privacy, as understanding how AI systems work can help to identify potential privacy risks.

5. Conclusion

Healthcare is a very vulnerable sector for every person. Health care considers private data, where everyone has their own private zone and ownership, where one should not try to indulge or interfere without their consent. So, no one should disclose their personal data without informed consent. It has been observed that no research has been done regarding this in the industry. Chatbots are useful, but chatbots do not take permission before disclosing one's data and information to others. Generative AI is very useful in today's world, but using it may alter or modify the data automatically, which we do not want. While significant progress has been made in understanding the ethical application of AI in marketing, there remain major important gaps that need to be explored further. These gaps are evident in key areas such as emotional value, user consent, generative AI, healthcare marketing, and data protection through chatbots. Addressing these gaps is very crucial for developing a comprehensive framework for ethical AI marketing.

After going through a set of research papers, we have concluded that most of them were released during recent years and that in India, there are very few researchers who have researched this topic. We have also noticed in our Vos Viewer analysis that AI and informed consent have a connection that is unexplored, and no significant works regarding their relationship and interlink have been found; thus, our study concludes that AI ethics is related to informed consent. AI is a rational reality. But AI must be thoughtfully implemented, not willfully. In this decade, when cybersecurity is a concern across all digital platforms, progressive thinking must shift to regressive thinking.

References

Andrieux, P., Johnson, R. D., Sarabadani, J., & Van Slyke, C. (2024). Ethical considerations of generative AI-enabled human resource management. *Organizational Dynamics*, *53*(1), Article 101032. https://doi.org/10.1016/j.orgdyn.2024.101032

Arango, L., & Singaraju, S. P. (2023). Consumer responses to AI-generated charitable giving ads. *Journal of Advertising*, *52*(4), 486–503. https://doi.org/10.1080/00913367.2023.2183285

Babatunde, S., & Odejide, O. A. (2024). The role of AI in marketing personalization. *International Journal of Management and Entrepreneurship*, *6*(3), 936–949.

Barea Mendoza, J. A., Valiente Fernandez, M., Pardo Fernandez, A., & Gómez Álvarez, J. (2024). Current perspectives on the use of artificial intelligence in critical patient safety [Perspectivasactualessobreeluso de la inteligencia artificial en la seguridad del pacientecrítico]. *Medicina Intensiva (English Edition)*, *49*(3), 154–164. https://doi.org/10.1016/j.medine.2024.04.002

Bar-Gil, O., Ron, T., & Czerniak, O. (2024). AI for the people? Embedding AI ethics in HR and people analytics projects. *Technology in Society*, *77*, 102527.

Bartenschlager, C. C., Gassner, U. M., Römmele, C., Brunner, J. O., Schlögl-Flierl, K., & Ziethmann, P. (2024). The AI ethics of digital COVID-19 diagnosis and their legal, medical, technological, and operational managerial implications. *Artificial Intelligence in Medicine*, *152*, 102873. https://doi.org/10.1016/j.artmed.2024.102873

Bouhouita-Guermech, S., & Haidar, H. (2024). Scoping review shows the dynamics and complexities inherent to the notion of "responsibility" in artificial intelligence within the healthcare context. *Asian Bioethics Review*, *16*(3), 315–344. https://doi.org/10.1007/s41649-024-00292-7.

Deslée, A., & Cloarec, J. (2024). Safeguarding privacy: Ethical considerations in data-driven marketing. In L. Matosas-López (Ed.), *The impact of digitalization on current marketing strategies* (Marketing & Technology: New Horizons and Challenges, pp. 147–161). Emerald Publishing Limited. https://doi.org/10.1108/978-1-83753-686-320241009

Dignum, V. (2018). Ethics in artificial intelligence: Introduction to the special issue. *Ethics and Information Technology*, *20*, 1–3. https://doi.org/10.1007/s10676-018-9450-z

Drage, E., McInerney, K., & Browne, J. (2024). Engineers on responsibility: Feminist approaches to who's responsible for ethical AI. *Ethics and Information Technology*, *26*(1), 1–13. https://doi.org/10.1007/s10676-023-09739-1.

Du, S., & Xie, C. (2021). Paradoxes of artificial intelligence in consumer markets: Ethical challenges and opportunities. *Journal of Business Research*, *129*, 961–974.

Fassiaux, S. (2023). Preserving consumer autonomy through European Union regulation of artificial intelligence: A long-term approach. *European Journal of Risk Regulation*, *14*(4), 710–730.

Fitzek, S. (2024). Ethical challenges and transformative potential: Examining the impact of artificial intelligence on patient care, data security, and the healthcare workforce in Romania. *Journal of Community Positive Practices*, *24*(1), 59–86. https://doi.org/10.35782/JCPP.2024.1.04

Gangopadhyay, S., Guha, S., & Basu, P. (2024). Perceived value of prospect of AI enabled healthcare: View of Generation Z. In R. Singh, W. Shafik, D. Crowther, & V. Kumar (Eds.), *Transforming healthcare sector through artificial intelligence and environmental sustainability* (pp. 195–209). Springer Nature Singapore. https://doi.org/10.1007/978 981 97 9555 0_10

Gao, B., Wang, Y., Xie, H., Hu, Y., & Hu, Y. (2023). Artificial intelligence in advertising: Advancements, challenges, and ethical considerations in targeting, personalization, content creation, and ad optimization. *Sage Open*, *13*(4), Article 21582440231210759. https://doi.org/10.1177/21582440231210759

Goktas, P., Karakaya, G., Kalyoncu, A. F., & Damadoglu, E. (2023). Artificial intelligence chatbots in allergy and immunology practice: Where have we been and where are we going? *Journal of Allergy and Clinical Immunology: In Practice*, *11*(9), 2697–2700. https://doi.org/10.1016/j.jaip.2023.05.042

Gonçalves, R. A., Pinto, D. C., Rita, P., & Pires, T. (2023). Artificial intelligence and its ethical implications for marketing. *Emerging Science Journal*, *7*(2), 1070–1312. https://research.unl.pt/ws/portalfiles/portal/53855603/Artificial_Intelligence_Its_Ethical_Implications_for_Marketing.pdf

Gurjar, K., Jangra, A., Baber, H., Islam, M., & Sheikh, S. A. (2024). An analytical review on the impact of artificial intelligence on the business industry: Applications, trends, and challenges. *IEEE Engineering Management Review*, *52*(2), 84–102. https://doi.org/10.1109/EMR.2024.3355973

Hansen, L. R. (2023). On the existence of robot zombies and our ethical obligations to AI systems. *Journal of Social Computing*, *4*(4), 270–274.

Hermann, E. (2022). Leveraging artificial intelligence in marketing for social good—An ethical perspective. *Journal of Business Ethics*, *179*, 43–61. https://doi.org/10.1007/s10551-021-04843-y

Hicham, N., Nassera, H., & Karim, S. (2023). Strategic framework for leveraging artificial intelligence in future marketing decision-making. *Journal of Intelligent Management Decision*, *2*(3), 139–150. https://www.researchgate.net/profile/Nassera-Habbat/publication/373759557_Strategic_Framework_for_Leveraging_Artificial_Intelligence_in_Future_Marketing_Decision-Making/links/65dcba82c3b52a1170fbbff2/Strategic-Framework-for-Leveraging-Artificial-Intelligence-in-Future-Marketing-Decision-Making.pdf

Hua, S., Jin, S., & Jiang, S. (2024). The limitations and ethical considerations of ChatGPT. *Data Intelligence*, *6*(1), 201–239. https://doi.org/10.1162/dint_a_00243

Ivanov, S., & Umbrello, S. (2021). The ethics of artificial intelligence and robotization in tourism and hospitality: A conceptual framework and research agenda. *Journal of Smart Tourism*, *1*(4), 9–18. https://papers.ssrn.com/sol3/papers.cfm?abstract_id=4030669

Jobin, A., Ienca, M., & Vayena, E. (2019). The global landscape of AI ethics guidelines. *Nature Machine Intelligence*, *1*, 389–399. https://doi.org/10.1038/s42256-019-0088-2

Jones, V. (2018). Voice-activated change: Marketing in the age of artificial intelligence and virtual assistants. *Journal of Brand Strategy*, *7*(3), 233–245. https://www.ingentaconnect.com/content/hsp/jbs/2018/00000007/00000003/art00005

Karizat, N., Vinson, A. H., Parthasarathy, S., & Andalibi, N. (2024). Patent applications as glimpses into the sociotechnical imaginary: Ethical speculation on the imagined futures of emotion AI for mental health monitoring and detection. *Proceedings of the ACM on Human-Computer Interaction*, *8*, 106. https://doi.org/10.1145/3637383

Kuchipudi, R., Prathima, T., Palamakula, B. R., Murthy, S. T., & Rao, G. K. (2024). Private AI in e-commerce: Safeguarding consumer data in the digital marketplace. In V. Uma Maheswari & R. Aluvalu (Eds.), *Sustainable development using private AI* (pp. 232–239). CRC Press. https://doi.org/10.1201/9781032716749-12

Kumar, D., & Suthar, N. (2024). Ethical and legal challenges of AI in marketing: An exploration of solutions. *Journal of Information, Communication and Ethics in Society*, *22*(1), 124–144. https://doi.org/10.1108/JICES-05-2023-0068

Lo, L. S. (2023a). An initial interpretation of the U.S. Department of Education's AI report: Implications and recommendations for academic libraries. *Journal of Academic Librarianship*, *49*, 102761. https://doi.org/10.1016/j.acalib.2023.102761

Lo, L. S. (2023b). AI policies across the globe: Implications and recommendations for libraries. *IFLA Journal*, *49*(4), 645–649. https://doi.org/10.1177/03400352231196172

Lukaszewski, K. M., & Stone, D. L. (2024). Will the use of AI in human resources create a digital Frankenstein? *Organizational Dynamics*, *53*, 101033.

Mariani, M. M., Perez-Vega, R., & Wirtz, J. (2022). AI in marketing, consumer research and psychology: A systematic literature review and research agenda. *Psychology & Marketing*, *39*(4), 755–776. https://doi.org/10.1002/mar.21619

Mitov, A. (2021). *Ethical use of artificial intelligence through the utilitarianism perspective* [Bachelor's thesis, University of Twente]. University of Twente Student Theses Repository. https://purl.utwente.nl/essays/86726

Mouta, A., Torrecilla-Sánchez, E. M., & Pinto-Llorente, A. M. (2024). Comprehensive professional learning for teacher agency in addressing ethical challenges of AIED: Insights from educational design research. *Education and Information Technologies*, *30*(3), 3343–3387. https://doi.org/10.1007/s10639-024-12946-y

Nazer, L. H., Zatarah, R., Waldrip, S., Ke, J. X. C., Moukheiber, M., Khanna, A. K., et al. (2023). Bias in artificial intelligence algorithms and recommendations for mitigation. *PLOS Digital Health*, *2*(6), e0000278. https://doi.org/10.1371/journal.pdig.0000278

Neves, B. B., Omori, M., Petersen, A., Vered, M., & Carter, A. (2024). Navigating artificial intelligence in care homes: Competing stakeholder views of trust and logics of care. *Social Science & Medicine*, *358*, 117187. https://doi.org/10.1016/j.socscimed.2024.117187

Pierson, C. M., & Hildt, E. (2023). From principles to practice: Comparative analysis of European and United States ethical AI frameworks for assessment and methodological application. *Proceedings of the Association for Information Science and Technology*, *60*(1), 327–337. https://doi.org/10.1002/pra2.792

Pruski, M. (2024). AI-enhanced healthcare: Not a new paradigm for informed consent. *Journal of Bioethical Inquiry*, *21*(3), 475–489. https://doi.org/10.1007/s11673-023-10320-0

Rana, N. (2024). Ethical AI integration in marketing strategies for sustainable e commerce fashion designing. In K. Kankaew, S. Chaudhary, & S. Widtayakornbundit (Eds.), *Contemporary management and global leadership for sustainability* (pp. 218–233). IGI Global. https://doi.org/10.4018/979 8 3693 1273 5.ch013.

Rivas, P., & Zhao, L. (2023). Marketing with ChatGPT: Navigating the ethical terrain of GPT-based chatbot technology. *AI*, *4*(2), 375–384. https://doi.org/10.3390/ai4020019

Romagnoli, A., Ferrara, F., Langella, R., & Zovi, A. (2024). Healthcare systems and artificial intelligence: Focus on challenges and the international regulatory framework. *Pharmaceutical Research*, *41*(4), 721–730. https://doi.org/10.1007/s11095-024-03685-3

Sáez Ortuño, L., Sánchez García, J., Forgas Coll, S., Huertas García, R., & Puertas Prat, E. (2023). Impact of artificial intelligence on marketing research: Challenges and ethical considerations. In L.. Moutinho, L. Cavique, & E. Bigné (Eds.), *Philosophy of artificial intelligence and its place in society* (pp. 18–42). IGI Global. https://doi.org/10.4018/978-1-6684-9591-9.ch002

Salgado-Criado, J., Mataix-Aldeanueva, C., Nardini, S., López-Pablos, C., Balestrini, M., & Rosales-Torres, C. S. (2024). How should we govern digital innovation? A venture capital perspective. *Technological Forecasting and Social Change*, *200*, 123198.

Sara, T., & Mandour, Y. (2024). Can the pioneering impact of artificial intelligence in anaesthetic practice uphold good medical practice? *British Journal of Hospital Medicine*, *85*(8), 1–5. https://doi.org/10.12968/hmed.2024.0084

Schiff, D. S. (2023). Looking through a policy window with tinted glasses: Setting the agenda for U.S. AI policy. *Review of Policy Research*, *40*(5), 729–756. https://doi.org/10.1111/ropr.12535

Schmid, J. M., Vanderelst, D., Vogel, D., & Ebinger, F. (2022). AI-driven public services and the privacy paradox: Do citizens really care about their privacy? *Public Management Review*, *25*(11), 2116–2134.

Song, N. (2024). Higher education crisis: Academic misconduct with generative AI. *Journal of Contingencies and Crisis Management*, *32*, e12532.

Tóth, Z., & Blut, M. (2024). Ethical compass: The need for corporate digital responsibility in the use of artificial intelligence in financial services. *Organizational Dynamics*, *53*, 101041. https://doi.org/10.1016/j.orgdyn.2024.101041

Williamson, M. S., & Prybutok, V. (2024). Balancing privacy and progress: A review of privacy challenges, systemic oversight, and patient perceptions in AI-driven healthcare. *Applied Sciences*, *14*(2), 675.

Yu, L., & Zhai, X. (2025). Use of artificial intelligence to address health disparities in low- and middle-income countries: A thematic analysis of ethical issues. *Public Health*, *34*(5), 123–137.

Zebec, A., & Indihar Štemberger, M. (2024). Creating AI business value through BPM capabilities. *Business Process Management Journal*, *30*(8), 1–26. https://doi.org/10.1108/BPMJ-07-2023-0566

Zhui, L., Fenghe, L., Xuehu, W., Qining, F., & Wei, R. (2024). Ethical considerations and fundamental principles of large language models in medical education: Viewpoint. *Journal of Medical Internet Research*, *26*, e60083. https://doi.org/10.2196/60083

Chapter 5

Harnessing AI for Waste Management and Circular Economy: Enhancing Recycling and Resource Efficiency

Mainak Saha[a], *Rabin Bhaumik*[a] *and Shriya Chakraborty*[b]

[a]*National Institute of Technology Agartala, Jirania, Agartala, Tripura, India*
[b]*Techno College of Engineering, Maheshkhola, Agartala, Tripura, India*

Abstract

Plastic waste from single-use items, like drink cans, presents a pressing environmental issue that calls for innovative solutions in waste management. This chapter explores the transformative role of artificial intelligence (AI) in advancing circular economy principles, where materials are continuously reused, waste is minimized, and recycling is prioritized. By integrating AI-driven systems for smart waste collection, precise sorting, and lifecycle assessment (LCA), waste management processes can optimize recycling, enhance resource recovery, and significantly reduce landfill contributions. Case studies from cities such as Amsterdam and San Francisco demonstrate the practical potential of AI in optimizing waste management systems. Amsterdam utilizes AI to streamline waste collection routes and reduce emissions, while San Francisco's smart recycling initiatives have improved sorting accuracy and public engagement. However, challenges such as high initial costs, technological infrastructure needs, and complexities in sorting mixed-material waste remain obstacles. Addressing these issues is crucial to fully harness AI's potential in waste management systems aligned with circular economy goals. This study highlights AI's current applications in enhancing recycling efficiencies, offers solutions to overcome implementation barriers, and outlines pathways for future research to foster widespread adoption of AI for a sustainable, resource-efficient future.

Keywords: Artificial Intelligence; waste management; recycling; plastic pollution; circular; economy; sustainable practices

Harnessing the Potential of Artificial Intelligence to Promote Environmental Sustainability, 71–87

doi:10.1108/978-1-83662-996-220251005

Introduction

Background

Plastic pollution has become one of the most pressing environmental challenges, driven largely by the proliferation of single-use plastics like drink cans. These items, which are lightweight, durable, and cost-effective, have become integral to daily life across industries from packaging to consumer goods. However, this widespread use brings significant environmental costs, especially since traditional waste management systems follow a linear "take, make, dispose" model (Ellen MacArthur Foundation, 2023; Plastics Europe, 2023). This approach depletes resources, generates substantial waste, and lacks sufficient recycling practices, particularly for single-use plastics. The environmental impact of such waste is profound: as plastics degrade, they fragment into microplastics, contaminating ecosystems and posing health risks to wildlife and humans alike (Geyer et al., 2020; Smith et al., 2018). Furthermore, the production and incineration of plastics release greenhouse gases, contributing to climate change and exacerbating global environmental challenges (Zheng & Suh, 2021).

In contrast, the concept of a circular economy offers a sustainable alternative, emphasizing resource conservation by reusing, recycling, and repurposing materials (Geissdoerfer et al., 2017). A circular economy seeks to keep resources in use, thereby reducing waste and minimizing environmental harm. AI has emerged as a promising tool for enabling these principles in waste management. AI technologies including data-driven sorting, smart waste collection, and lifecycle analysis can optimize the processes within a circular economy, enhancing recycling efficiency, minimizing waste, and reducing carbon emissions associated with waste management (European Environment Agency, 2023; Yarlagadda, n.d.).

Motivation and Research Objectives

This research seeks to explore AI's transformative role in advancing circular economy goals within plastic waste management, specifically targeting single-use items like drink cans. By examining AI applications in waste collection, automated sorting, and LCAs, this study aims to demonstrate how AI can enhance recycling processes and facilitate sustainable practices (Lanzalonga et al., 2024). The integration of AI in waste management holds the potential to revolutionize recycling by improving sorting accuracy, reducing contamination, and enabling data-driven decision-making in resource recovery.

The study also discusses the challenges AI faces in this context, such as the initial costs of AI technology, limitations in data infrastructure, and complexities associated with mixed-material waste sorting. By analyzing real-world case studies, including AI-driven waste management practices in Amsterdam and San Francisco, this chapter provides insights into AI's practical applications and limitations (Sarc et al., 2019). Through a comprehensive examination of AI's capabilities, this research contributes to the understanding of how technology can drive a sustainable shift toward a circular economy.

Ultimately, this chapter aims to offer a framework for future research and implementation, encouraging the integration of AI-driven solutions in waste management to create a cleaner, resource-efficient, and sustainable future.

Literature Review

Waste Management Models: Linear Versus Circular Economy

The linear waste management model, characterized by "take, make, dispose," has led to unsustainable resource depletion and environmental degradation due to excessive extraction, production, and disposal. In contrast, circular economy models prioritize resource efficiency, recycling, and waste minimization. Studies indicate that transitioning from linear to circular approaches could reduce global plastic waste by up to 30% (Lanzalonga et al., 2024; Sarc et al., 2019). AI is instrumental in facilitating this shift by enabling efficient reuse and recycling of materials, thereby supporting a closed-loop system and reducing the need for virgin resources (Sariatli, 2017).

AI in Waste Management: Advances and Applications

AI applications in waste management are diverse, encompassing smart bins, route optimization, and advanced sorting mechanisms. AI-powered optical sorters, for example, achieve over 90% accuracy in identifying and separating materials, significantly reducing contamination in recycling streams and improving the recovery of recyclable items such as Polyethylene Terephthalate (PET), High-Density Polyethylene (HDPE), and aluminum (Abdallah et al., 2020). Machine learning algorithms in these systems enable efficient categorization, enhancing the purity of recycled materials and contributing to circular economy goals by increasing recovery rates (Yarlagadda, n.d.).

AI and LCA in Waste Management

LCA tools evaluate the environmental impact of products across their entire lifecycle, from production to disposal. AI-enhanced LCA models offer dynamic data analysis, empowering stakeholders to make informed decisions on material use, packaging, and waste treatment. For instance, AI-based LCAs can help reduce material costs by 15% by optimizing resource allocation and minimizing waste (Christensen et al., 2020). By providing actionable insights, AI-driven LCA supports sustainable product design, material efficiency, and waste reduction.

Smart Waste Collection and Routing Optimization

AI-driven waste collection systems, particularly in urban areas, use smart bins equipped with sensors that monitor fill levels in real-time. These systems facilitate efficient routing, enabling waste collection services to optimize schedules and reduce operational costs. A study in Amsterdam demonstrated that AI-optimized collection routes reduced fuel consumption and emissions by 20%, contributing to both environmental and economic sustainability (Amsterdam Smart City, 2023). Through predictive analytics, AI can further refine waste collection patterns to anticipate peak disposal times and seasonal trends, enhancing the overall efficiency of waste management.

AI-powered Sorting Technologies and Robotics

Advanced sorting technologies powered by AI have revolutionized recycling processes by enabling precise material separation, even for complex waste streams. Automated robotic arms, guided by computer vision and machine learning, can accurately sort different types of plastics and metals. Studies indicate that AI-driven sorters reduce sorting time by 50% and minimize errors, resulting in higher recovery rates and reduced contamination (Lubongo et al., 2024). This precision in sorting not only improves recycling efficiency but also supports circular economy goals by reducing the volume of materials sent to landfills.

Consumer Behavior Analysis and Engagement in Waste Management

AI's ability to analyze data at scale makes it a powerful tool for understanding and influencing consumer behavior related to waste disposal and recycling. By analyzing patterns in consumer waste habits, AI can help design targeted public awareness campaigns that promote sustainable behaviors. For example, AI-based applications can send reminders to consumers to recycle and offer rewards for responsible waste disposal, thus fostering a culture of sustainability (Islam et al., 2021). Furthermore, AI can be used in educational programs to inform the public about recycling best practices, encouraging active participation in circular waste management initiatives.

AI in Product Design for Recyclability

Product design plays a critical role in facilitating recycling and resource efficiency. AI and Machine Learning (ML) can assist designers in evaluating materials and structural choices, suggesting sustainable alternatives that enhance recyclability and align with circular economy principles. Research shows that AI-based design tools can reduce material waste by 10–20% by optimizing product packaging and encouraging the use of recyclable materials (Erkinay Ozdemir et al., 2021). Through simulation and analysis, AI and ML can help identify environmentally friendly materials and streamline the design process for sustainable outcomes.

AI in Predictive Maintenance for Waste Management Infrastructure

Maintaining waste management infrastructure, such as sorting machines and collection vehicles, is essential for operational efficiency. AI-based predictive maintenance systems analyze equipment performance data to forecast potential failures and schedule timely repairs. This predictive approach minimizes downtime, reduces maintenance costs, and extends equipment lifespan, thereby supporting resource efficiency and lowering environmental impact (Rutqvist et al., 2020). Such systems can be integrated with waste management facilities to ensure continuous operation and optimal performance, aligning with circular economy goals by minimizing resource input and waste output.

Ethical and Regulatory Considerations in AI-driven Waste Management

The use of AI in waste management raises ethical concerns and regulatory challenges, particularly around data privacy, transparency, and accessibility. Ensuring that AI systems are fair and unbiased is crucial to maintaining public trust and equitable access to technology. Additionally, regulatory frameworks for waste management and AI integration are still evolving, with an emphasis on promoting responsible use while protecting individual privacy rights. A review by Fan et al. (2023) highlights the importance of transparent AI policies to ensure compliance with environmental and data protection standards.

Methodology

Data Collection and Processing

The data required for AI-driven waste management was collected from a variety of sources, including smart waste bins, recycling facilities, and consumer surveys. Smart waste bins equipped with fill-level sensors collected data on waste volume, types, and disposal patterns in real-time. These bins provided insights into waste generation trends across different locations and times, allowing for more accurate predictions in waste collection and recycling processes (Vu & Kaddoum, 2017). The data collected from smart bins was then transmitted to a central database, where it was preprocessed for machine learning applications.

Additionally, high-resolution cameras and optical sensors installed in sorting facilities captured images and physical characteristics of waste materials as they moved along conveyor belts. These images, covering various material types such as PET, HDPE, Polyvinyl Chloride (PVC), and aluminum-lined plastics, formed a large dataset used to train AI models for accurate sorting (Sirawattananon et al., 2021). To improve data quality, preprocessing steps such as image normalization, noise reduction, and labeling were conducted, ensuring the model's accuracy and robustness.

To gain insights into consumer behavior, surveys were also conducted to understand household waste disposal habits and attitudes toward recycling (Sarbassov et al., 2019). This behavioral data was used to identify patterns and further enhance the AI models' predictive capabilities. Altogether, the data collected was divided into training, validation, and testing sets to facilitate model development and performance evaluation.

AI Model Design and Training

AI model development focused on designing algorithms capable of accurately identifying, classifying, and sorting different types of waste. For this purpose, convolutional neural networks (CNNs) and support vector machines (SVMs) were selected due to their high performance in image recognition and classification tasks. CNNs were used to process the high-resolution images from sorting lines, leveraging their ability to capture spatial hierarchies in data and recognize complex patterns in different types of plastics and metals (Toğaçar et al., 2020). The CNN model was trained on labeled images, with each type of material assigned specific tags for classification purposes. During training, data augmentation techniques such as rotation, scaling, and flipping were employed to increase the robustness of the model by exposing it to various perspectives and lighting conditions. The use of transfer learning where a pre-trained CNN model is fine-tuned with domain-specific data accelerated the training process and enhanced classification accuracy. SVMs were used for fine-grained classification tasks on smaller datasets, specifically to detect material layers like plastic linings in aluminum cans. SVM models were trained with cross-validation and hyperparameter tuning to prevent overfitting, achieving over 90% classification accuracy (Pasadas et al., 2020). Key evaluation metrics included accuracy, precision, recall, and $F1$-score, with iterative training cycles to optimize model performance, ensuring reliable real-world waste sorting applications.

System Integration and Testing

AI models were integrated into the waste management infrastructure to enable real-time sorting through robotic arms equipped with sensors and cameras. These arms used AI-driven algorithms to accurately separate materials based on type and recyclability, such as directing aluminum cans with plastic linings to specific processing stations. A pilot study was conducted across multiple recycling streams, evaluating sorting speed, accuracy, and efficiency under various conditions. The system achieved a 92% sorting accuracy rate, reduced contamination, and improved processing efficiency (Rahman et al., 2020). Key performance indicators such as sorting accuracy, processing time, and contamination reduction were used to measure success. Regular maintenance and recalibration protocols were established to ensure continued optimal performance.

Real-time Monitoring and Adaptive Learning

To ensure ongoing optimization, a real-time monitoring module was implemented to continuously track the performance of AI-driven sorting operations. This module collected data on sorting accuracy and operational efficiency, which was fed back into the AI model to facilitate adaptive learning. By continuously updating the model with new data, the system was able to improve its classification accuracy and dynamically respond to changes in waste composition over time (Sirawattananon et al., 2021). Adaptive learning allowed the system to refine its sorting algorithms based on real-world feedback loops. For instance, if a particular material type was frequently misclassified, the monitoring system flagged the issue and prompted model retraining with additional labeled data to correct the misclassification. Furthermore, automated machine learning (AutoML) was employed to enhance the classification accuracy and recall of the recycling container emptying detection model, utilizing a Random Forest classifier to improve performance (Rutqvist et al., 2020). This adaptive capability not only improved sorting accuracy but also enabled the system to handle evolving waste streams and material variations, aligning with circular economy goals by optimizing resource recovery.

AI Applications in Plastic Waste Management

Smart Waste Collection and Routing

AI-based smart waste collection systems use fill-level sensors installed in waste bins to monitor and report fill levels in real-time. By continuously assessing the status of each bin, these systems provide data for dynamic scheduling and route optimization, ensuring that waste collection only occurs when bins are near capacity (Sirawattananon et al., 2021; Vu & Kaddoum, 2017). This data-driven approach prevents unnecessary pickups, conserves fuel, and reduces both operational costs and carbon emissions. For example, an AI-driven waste collection initiative in Amsterdam resulted in a 20% reduction in collection costs and a 15% decrease in CO_2 emissions by optimizing collection routes (Amsterdam Smart City, 2023).

In addition to optimizing routes, AI-enabled waste collection systems use predictive analytics to anticipate waste generation patterns, enabling waste management companies to allocate resources based on peak disposal times and seasonal fluctuations. This predictive capability reduces the frequency of overflows, enhances service efficiency, and minimizes the environmental impact associated with waste collection vehicles (Abdallah et al., 2020). Furthermore, smart bins can distinguish between recyclable and non-recyclable waste, segregating materials at the point of disposal, which supports recycling processes by reducing initial sorting needs.

Enhanced Sorting and Recycling

AI-driven sorting technologies play a crucial role in automating and optimizing the recycling process. Optical sorters powered by AI use high-resolution cameras and sensors to identify different types of plastics, metals, and composite materials in waste streams. Image recognition algorithms enable these systems to distinguish between various materials, allowing for precise sorting, even in complex cases like drink cans that combine aluminum with plastic linings (Rahman et al., 2020). This precise sorting is vital for enhancing the quality of recycled materials and reducing contamination rates, which are typically a major barrier to efficient recycling.

Studies have shown that AI-powered sorting systems can reduce contamination rates by 40%, significantly improving the purity and marketability of recycled materials. The AI algorithms used in these systems are continually refined through machine learning, which allows them to adapt to new material compositions and contamination patterns over time (Guo et al., 2020). In some facilities, robotic arms controlled by AI-powered sorting algorithms separate materials with an accuracy of up to 92%, enabling higher recovery rates for recyclable plastics and metals. By increasing the amount of recyclable material recovered from waste, these systems align with circular economy goals by reducing the reliance on virgin resources and extending the lifecycle of existing materials (Rahman et al., 2020).

Additionally, AI-driven sorters can operate continuously, reducing the need for manual sorting and allowing recycling facilities to process higher volumes of waste with fewer human resources. Some systems also incorporate infrared and X-ray technologies in conjunction with AI, which further improves material recognition by analyzing the chemical composition of waste (Abdallah et al., 2020). This combination allows facilities to manage diverse waste streams with high precision, including the accurate separation of plastics like PET, HDPE, and PVC (Sirawattananon et al., 2021).

LCA and Redesigning Packaging

LCAs are crucial for evaluating the environmental impact of products from raw material extraction to disposal. AI-enhanced LCAs provide manufacturers with real-time insights into sustainability by analyzing large datasets on material sourcing, energy use, and waste generation. This helps identify areas for improvement and encourages redesigning packaging with recyclability and sustainability in mind. AI-powered LCAs can simulate various design and material options, enabling data-driven decisions that align with circular economy principles (Christensen et al., 2020). For example, if a packaging material proves hard to recycle or generates high emissions, AI can recommend alternative materials or design changes to minimize environmental impact, promoting the use of monomaterial packaging or biodegradable polymers.

In addition to material recommendations, AI-driven LCAs can suggest packaging designs that use less material, improve product durability, or facilitate disassembly, making recycling more efficient. For instance, drink cans with removable plastic linings allow recycling facilities to separate and process aluminum and plastic more easily, reducing contamination and improving the quality of recycled output. According to studies, AI-based LCA applications can reduce material costs by up to 15% by promoting efficient resource allocation and waste reduction (Nordahl & Scown, 2024). Ultimately, this helps manufacturers align with circular economy objectives, supporting both environmental sustainability and cost savings.

AI-driven Material Innovation for Sustainable Packaging

AI can also assist manufacturers in developing sustainable materials that are easier to recycle or biodegrade, reducing the environmental footprint of packaging. Machine learning models can analyze the chemical and physical properties of materials, identifying those that align best with recyclability standards while maintaining product safety and durability (D'Almeida & de Albuquerque, 2024).

For instance, AI can recommend additives that improve the recyclability of plastics or suggest alternative formulations that reduce reliance on virgin plastics. Some manufacturers are using AI to explore plant-based materials or bio-plastics as alternatives to conventional plastics, aligning with consumer demand for sustainable products and packaging.

Case Studies

Amsterdam's AI-driven Waste Management

Amsterdam has adopted a comprehensive AI-driven waste management system that leverages smart bins equipped with fill-level sensors and image recognition software. These smart bins continuously monitor waste levels and transmit real-time data to waste management authorities, enabling dynamic route planning and optimizing collection frequency based on actual needs rather than fixed schedules (Reza & Hassan, 2023). This AI-based approach has reduced the frequency of unnecessary pickups, lowering fuel consumption by 18% and cutting operational costs. Furthermore, the system's advanced image recognition technology assists in identifying and separating recyclables, leading to higher recycling rates by effectively segregating materials before they reach processing facilities. Amsterdam's AI-enabled waste management framework has served as a model for other cities, demonstrating how technology can streamline urban waste systems, reduce emissions, and enhance resource recovery (Amsterdam Smart City, 2023).

San Francisco's Zero Waste Initiative

San Francisco's commitment to achieving zero waste by 2030 led to the integration of AI-powered bins across the city. These bins are designed with real-time sorting capabilities, utilizing image recognition and sensor-based technology to guide users on proper disposal. When a user disposes of an item, the bin provides interactive feedback on whether the item is recyclable, compostable, or landfill waste, improving accuracy in waste sorting at the source (City of San Francisco, 2024). Coupled with extensive public awareness campaigns, this initiative has resulted in a 25% increase in recycling rates since its launch and has effectively reduced contamination in recycling streams, enabling cleaner and more efficient recycling processes (City of San Francisco, 2024). Additionally, this initiative highlights the importance of engaging communities in sustainability efforts by making waste sorting a more interactive and informed process.

Challenges in Sorting Mixed Plastics: Case Study of New York City

New York City's waste management system faces distinct challenges in handling mixed plastic waste, particularly for drink cans that combine aluminum with plastic linings. While AI-enabled sorting technologies have improved separation accuracy by 85%, issues with material contamination and variability in plastic quality persist, limiting recycling efficiency. Due to the complexity of sorting materials with different properties, such as plastic-aluminum composites, New York's waste management facilities struggle with accurately separating recyclable components without contaminating the recycled output (Ventola et al., 2021). This case study underscores the need for advanced sorting algorithms and adaptive machine learning models that can handle heterogeneous waste streams more effectively (New York City Department of Sanitation, 2023).

Singapore's AI-enhanced Waste Collection and Sorting

Singapore has implemented AI-powered waste management solutions to address high waste generation rates in its densely populated urban environment. The city's AI-driven waste collection system uses fill-level sensors installed in bins across residential and commercial areas, which transmit data to waste collection services for real-time route optimization. This approach has reduced the number of collection trips by 15%, leading to a 10% reduction in fuel consumption and CO_2 emissions (Fan et al., 2019). Additionally, Singapore's recycling facilities utilize AI-enhanced sorting machines that accurately separate plastics and metals, achieving over 90% sorting accuracy. This efficient sorting has significantly reduced contamination rates in recycling streams, supporting the country's goal of achieving a recycling rate of 70% by 2030.

Tokyo's AI-powered Waste Sorting for Clean Resource Recovery

Tokyo, Japan, has integrated AI-based sorting technology in its recycling facilities to enhance the recovery of clean resources and manage high urban waste volumes. The AI-enabled sorting system uses high-resolution cameras and infrared sensors to differentiate between plastics, metals, and paper products, with an accuracy rate exceeding 93%. This sorting technology has helped Tokyo increase its recycling rates by 20% over the past 5 years, especially for challenging waste streams like plastic containers and packaging (Tokyo Metropolitan Government, 2024). The city has also incorporated robotic arms controlled by AI that autonomously handle delicate sorting tasks, reducing the need for human labor and ensuring high sorting accuracy. Tokyo's use of AI in waste management has set a standard for cities dealing with high-density waste generation and limited landfill space, emphasizing AI's role in resource efficiency and clean recycling (Tokyo Metropolitan Government, 2024).

Barcelona's Smart Waste Management and Recycling Initiative

Barcelona has embraced AI-driven waste management to streamline operations and improve recycling efficiency. In this system, AI-powered smart bins monitor waste levels and waste composition, providing data that optimizes collection schedules and ensures efficient resource allocation. Barcelona's waste management system has reduced collection costs by 15% and increased recycling rates by 18% since implementing the AI-based model (Barcelona Smart City Report, 2024). Additionally, AI-based sorting facilities in the city separate different types of plastics and metals with 92% accuracy, contributing to a cleaner recycling stream and reducing the amount of waste sent to landfills (Barcelona Smart City Report, 2024). This initiative underscores the value of AI in creating sustainable urban waste management systems and promoting circular economy practices.

Berlin's Circular Economy Initiative Using AI in Waste Segregation

Berlin has implemented an AI-based waste segregation program as part of its circular economy initiative to reduce landfill dependence and promote resource recovery. AI-driven sorting systems in Berlin's recycling facilities use machine learning to accurately separate materials such as PET, HDPE, and aluminum, achieving over 90% accuracy in classification. These facilities are also equipped with adaptive learning algorithms that improve sorting precision based on real-time waste stream data, reducing material contamination and enhancing the quality of recyclable output (Berlin Waste Management Authority, 2023). Since adopting this AI-based approach, Berlin has seen a 25% improvement in recycling rates, contributing to its goal of achieving zero waste by 2050 (Berlin Waste Management Authority, 2023).

Challenges and Community Engagement in AI-enabled Waste Management

Financial Constraints and Accessibility

Implementing AI in waste management requires substantial upfront investment, including costs for advanced hardware, such as cameras, sensors, and computing power, as well as ongoing software maintenance and system updates (Sirawattananon et al., 2021). This financial burden often poses a significant barrier, especially for smaller facilities or communities with limited budgets. Developing regions face additional challenges, as the resources needed to install and sustain AI-driven infrastructure may be prohibitive without financial support or government incentives. To make AI more accessible, governments and private sectors can collaborate to provide funding initiatives, subsidies, or public-private partnerships, enabling more facilities to benefit from AI's efficiency and environmental impact (Abdallah et al., 2020). For broader adoption, establishing cost-sharing models or leasing programs for AI equipment can also help reduce the initial financial burden.

Infrastructure and Technological Barriers

The lack of necessary technological infrastructure in waste facilities, especially in remote or rural areas, hampers AI integration. AI-based waste management systems require a stable internet connection, reliable power supply, and access to high-quality data, all of which are sometimes lacking in these regions (Abdallah et al., 2020). Connectivity issues disrupt real-time data transmission from smart bins and sorting systems, preventing AI algorithms from functioning effectively. To address this challenge, there is a need for investment in internet connectivity and digital infrastructure in underserved areas. Moreover, developing scalable

AI systems that can operate effectively even with intermittent connectivity could expand the reach of AI-driven waste management solutions (Sharma et al., 2020). Creating adaptive, low-power AI systems that can process data locally, reducing dependency on cloud-based systems, may also improve the feasibility of deploying AI in regions with limited infrastructure.

Data Quality, Consistency, and Management

AI models in waste management heavily rely on high-quality, consistent data to perform effectively. However, incomplete or inconsistent data can degrade AI model accuracy, leading to misclassification and errors in sorting and routing. Waste composition and contamination levels vary by location and time, adding to the complexity of maintaining consistent data (Sirawattananon et al., 2021). Establishing standardized data collection practices across facilities can help mitigate these challenges. For instance, implementing uniform labeling and categorization of waste types across regions can improve data accuracy, thereby enhancing the AI system's predictive capabilities (Namoun et al., 2022). Moreover, robust data management practices, including regular updates and validation of data inputs, are essential for ensuring the reliable operation of AI algorithms.

Technical Challenges: Sorting Mixed and Multi-material Waste

One of the more complex technical challenges faced by AI in waste management is accurately sorting mixed-material waste, especially plastics combined with other materials, like aluminum-lined drink cans (Lanzalonga et al., 2024; Rahman et al., 2020). These items require precise identification and separation due to their multi-layered composition, which can lead to contamination if not handled properly. Current AI sorting algorithms may struggle with these mixed-material items, as they vary significantly in texture, thickness, and chemical composition. To address this, advancements in sorting algorithms and the integration of multi-sensor technology, such as X-ray and infrared spectroscopy, can improve AI's ability to differentiate and separate materials effectively (Guo et al., 2022). Research into machine learning models capable of handling heterogeneous waste streams will also be critical for advancing AI's applicability in complex recycling environments.

Addressing Challenges and Encouraging Community Involvement

Overcoming the challenges associated with AI in waste management requires a multi-faceted approach, combining technological innovation, infrastructure investment, and community engagement. Building affordable, scalable AI systems that can adapt to diverse waste streams, alongside implementing public awareness campaigns, will increase the reach and efficacy of AI in promoting sustainable waste management practices (Onyeaka et al., 2023). Collaborations between government entities, private companies, and local communities can also provide the support necessary to address financial and technological barriers. Ultimately, a combination of robust AI systems and an informed, engaged public offers the most sustainable path forward for waste management and the circular economy, fostering an ecosystem where technological advancements and community responsibility work in tandem to create lasting environmental impact (Abdallah et al., 2020).

Results and Discussion

Enhanced Recycling Efficiency and Contamination Reduction

AI-enabled sorting systems have achieved remarkable advancements in recycling accuracy, with an 85% success rate across diverse material types, including plastics, metals, and mixed-material items like drink cans lined with plastic (Lanzalonga et al., 2024). This level of accuracy represents a substantial improvement over traditional methods, which often struggle to achieve precise separation due to the complexity of material properties and the limitations of manual or semi-automated processes. AI-powered sorting technologies, such as high-resolution optical sorters and machine learning algorithms, allow facilities to process waste at a faster pace, significantly improving sorting consistency and quality (Rahman et al., 2020).

One of the most notable benefits of AI-enhanced sorting is the reduction in contamination levels within recycling streams. Contamination is a major issue in recycling, as even small amounts of non-recyclable materials can compromise the quality of an entire batch, rendering it unsuitable for reuse. By precisely identifying and separating materials, AI systems significantly reduce contamination, which in turn increases the purity of recycled products (Guo et al., 2022). This high-quality output is suitable for reintegration into production cycles without the need for extensive reprocessing, lowering both environmental impact and operational costs. Facilities implementing AI sorting have reported up to a 40% improvement in material quality, enhancing the viability and profitability of recycled materials in industrial applications (Fan et al., 2023).

Cost Reduction and Operational Efficiency

The integration of AI in waste management has led to notable reductions in operational costs, primarily due to optimized waste collection and sorting processes (Abdallah et al., 2020). AI-driven waste collection systems use real-time data from smart bins to streamline collection routes, reducing the number of pickups and associated labor, fuel, and maintenance costs. Cities like Amsterdam (Amsterdam Smart City, 2023; Reza & Hassan, 2023) and San Francisco (City of San Francisco, 2024), which have implemented AI-optimized routing, have reported up to a 20% decrease in operational expenses (Amsterdam Smart City, 2023; City of San Francisco, 2024). By ensuring that waste is collected only when bins are nearing capacity, these AI systems prevent unnecessary trips, further minimizing fuel consumption and greenhouse gas emissions.

Within recycling facilities, AI-driven automation has reduced dependency on manual labor, lowering labor costs and minimizing the risk of human error in sorting operations. Facilities equipped with robotic sorting arms powered by AI algorithms operate continuously with minimal downtime, processing higher volumes of waste at a faster rate than traditional methods (Fan et al., 2023; Rutqvist et al., 2020). This continuous operation increases throughput and efficiency, particularly in high-volume facilities, where managing fluctuating waste inputs can be challenging. Some recycling facilities have also experienced energy savings of up to 15% due to optimized sorting processes, which reduce idle time and enhance equipment longevity (Lubongo & Alexandridis, 2022).

Environmental Impact: Carbon Footprint and Waste Reduction

The environmental benefits of AI-driven waste management are multi-faceted, extending beyond operational efficiency to address pressing ecological concerns such as carbon emissions and waste diversion from landfills. By reducing landfill contributions by 25%, AI-enhanced recycling efforts have decreased methane emissions, one of the most potent greenhouse gases associated with landfill decomposition (Shen, 2023). The diversion of waste from landfills not only helps reduce environmental pollution but also mitigates the strain on landfill capacity, particularly in urban areas facing landfill scarcity.

LCAs have further demonstrated that AI-optimized recycling processes reduce reliance on virgin materials, leading to a 30% decrease in plastic waste generation. This reduction is significant, as it translates into fewer resources required for material production, which in turn decreases energy consumption and emissions across the production lifecycle (Abdallah et al., 2020). By extending the lifecycle of materials through recycling and reuse, AI-driven waste management contributes to circular economy goals, aligning with broader environmental objectives such as resource conservation and reduced ecological footprint.

Contribution to Circular Economy Goals

AI's contributions to waste management align closely with circular economy goals, promoting material reuse, resource conservation, and waste minimization. By enhancing sorting accuracy, AI enables more materials to reenter the production cycle rather than being discarded, reducing dependence on raw materials and fostering a closed-loop system (Lanzalonga et al., 2024). Furthermore, AI-powered LCAs provide crucial insights for manufacturers to design products with recyclability in mind, encouraging sustainable production and packaging.

AI's ability to continuously analyze and optimize processes strengthens these goals by adapting to changing waste compositions and advancing sustainable resource management (Sarc et al., 2019). Through precise recycling and waste reduction, AI-driven waste management systems enhance resource recovery and enable industries to adopt sustainable practices aligned with circular economy principles. This holistic approach supports environmental, economic, and social sustainability by minimizing waste, conserving resources, and promoting a cleaner ecosystem (Sariatli, 2017).

Conclusion

The integration of AI in plastic waste management showcases its transformative potential in enhancing recycling efficiency, reducing operational costs, and advancing circular economy goals. AI's ability to optimize waste collection, automate sorting processes, and conduct LCAs demonstrates its value in creating a more sustainable, efficient, and environmentally responsible waste management system. The case studies of cities such as Amsterdam, San Francisco, and Tokyo illustrate the practical benefits and impacts of AI-driven waste management, including reductions in fuel consumption, carbon emissions, and contamination within recycling streams.

Despite its benefits, implementing AI in waste management is not without challenges. High initial costs for infrastructure, data management issues, and the complexity of sorting mixed-material waste present obstacles that need to be addressed for wider adoption. Future research should focus on developing scalable AI solutions that can be implemented across a diverse range of facilities, from urban to remote settings. Improvements in data quality, adaptive algorithms for handling heterogeneous waste, and enhanced public awareness programs are essential to maximizing AI's potential in waste management.

Additionally, fostering community engagement and increasing public participation in sustainable practices will complement AI-driven efforts, creating a synergy between technology and social responsibility. By promoting circular economy principles through resource recovery and waste reduction, AI has the potential to drive systemic change in how society manages plastic waste, contributing to a cleaner, more resource-efficient future. Through continuous innovation and collaboration, AI in waste management can pave the way toward a sustainable, circular economy that benefits both society and the environment.

References

Abdallah, M., Talib, M., Feroz, S., Nasir, Q., Abdalla, H., & Mahfood, B. (2020). Artificial intelligence applications in solid waste management: A systematic research review. *Waste Management*, *109*, 231–246. https://doi.org/10.1016/j.wasman.2020.04.057

Amsterdam Smart City. (2023). *Smart waste management for sustainable urban living*. https://amsterdamsmartcity.com/

Barcelona Smart City Report. (2024). *Barcelona's smart waste management and recycling initiative*. https://www.barcelonasmartcity.com/smart-waste-management

Berlin Waste Management Authority. (2023). *Abfallwirtschaftskonzept für Siedlungs- und BauabfällesowieKlärschlämme für den Planungszeitraum 2020 bis 2030*. Berlin.de. https://www.berlin.de

Christensen, T., Damgaard, A., Levis, J., Zhao, Y., Björklund, A., Arena, U., Barlaz, M., Starostina, V., Boldrin, A., Astrup, T., & Bisinella, V. (2020). Application of LCA modelling in integrated waste management. *Waste Management*, *118*, 313–322.

City of San Francisco. (2024). *Zero waste initiative: AI-powered waste management in San Francisco*. City of San Francisco Report. https://www.sfgov.org/services/recycling-zero-waste

D'Almeida, A. P., & de Albuquerque, T. L. (2024). Innovations in food packaging: From bio-based materials to smart packaging systems. *Processes*, *12*(10), 2085.

Ellen MacArthur Foundation. (2023). *The circular economy in detail*. ellenmacarthurfoundation.org

Erkinay Ozdemir, M., Ali, Z., Subeshan, B., & Asmatulu, E. (2021). Applying machine learning approach in recycling. *Journal of Material Cycles and Waste Management*, *23*, 855–871.

European Environment Agency. (2023). *Artificial intelligence for circular economy*. eea.europa.eu

Fan, B., Yang, W., & Shen, X. (2019). A comparison study of 'motivation–intention–behavior' model on household solid waste sorting in China and Singapore. *Journal of Cleaner Production*, *211*, 442–454. https://doi.org/10.1016/J.JCLEPRO.2018.11.168

Fan, Z., Yan, Z., & Wen, S. (2023). Deep learning and artificial intelligence in sustainability: A review of SDGs, renewable energy, and environmental health. *Sustainability*, *15*(18), 13493.

Geissdoerfer, M., Savaget, P., Bocken, N. M. P., & Hultink, E. J. (2017). The circular economy – A new sustainability paradigm? *Journal of Cleaner Production*, *143*, 757–768.

Geyer, R., Jambeck, J. R., & Law, K. L. (2020). Production, use, and fate of all plastics ever made. *Science Advances*, *3*(7), e1700782.

Guo, D., Liu, H., Fang, B., Sun, F., & Yang, W. (2022). Visual affordance guided tactile material recognition for waste recycling. *IEEE Transactions on Automation Science and Engineering*, *19*, 2656–2664. https://doi.org/10.1109/TASE.2021.3065991

Guo, H., Wu, S., Tian, Y., Zhang, J., & Liu, H. (2020). Application of machine learning methods for the prediction of organic solid waste treatment and recycling processes: A review. *Bioresource Technology*, *319*, 124114. https://doi.org/10.1016/j.biortech.2020.124114

Islam, M. T., Huda, N., Baumber, A., Shumon, R., Zaman, A., Ali, F., Hossain, R., & Sahajwalla, V. (2021). A global review of consumer behavior towards e-waste and implications for the circular economy. *Journal of Cleaner Production*, *316*, 128297.

Lanzalonga, F., Marseglia, R., Irace, A., & Biancone, P. P. (2024). The application of artificial intelligence in waste management: Understanding the potential of data-driven approaches for the circular economy paradigm. *Management Decision*. https://doi.org/10.1108/MD-10-2023-1733.

Lubongo, C., & Alexandridis, P. (2022). Assessment of performance and challenges in use of commercial automated sorting technology for plastic waste. *Recycling*, *7*(2), 11. https://doi.org/10.3390/recycling7020011

Lubongo, C., Bin Daej, M. A., & Alexandridis, P. (2024). Recent developments in technology for sorting plastic for recycling: The emergence of artificial intelligence and the rise of the robots. *Recycling*, *9*(4), 59.

Namoun, A., Tufail, A., Khan, M., Alrehaili, A., Syed, T., & Benrhouma, O. (2022). Solid waste generation and disposal using machine learning approaches: A survey of solutions and challenges. *Sustainability*, *14*(20), 13578. https://doi.org/10.3390/su142013578

Nordahl, S. L., & Scown, C. D. (2024). Recommendations for life-cycle assessment of recyclable plastics in a circular economy. *Chemical Science*, *15*(25), 9397–9407.

Onyeaka, H., Tamasiga, P., Nwauzoma, U., Miri, T., Juliet, U., Nwaiwu, O., & Akinsemolu, A. (2023). Using Artificial Intelligence to tackle food waste and enhance the circular economy: Maximising resource efficiency and minimising environmental impact: A review. *Sustainability*, *15*(13), 10482. https://doi.org/10.3390/su151310482

Pasadas, D., Baskaran, P., Ramos, H., & Ribeiro, A. (2020). Detection and classification of defects using ECT and multi-level SVM model. *IEEE Sensors Journal*, *20*, 2329–2338. https://doi.org/10.1109/JSEN.2019.2951302

Plastics Europe. (2023). *Plastics – The facts*. plasticseurope.org

Rahman, M., Islam, R., Hasan, A., Bithi, N., Hasan, M., & Rahman, M. (2020). Intelligent waste management system using deep learning with IoT. *Journal of King Saud University – Computer and Information Science, 34*, 2072–2087. https://doi.org/10.1016/j.jksuci.2020.08.016

Reza, M., & Hassan, M. (2023). AI-Driven solutions for enhanced waste management and recycling in urban areas. *International Journal of Sustainable Infrastructure for Cities and Societies, 8*(2), 1–13.

Rutqvist, D., Kleyko, D., & Blomstedt, F. (2020). An automated machine learning approach for smart waste management systems. *IEEE Transactions on Industrial Informatics, 16*(1), 384–392. https://doi.org/10.1109/TII.2019.2915572

Sarbassov, Y., Sagalova, T., Tursunov, O., Venetis, C., Xenarios, S., & Inglezakis, V. (2019). Survey on household solid waste sorting at source in developing economies: A case study of Nur-Sultan city in Kazakhstan. *Sustainability, 11*(22), 6496. https://doi.org/10.3390/su11226496

Sarc, R., Curtis, A., Kandlbauer, L., Khodier, K., Lorber, K., & Pomberger, R. (2019). Digitalisation and intelligent robotics in value chain of circular economy oriented waste management – A review. *Waste Management, 95*, 476–492. https://doi.org/10.1016/J.WASMAN.2019.06.035

Sariatli, F. (2017). Linear economy versus circular economy: A comparative and analyzer study for optimization of economy for sustainability. *Visegrad Journal on Bioeconomy and Sustainable Development, 6*, 31–34. https://doi.org/10.1515/vjbsd-2017-0005

Sharma, M., Joshi, S., Kannan, D., Govindan, K., Singh, R., & Purohit, H. (2020). Internet of Things (IoT) adoption barriers of smart cities' waste management: An Indian context. *Journal of Cleaner Production, 270*, 122047. https://doi.org/10.1016/j.jclepro.2020.122047

Shen, R. (2023). Utilizing artificial intelligence and machine learning to facilitate achieving carbon neutrality. *Science and Technology of Engineering, Chemistry and Environmental Protection, 1*(1), 11–14.

Sirawattananon, C., Muangnak, N., & Pukdee, W. (2021). Designing of IoT-based smart waste sorting system with image-based deep learning applications. In *2021 18th international conference on electrical engineering/electronics, computer, telecommunications and information technology (ECTI-CON)* (pp. 383–387). IEEE. https://doi.org/10.1109/ECTI-CON51831.2021.9454826.

Smith, M., Love, D. C., Rochman, C. M., & Neff, R. A. (2018). Microplastics in seafood and the implications for human health. *Current Environmental Health Reports, 5*(3), 375–386.

Toğaçar, M., Ergen, B., & Cömert, Z. (2020). Waste classification using AutoEncoder network with integrated feature selection method in convolutional neural network models. *Measurement, 153*, 107459. https://doi.org/10.1016/j.measurement.2019.107459

Tokyo Metropolitan Government. (2024). *Tokyo's AI-powered waste sorting for clean resource recovery*. Tokyo Metropolitan Government [online]. Retrieved November 6, 2024, from https://www.japan.go.jp/technology/advanced_waste_disposal.html

Ventola, V., Brenman, E., Chan, G., Ahmed, T., & Castaldi, M. (2021). Quantitative analysis of residential plastic recycling in New York City. *Waste Management & Research, 39*, 703–712. https://doi.org/10.1177/0734242X211009968

Vu, D. D., & Kaddoum, G. (2017, November). A waste city management system for smart cities applications. In *2017 advances in wireless and optical communications (RTUWO)* (pp. 225–229). IEEE. https://doi.org/10.1109/RTUWO.2017.8228538

Yarlagadda, S. C. The use of Artificial Intelligence and machine learning in creating a roadmap towards a circular economy for plastics. *International Journal on Recent and Innovation Trends in Computing and Communication, 11*(9s), 829–836.

Zheng, J., & Suh, S. (2021). Strategies to reduce the global carbon footprint of plastics. *Nature Climate Change, 9*(5), 374–378.

Chapter 6

Optimized Plant Identification Through Leaf Feature Extraction Using Deep Learning and Advanced Digital Image Processing Techniques

Mainak Saha and Sushanta Das

National Institute of Technology Agartala, Jirania, Agartala, Tripura, India

Abstract

In pursuit of sustainable agriculture and optimized resource management, this chapter presents an advanced approach to automated plant species identification using digital image processing (DIP) and machine learning (ML) techniques. Leveraging the Flavia Leaves dataset encompassing 32 plant species, the system effectively classifies plants based on distinct leaf attributes, including shape, size, color, and texture. The processing pipeline begins with pre-processing steps, such as background subtraction and image enhancement to isolate leaves, followed by feature extraction, capturing essential metrics, such as aspect ratio, circularity, Red, Green, Blue (RGB) color components, and texture features derived from the gray level co-occurrence matrix (GLCM). A support vector machine (SVM) classifier, chosen for its robustness in high-dimensional data spaces, achieves a classification accuracy of 90.05%, with minor errors occurring in species with overlapping textures or similar morphological traits. This system's high accuracy highlights the potential of DIP and ML in efficient and sustainable plant classification, with direct applications in biodiversity conservation, agricultural resource management, and ecosystem monitoring. Future work aims to enhance the model's adaptability and precision by integrating deep learning techniques and expanding

Harnessing the Potential of Artificial Intelligence to Promote Environmental Sustainability, 89–104

Published under exclusive licence by Emerald Publishing Limited
doi:10.1108/978-1-83662-996-220251006

dataset diversity, thereby strengthening its applicability in sustainable agriculture and resource management initiatives.

Keywords: Digital image processing; machine learning; plant leaf classification; feature extraction; SVM classifier

Introduction

The identification of plant species is a fundamental task in botany, agriculture, and biodiversity conservation, playing an essential role in understanding and managing ecosystems (Sachar & Kumar, 2021). Leaves, as one of the most characteristic features of plants, offer valuable insights for classification and identification purposes due to their diverse morphologies, colors, and textures. Traditional methods of leaf identification, however, often rely on manual examination and expertise, which can be time-consuming, subjective, and prone to error, especially with species that exhibit overlapping characteristics or subtle morphological differences. These limitations present a considerable challenge in large-scale ecological studies and agricultural resource management, where accurate and efficient species identification is essential (Thenmozhi et al., 2021). The urgency for effective identification techniques grows as agriculture shifts toward sustainable practices and conservation efforts intensify to combat biodiversity loss. With millions of plant species yet to be documented, leveraging advanced technological tools for species identification becomes increasingly vital.

Recent advancements in automation, specifically DIP and ML, have opened new possibilities for automating plant classification, providing solutions that are both highly accurate and adaptable across a wide range of species (Nesteruk et al., 2021; Ngugi et al., 2021). Automation reduces the dependency on expert taxonomists and enables large-scale biodiversity assessments, which are crucial for conservation and sustainable agriculture. Several studies in the field demonstrate the promise of ML and DIP for plant classification, where DIP methods enhance image quality and isolate leaf features, while ML models classify species based on these characteristics with significant precision (Alyas & Mohammed, 2022; Bisen, 2021; Nesteruk et al., 2021). Yigit et al. (2019) demonstrated the efficacy of SVMs in classifying plant leaves with high accuracy in high-dimensional datasets, while Kim et al. (2002) research on texture-based leaf identification highlighted the value of texture features for distinguishing morphologically similar species. These works underscore the transformative role of ML and DIP in botanical studies, presenting scalable solutions for fieldwork and conservation.

In modern botany, the integration of ML and DIP techniques has revolutionized plant classification. Image processing techniques such as background subtraction, image enhancement, and segmentation allow for the isolation of leaf characteristics crucial for classification (Pooja et al., 2017). These techniques enable automated systems to assess unique features such as shape, size, color, and texture, transforming them into quantifiable data. In particular, ML algorithms, such as SVMs, *k*-nearest neighbor (*k*-NN), and convolutional neural networks (CNN), have been extensively applied to classify leaves based on extracted features. Each method offers distinct advantages: SVMs are effective in high-dimensional feature spaces, as demonstrated by Yigit et al. (2019) in an SVM-based leaf classification study; *k*-NN is intuitive and effective in smaller datasets, while CNN excel in complex feature hierarchies, making them suitable for large-scale image datasets (Barbedo, 2019). By combining these techniques, automated systems achieve rapid, accurate identification, enabling large-scale studies that were once impractical with traditional methods.

This chapter explores the implementation of DIP and ML for automated plant leaf classification, focusing on a model that leverages these technologies to improve accuracy and efficiency in species identification. By discussing the strengths of SVM for high-dimensional datasets, along with texture-based identification methods and other ML approaches, this study contributes to ongoing research in sustainable agriculture and conservation. The proposed approach addresses traditional classification challenges by offering a scalable, precise solution applicable to a broad range of species, with potential for future enhancement through deep learning and broader datasets. As technological advancements continue to shape botanical research, automated plant classification stands as a promising tool for addressing the pressing needs of agriculture.

Literature Review

The early development of automated plant leaf classification focused on straightforward DIP techniques to differentiate plant species. Initial efforts applied edge detection, shape analysis, and color histogram analysis to extract defining features from leaf images (Wei Tan et al., 2020). These studies relied on visual attributes, such as leaf contours and colors, as primary classification criteria, establishing a foundational approach for more advanced methodologies.

As image processing evolved, researchers began integrating statistical and ML techniques to improve classification outcomes. Early ML methods, such as *k*-NNs and SVMs, were introduced for their ability to analyze feature vectors generated from morphological characteristics (Kim et al., 2002). These methods marked a transition toward data-driven models, bringing higher accuracy to classification tasks by efficiently handling leaf shape, size, and texture metrics (Yigit et al., 2019).

In recent years, a range of ML algorithms has been applied to leaf classification, each demonstrating unique strengths and limitations (Ariyapadath, 2021). Techniques like SVM, CNN, decision trees, *k*-NNs, and random forests have been widely employed for their distinct suitability to the field. SVM, for instance, performs well in classifying leaves when shape, color, and texture features are extracted using methods like GLCM analysis (Kim et al., 2002; Yigit et al., 2019). CNN, on the other hand, use layered convolutional structures to automatically extract complex, hierarchical features, excelling with large datasets and performing well in capturing intricate textures and patterns directly from image data (Wei Tan et al., 2020).

Decision trees and random forests offer simpler and more interpretable models, often effective on smaller datasets but generally achieving lower accuracy on high-dimensional data compared to SVM and CNN (Chen et al., 2020). Algorithms such as k-NN, although effective in straightforward classification tasks, struggle with high-dimensional leaf datasets, particularly where dataset complexity and variety increase.

These varied algorithmic approaches highlight the balance between training time, accuracy, and scalability, suggesting the need for careful selection based on data volume and task complexity in leaf classification studies.

Gaps in Current Research

While ML has enabled significant advancements in plant species identification, several limitations persist.

Dependency on Labeled Datasets: Many ML models, particularly deep learning models like CNN, rely heavily on large, labeled datasets. This dependency presents challenges, as obtaining comprehensive labeled datasets of diverse leaf types is labor-intensive and costly (Li et al., 2023). Additionally, the performance of these models is often tied closely to the dataset quality, limiting their adaptability in settings with fewer annotated data resources.

Handling of Complex Backgrounds: Existing methods often encounter difficulty in isolating leaves from complex backgrounds, affecting classification performance. Outdoor images, for instance, commonly include overlapping foliage, uneven lighting, and natural obstructions, which can interfere with the feature extraction process (Yang et al., 2020). Developing methods that effectively address complex backgrounds would improve model reliability in real-world environments.

Model Generalizability: Another critical limitation is that many models trained on specific datasets, such as the Flavia Leaves or Swedish Leaf datasets, exhibit reduced accuracy when applied to other datasets (Li et al., 2023; Yang et al., 2020). This reduced generalizability underscores the need for approaches that adapt across diverse environmental conditions, lighting variations, and plant species to ensure broad applicability.

This work seeks to address notable gaps in automated plant leaf classification by enhancing feature extraction and pre-processing methods to effectively manage complex backgrounds and minimize reliance on extensive, labeled datasets. By integrating advanced image processing with ML, this approach aims to develop a more robust and adaptable classification pipeline, capable of maintaining high accuracy in diverse and challenging real-world environments. Additionally, the study considers future avenues for improvement through deep learning techniques, such as transfer learning, to facilitate broader generalizability across various plant species and environmental conditions. This approach not only aims to improve classification accuracy but also underscores the scalability and adaptability essential for real-world applications, contributing novel insights to the fields of automated plant identification, sustainable agriculture, and biodiversity management.

The progression of automated plant leaf classification research demonstrates a substantial evolution in accuracy and applicability, as ML and DIP techniques have advanced. However, challenges remain, notably the dependency on labeled datasets and the complexity of natural backgrounds. By addressing these limitations, this study contributes significantly to the advancement of ML in plant classification, highlighting its potential to enhance sustainability initiatives in agriculture and conservation. This work represents a meaningful step toward developing adaptable, high-precision classification systems that can support agricultural efficiency, biodiversity monitoring, and resource conservation on a broader scale.

Methodology

Data Collection and Preparation

Flavia Leaves Dataset

This study utilizes the Flavia Leaves dataset, which consists of images of 32 different plant species, capturing a total of approximately 4,000 images. Each species is represented by a diverse set of images, taken under controlled conditions to minimize variability in lighting and background (Su et al., 2020). The features selected for analysis in this dataset include shape, color, and texture characteristics of the leaves, which are crucial for effective classification.

Statistics:

Total species: 32.
Total images: ∼4,000.
Average images per species: approximately 125.

Distribution of species varies, with some species having a more substantial representation than others, aiding in ensuring robust training and validation of the classification model.

Data Augmentation

To enhance the model's robustness against real-world variations, data augmentation techniques were employed. These methods help increase the diversity of the training set without the need for additional data collection (Bravin et al., 2023). The following augmentation strategies were applied:

Rotations: Random rotations within a specified range (e.g., ±30 degrees) to account for various orientations in natural environments.

Scaling: Adjustments in size to simulate varying distances from the camera.

Cropping: Random cropping of images to focus on different parts of the leaves, allowing for better feature representation.

Pre-processing Techniques

The pre-processing phase is essential for enhancing image quality and preparing the dataset for feature extraction. It consists of several key steps:

Image Acquisition

Images are imported from the Flavia Leaves dataset and organized for efficient processing.

Background Subtraction

To isolate the leaves from background noise, morphological transformations were applied. The primary techniques include:

Dilation: Expanding the boundaries of the foreground (leaves) to fill small holes and gaps.

Erosion: Shrinking the boundaries to remove small noise and irrelevant artifacts from the background.

These transformations effectively isolate the leaf features from their complex backgrounds, enhancing subsequent analysis.

Image Enhancement

Image enhancement techniques, such as Gaussian filtering and Otsu's thresholding, are used to improve feature contrast and facilitate better segmentation:

Gaussian filtering: A smoothing technique that reduces noise and detail in the image, aiding in clearer feature extraction.

Otsu's thresholding: An adaptive method that determines an optimal threshold value to segment the leaf from the background, thus improving the clarity of the image.

Feature Extraction

Feature extraction is crucial in transforming raw image data into meaningful representations that can be utilized by the classification model. This study focuses on three primary categories of features: shape, color, and texture.

Shape-based Features

Shape metrics are calculated to distinguish species based on leaf morphology:

Aspect ratio: Defined as the ratio of the width to the height of the bounding rectangle of the leaf.

$$\text{Aspect ratio} = \frac{\text{Width}}{\text{Height}}$$

Rectangularity: A measure of how closely the shape of the leaf resembles a rectangle.

$$\text{Rectangularity} = \frac{\text{Area of leaf}}{\text{Area of bounding rectangle}}$$

Circularity: A metric indicating how circular the leaf is.

$$\text{Circularity} = \frac{4\pi \times \text{area}}{\text{Perimeter}^2}$$

These shape descriptors facilitate the differentiation of species based on their unique geometric properties.

Color-based Features

Color features are analyzed using color models, primarily RGB and Hue, Saturation, Value (HSV). The use of these models allows for a comprehensive understanding of color differences among species:

Color histograms: Histograms representing the distribution of colors in the leaf images are generated to capture color variance.

Texture-based Features

Texture analysis employs Haralick moments, which are derived from the GLCM to capture textural variance (Aouat et al., 2021):

Contrast: Measures the intensity contrast between a pixel and its neighbor.

$$\text{Contrast} = \sum_{i,j} (i - j)^2 \times P(i,j)$$

Correlation: Evaluates the joint probability distribution of the pixels.

$$\text{Correlation} = \frac{\sum_{i,j} (i - \mu_x)(j - \mu_y)P(i - j)}{\sigma_x \sigma_y}$$

Entropy: Represents the complexity or randomness of the texture.

$$\text{Entropy} = -\sum_{i,j} P(i - j)\log(P(i,j))$$

Feature vectors: The extracted features are combined into feature vectors that represent each leaf, providing a comprehensive set of characteristics for classification.

Classification Model: SVM

Overview of SVM

SVM serves as the core classification algorithm in this study due to its effectiveness in handling high-dimensional data. SVM works by finding the hyperplane that best separates the different classes in the feature space (Gholami & Fakhari, 2017). The key components include:

Kernel functions: SVM utilizes various kernel functions to enable classification in nonlinear spaces. Common kernels include:

Linear kernel: For linearly separable data.
Polynomial kernel: For capturing polynomial relationships.
Radial basis function (RBF) kernel: For complex datasets where classes are not linearly separable.

Model Training and Testing

The dataset is split into training and testing sets, typically using an 80–20% ratio. The training set is utilized to develop the SVM model, while the testing set evaluates its performance. Model tuning is performed through hyperparameter optimization, ensuring the SVM classifier achieves optimal performance.

Cross-validation: k-Fold cross-validation is employed to enhance model reliability, helping to mitigate overfitting by assessing the model's performance across multiple subsets of the data.

Mathematical formulation: The SVM classifier can be mathematically represented as follows:

$$f(x) = \text{sign}(\omega \cdot x + b)$$

where ω represents the weight vector, x the input feature vector, and b the bias term.

Experimental Setup and Implementation

Environment

The implementation of the automated plant leaf classification system was conducted with Python, using key libraries for DIP and ML to streamline and optimize the workflow:

- *Programming language*: Python
- *Libraries*:
  - *OpenCV*: Used for image processing, including tasks such as filtering, edge detection, and morphological transformations, which help in feature isolation and enhancement.
  - *Scikit-learn*: Facilitated the application of ML algorithms, particularly SVM for classification.
  - *NumPy*: Provided tools for numerical computation, particularly in handling and processing arrays.
  - *Pandas*: Assisted in data manipulation, organization, and management for efficient handling of dataset attributes.
  - *Matplotlib*: Enabled visualization of data distribution, results, and performance metrics.
  - *Mahotas*: Provided advanced image processing functions beneficial for specific feature extraction techniques.

Installation

The software environment was configured with Python and essential libraries, installed using pip: pip install OpenCV-python scikit-learn NumPy pandas matplotlib Mahotas.

This setup was chosen for its cross-platform compatibility and support for ML and image processing tasks, optimizing the project's reproducibility and ease of use.

Implementation Steps

The implementation of the automated classification model involved structured stages, each critical to achieving accurate classification of plant leaves.

Data Loading

The dataset comprises leaf images from various plant species, structured by species into directories, allowing easy labeling and preparation for classification.

Pre-processing

Pre-processing steps were applied to enhance image quality and standardize data before feature extraction:

- *Resizing*: Each image was resized to a consistent dimension, creating uniform input data and reducing computational load.
- *Grayscale conversion*: Converted images to grayscale, simplifying data and focusing on shape and texture.
- *Gaussian smoothing*: Applied Gaussian filtering to reduce image noise, facilitating more accurate feature extraction.

Feature Extraction

Three categories of features – shape, color, and texture – were extracted from each image to capture unique leaf characteristics and improve classification performance:

- *Shape features*: Shape descriptors, such as area, perimeter, circularity, and aspect ratio, were calculated to represent structural attributes that distinguish different leaf types.
- *Color features*: Color histograms captured the distribution of colors within each leaf, aiding in differentiating species with similar shapes but different color patterns.
- *Texture features*: Texture was quantified using Haralick moments, which capture variance in texture characteristics like contrast and correlation. These features are particularly helpful for distinguishing leaves with similar shapes but different textures.

Model Training

The SVM classifier was chosen for its effectiveness in handling high-dimensional data. Model training involved the following:

- *Data split*: The dataset was divided into training and testing sets (typically 80% training, 20% testing), ensuring a balanced evaluation.
- *Training*: The SVM model was trained using the extracted features, with cross-validation used to optimize hyperparameters and improve generalization.

Model Testing

The trained SVM model was evaluated using the testing set:

- *Prediction*: The model generated predictions for each test sample based on learned features.
- *Evaluation*: Metrics such as accuracy, precision, recall, and *F*1 score were calculated to assess classification effectiveness.

Evaluation Metrics

The model's performance was evaluated comprehensively using several key metrics. Accuracy measures the overall effectiveness of the model by calculating the ratio of correctly classified samples to the total samples, offering an intuitive sense of the model's general performance. Precision evaluates the proportion of positive identifications that are actually correct, which is particularly relevant in applications where the cost of false positives is high. In contrast, Recall (also known as sensitivity) assesses the model's capacity to identify all relevant instances within the dataset, thereby measuring its effectiveness in minimizing false negatives. To balance both precision and recall, the *F*1 score is used, representing the harmonic mean of these two metrics. This score is particularly useful when both false positives and false negatives carry significant costs, as it provides a nuanced assessment of the model's reliability across different scenarios. Together, these metrics provide a well-rounded evaluation of the model's accuracy, precision, recall, and balanced performance.

Relevance of Evaluation Metrics in Classification Tasks

Each metric offers distinct insights:

- Accuracy provides a general measure of success but may be misleading in cases of class imbalance.
- Precision is critical when false positives need to be minimized, as misclassification can have high consequences.
- Recall is significant when failing to identify positive instances poses risks, especially for rare or endangered species.
- *F*1 score balances precision and recall, making it ideal for evaluating classifiers where both types of misclassifications have implications.

These metrics were essential in assessing the effectiveness of the SVM classifier within the automated plant leaf classification pipeline, ensuring robust, reproducible results aligned with real-world applications of plant species classification. This approach emphasizes the potential for combining ML and DIP to advance automated plant classification and support broader applications in biodiversity monitoring, environmental conservation, and sustainable agriculture.

Results and Analysis

Classification Results

The SVM classifier achieved an accuracy of 90.05% on the test dataset, demonstrating a significant improvement over baseline models, such as *k*-NN and decision trees, which yielded lower accuracy levels of 81.2% and 85.6%, respectively. This high accuracy indicates the effectiveness of the selected feature extraction techniques – shape, color, and texture descriptors – in distinguishing different plant species based on their leaf characteristics.

To further evaluate performance, Table 6.1 presents a comparison of key classification metrics – accuracy, precision, recall, and *F*1 score – across the three models. The SVM outperformed others in all metrics. Specifically, it achieved an average precision of 89.3% and recall of 88.7%, highlighting its ability to correctly identify true positives while maintaining a low false positive rate. The *F*1 score, averaging 88.9%, underscores the model's balanced and robust performance, confirming its suitability for automated plant leaf classification tasks.

Error Analysis

To further understand the model's limitations, an error analysis was conducted on misclassified samples. Several common types of misclassifications were identified, particularly among species with similar textures or overlapping shape characteristics. For instance, leaves with smooth edges and similar shades of green were often confused with one another, primarily due to minimal shape and color differences. Textural overlap also presented challenges, as species with similar vein patterns and surface textures had higher misclassification rates.

Such errors suggest that the model could benefit from more advanced techniques, such as incorporating additional, deeper texture descriptors or using

Table 6.1. Comparison of Classification Performance Metrics Across Models.

Metric	SVM Model (%)	*k*-NN (%)	Decision Tree (%)
Accuracy	90.05	81.2	85.6
Precision	89.3	80.5	85.0
Recall	88.7	81.0	85.4
*F*1 score	88.9	80.7	85.2

higher-level neural network architectures capable of capturing subtler inter-species differences. Additionally, the performance might be enhanced by using domain-specific augmentation techniques to increase the dataset's variability and simulate real-world scenarios.

Confusion Matrix

The confusion matrix provides a visual summary of the classifier's performance across all species, highlighting both correct and incorrect classifications. Diagonal elements represent accurate classifications, while off-diagonal elements correspond to misclassifications.

As shown in Table 6.2, the SVM classifier demonstrates strong performance, with high diagonal values for most species. For example, Species A was correctly classified 92 times, with only minor misclassifications into Species B and C. Similarly, Species B and C achieved high correct classification counts of 88 and 90, respectively.

Despite the overall effectiveness, some misclassifications occurred, particularly between species B and C, which is consistent with observations from the error analysis. These overlaps suggest that these species share similar features, and refining the feature extraction pipeline – possibly by enhancing shape or texture descriptors – could reduce such confusion.

Evaluation Metrics Visualization

To provide a clearer overview of the model's performance across different categories, additional visualizations were created, including bar charts for each metric. These charts illustrate the precision, recall, and *F*1 score achieved by the model for each species, enabling a detailed assessment of strengths and areas needing improvement.

From the visualizations, it's evident that while accuracy is consistently high, precision and recall vary slightly across species. Species with similar morphological characteristics tend to have lower recall scores, indicating a need for further feature refinement. These insights help guide future improvements, particularly in refining feature selection or integrating more complex classification architectures.

This comprehensive analysis supports the robustness of the SVM classifier while identifying specific areas for optimization. Together, these findings emphasize the promise of combining DIP and ML techniques in advancing automated plant classification applications.

Table 6.2. Confusion Matrix for SVM Classifier.

Actual/Predicted	Species A	Species B	Species C
Species A	92	4	3
Species B	5	88	7
Species C	4	6	90

Discussion

Strengths of SVM in Leaf Classification

SVM was selected as the primary classifier for this study due to its strong suitability for high-dimensional feature spaces and its ability to construct clear decision boundaries. SVM's robustness against overfitting, especially when applied to feature-rich datasets, makes it well-suited for tasks like leaf classification, where each instance is described by complex attributes such as shape, color, and texture (Jayanthi & Shashikumar, 2020). The kernel functions within SVM allow it to model nonlinear relationships effectively, enabling better separation between leaf species with similar characteristics. Compared to simpler classifiers like *k*-NNs or decision trees, which often suffer from high sensitivity to noise or perform poorly with overlapping feature spaces, SVM consistently delivers higher accuracy in this domain by leveraging its margin-maximization approach.

SVM's superior performance in handling multidimensional data has proven particularly advantageous here, as it manages to capture subtle interspecies variations within a feature space that includes shape descriptors, color histograms, and texture measurements. This strength supports the selection of SVM as an ideal classifier for this study's high-dimensional, feature-rich dataset, reaffirming its application in automated leaf classification.

Comparison with Existing Literature

The classification accuracy achieved in this study, at 90.05%, aligns well with the accuracy rates reported in the existing literature for leaf classification tasks. Compared to baseline models like *k*-NN, which achieved around 81.2%, and decision trees at 85.6% in this study, SVM's performance demonstrates a notable improvement. Previous studies employing CNN for similar tasks have reported accuracy levels between 85% and 93%, largely depending on dataset complexity and size. While CNN are known for their powerful feature extraction capabilities in large datasets, they often require significant computational resources and large labeled datasets to perform optimally.

In contrast, SVM achieves comparable accuracy without the extensive labeled data and computational overhead that CNN typically require. This positions SVM as an efficient and accurate choice for tasks like leaf classification, where a balanced tradeoff between computational efficiency and classification accuracy is desirable. Moreover, the combination of DIP techniques, such as background subtraction and color segmentation, with SVM offers a promising alternative to deep learning models, especially in applications with limited resources or smaller datasets.

Limitations and Challenges

While the SVM classifier demonstrated robust performance, several challenges were encountered throughout the classification pipeline. A primary issue was the impact of background noise in the images. Leaves with complex backgrounds or varying lighting conditions introduced noise, which complicated feature extraction and sometimes led to misclassifications. To address this, image pre-processing techniques such as background subtraction, Gaussian filtering, and morphological transformations were applied to minimize the influence of background elements and to isolate leaf features more effectively (Fu et al., 2022). These steps contributed to improved feature quality, though they did not fully eliminate the challenges posed by intricate backgrounds.

Another limitation observed in this study was the inherent difficulty of distinguishing species with overlapping morphological or color characteristics. Despite the effectiveness of shape and texture features, certain species with similar textures or minimal color variation remained challenging to classify accurately. Future work may address this by integrating additional feature sets, such as venation patterns or deeper texture descriptors, or by applying transfer learning with fine-tuned CNN architectures.

Conclusion

This study presents an effective and automated approach for plant leaf classification, combining DIP techniques with SVM classification to achieve a commendable accuracy rate of 90.05%. The results underscore the strengths of SVM in handling high-dimensional data and leveraging shape, color, and texture-based features to differentiate species. Through a meticulously designed pre-processing pipeline involving background subtraction and texture extraction, the model attains high accuracy, demonstrating its viability as a streamlined tool for plant species identification. This approach balances accuracy with computational efficiency, reducing the reliance on complex deep learning networks while still providing reliable performance.

The findings suggest that automated leaf classification has significant practical implications for agricultural management, ecological studies, and botanical research. In agriculture, this classification system could support automated plant monitoring, aiding farmers in identifying crop types and promoting diversity management for optimized yields. In environmental conservation, the system holds potential for efficiently tracking plant biodiversity in natural habitats, especially for monitoring endangered species. For botanical research, it offers a rapid and accurate method for species identification, aiding in the study and documentation of flora in both laboratory and field settings.

Several promising directions for future research could enhance the model's performance and expand its utility. Integrating deep learning architectures like CNN could enhance feature extraction and improve adaptability across diverse datasets. Transfer learning could further refine the model's capacity to handle a variety of plant species and environmental conditions. Additionally, experimenting with three-dimensional imaging could provide richer leaf feature data, potentially boosting classification accuracy. Expanding the dataset to cover a broader range of plant species and environmental contexts, along with employing advanced pre-processing techniques, could also strengthen the model's generalizability and precision.

References

Alyas, R. M., & Mohammed, A. S. (2022, July). Detection of plant diseases using image processing with machine learning. In *2022 2nd International Conference on Computing and Machine Intelligence (ICMI)* (pp. 1–6). IEEE. https://doi.org/10.1109/ICMI55296.2022.9873793.

Aouat, S., Ait-hammi, I., & Hamouchene, I. (2021). A new approach for texture segmentation based on the gray level co-occurrence matrix. *Multimedia Tools and Applications*, *80*, 24027–24052. https://doi.org/10.1007/s11042-021-10634-4

Ariyapadath, S. (2021). Plant leaf classification and comparative analysis of combined feature set using machine learning techniques. *Traitement du Signal*, *38*, 1587–1598.

Barbedo, J. G. A. (2019). Plant disease identification from individual lesions and spots using deep learning. *Biosystems Engineering*, *180*, 96–107.

Bisen, D. (2021). Deep convolutional neural network based plant species recognition through features of leaf. *Multimedia Tools and Applications*, *80*(4), 6443–6456.

Bravin, R., Nanni, L., Loreggia, A., Brahnam, S., & Paci, M. (2023). Varied image data augmentation methods for building ensemble. *IEEE Access*, *11*, 8810–8823. https://doi.org/10.1109/ACCESS.2023.3239816

Chen, R. C., Dewi, C., Huang, S. W., & Caraka, R. E. (2020). Selecting critical features for data classification based on machine learning methods. *Journal of Big Data*, *7*, 1–26.

Fu, H., Zhang, A., Sun, G., Ren, J., Jia, X., Pan, Z., & Ma, H. (2022). A novel band selection and spatial noise reduction method for hyperspectral image classification. *IEEE Transactions on Geoscience and Remote Sensing*, *60*, 1–13. https://doi.org/10.1109/TGRS.2022.3189015

Gholami, R., & Fakhari, N. (2017). *Support vector machine: Principles, parameters, and applications* (pp. 515–535). Academic Press. https://doi.org/10.1016/B978-0-12-811318-9.00027-2

Jayanthi, M. G., & Shashikumar, D. (2020). Automatic tomato plant leaf disease classification using multi-kernel support vector machine. *International Journal of Engineering and Advanced Technology*, *9*(5), 560–565. https://doi.org/10.35940/ijeat.e9689.069520

Kim, K. I., Jung, K., Park, S. H., & Kim, H. J. (2002). Support vector machines for texture classification. *IEEE Transactions on Pattern Analysis and Machine Intelligence*, *24*(11), 1542–1550.

Li, J., Chen, D., Qi, X., Li, Z., Huang, Y., Morris, D., & Tan, X. (2023). *Label-efficient learning in agriculture: A comprehensive review*. ArXiv, abs/2305.14691. https://doi.org/10.48550/arXiv.2305.14691

Nesteruk, S., Shadrin, D., Pukalchik, M., Somov, A., Zeidler, C., Zabel, P., & Schubert, D. (2021). Image compression and plants classification using machine learning in controlled-environment agriculture: Antarctic station use case. *IEEE Sensors Journal*, *21*(16), 17564–17572.

Ngugi, L. C., Abelwahab, M., & Abo-Zahhad, M. (2021). Recent advances in image processing techniques for automated leaf pest and disease recognition – A review. *Information Processing in Agriculture*, *8*(1), 27–51.

Pooja, V., Das, R., & Kanchana, V. (2017). Identification of plant leaf diseases using image processing techniques. *In 2017 IEEE Technological Innovations in ICT for Agriculture and Rural Development (TIAR)* (pp. 130–133). IEEE. https://doi.org/10.1109/TIAR.2017.8273700

Sachar, S., & Kumar, A. (2021). Survey of feature extraction and classification techniques to identify plant through leaves. *Expert Systems with Applications*, *167*, 114181.

Su, J., Wang, M., Wu, Z., & Chen, Q. (2020). Fast plant leaf recognition using improved multiscale triangle representation and KNN for optimization. *IEEE Access*, *8*, 208753–208766. https://doi.org/10.1109/ACCESS.2020.3037649

Thenmozhi, S., Lakshmi, R. J., Kumudavalli, M. V., Ibrahim, I., & Mohan, R. (2021). A novel plant leaf ailment recognition method using image processing algorithms. *Journal of Scientific & Industrial Research*, *80*(11), 979–984.

Wei Tan, J., Chang, S. W., Abdul-Kareem, S., Yap, H. J., & Yong, K. T. (2018). Deep learning for plant species classification using leaf vein morphometric. *IEEE/ACM Transactions on Computational Biology and Bioinformatics*, *17*(1), 82–90. https://doi.org/10.1109/TCBB.2018.2848653

Yang, K., Zhong, W., & Li, F. (2020). Leaf segmentation and classification with a complicated background using deep learning. *Agronomy*, *10*(11), 1721. https://doi.org/10.3390/agronomy10111721

Yigit, E., Sabanci, K., Toktas, A., & Kayabasi, A. (2019). A study on visual features of leaves in plant identification using artificial intelligence techniques. *Computers and Electronics in Agriculture*, *156*, 369–377.

Chapter 7

Exploring the Role of Virtual Reality in Promoting Sustainable Tourism Practices Amidst COVID-19 Pandemic

Doyel Mukherjee Prodhan[a], *Archan Mitra*[b], *Amrita Mitra Mukherjee*[c] *and Soumik Gangopadhyay*[a]

[a]*Institute of Engineering & Management, University of Engineering and Management, Kolkata, West Bengal, India*
[b]*Nitte Institute of Communication, Nitte Deemed to be University, Karnataka, India*
[c]*Globsyn Business School, Kolkata, India*

Abstract

Virtual reality (VR) technology is revolutionising the tourism industry by enhancing customer relationships, marketing tourist destinations, and improving overall travel experiences. Studies show that VR applications create positive images of destinations and effectively communicate these to potential customers. Additionally, VR and augmented reality (AR) technologies are valuable for planning, marketing, education, and preservation in tourism, offering benefits such as cost reduction, tourist attraction through gamification, and brand loyalty building. However, the high cost of these technologies can limit their accessibility and marketing efforts. Tourism 4.0 aims to leverage VR, AR, Internet of Things, and artificial intelligence to enhance tourism experiences while minimising negative impacts through data-driven strategic planning aligned with sustainable development goals. During the COVID-19 pandemic, VR has emerged as a viable tool for sustainable tourism, serving as a substitute for physical travel when restrictions are in place and allowing tourists to enjoy virtual holiday experiences. This increased use of VR, driven by its ease of use, usefulness, and authenticity, helps reduce virus transmission risks, alleviate pressure on the tourism sector, and promote sustainability.

Harnessing the Potential of Artificial Intelligence to Promote Environmental Sustainability, 105–118

Published under exclusive licence by Emerald Publishing Limited
doi:10.1108/978-1-83662-996-220251007

The United Nations highlights the importance of rebuilding the tourism sector in a safe, equitable, and climate-friendly manner post-pandemic. This research explores the impact of VR on sustainable tourism during the COVID-19 pandemic. Through a comprehensive review of literature and case studies, this research evaluates VR's role in shaping a sustainable future for tourism, offering a new model for immersive and responsible travel experiences while addressing the challenges posed by the pandemic.

Keywords: Virtual reality; augmented reality; sustainable tourism; COVID-19; pandemic; immersive travel experiences

1. Introduction

1.1. Background

The COVID-19 pandemic has caused unprecedented adverse impact on global tourism, leading to significant losses in revenue and demand and the cancellation of millions of international trips due to stringent travel restrictions and lower travel appetite (Khalid et al., 2021; Ozbay et al., 2022). Moreover, many protected and conserved areas have suffered (Khalid et al., 2021), negatively affecting conservation investments and tourism businesses (Ozbay et al., 2022). To tackle these challenges, VR technology has emerged as a revolutionary solution especially during the pandemic situation by offering an alternative solution for traditional tourism (Spenceley et al., 2021; Yasin et al., 2022). In recent years, VR had been applied to destination promotion, user sentiments evaluation and sustainable development encompassing environmental, cultural and economic aspects (Lu et al., 2022).The pandemic augmented the VR use and practice by showcasing its prowess to considerably shrink carbon footprints, make tourism more accessible and assist with sustainable travel options. Tourism research has investigated the socio-economic benefits of VR implementation as a tourism tool to stimulate more sustainable tourism while improving the resilience of this sector (Gegung, 2021).

1.2. Problem Statement

The tourism sector has struggled with unprecedented operational challenges triggered by worldwide travel prohibitions and reinforced sophistication of health worries, markedly limited mobility and impaired traditional tourism events. These restrictions have not only damaged the sector's economic sustainability but also interrupted cultural interactions and local economies that rely on tourism. Hence, the implementation of novel measures like VR has turned out to be one of the crucial tactics to ensure a sustainable tourism industry. VR experiences can transport the viewer anywhere, allowing exploration of destinations without leaving home, which reduces the carbon footprint associated with traditional travel, and offers a way to keep the tourism sector alive while sustainable solutions to travel can be explored. This technological evolution has the capability to reshape the future of tourism and make it more resilient and adaptable to ongoing challenges.

1.3. Research Objectives

- To explore the role of VR in promoting sustainable tourism practices.
- To evaluate the benefits of VR for environmental conservation, educational value, and economic support for local communities.
- To discuss the challenges and future prospects of integrating VR into sustainable tourism.

2. Literature Review

2.1. COVID-19 Pandemic and Tourism

In December 2019, Wuhan, China, saw a pneumonia outbreak linked to the Huanan Seafood Wholesale Market (Schiopu et al., 2021), marking the onset of the global COVID-19 pandemic. This unprecedented crisis has wrought havoc across industries, with the hospitality sector suffering immense revenue losses (Ciotti et al., 2020; Hong et al., 2023). The (International Monetary Fund, 2022) reported a dramatic 3.0% global GDP decline in 2020, a stark reversal from the previous year's 2.8% growth (Gursoy & Chi, 2020). tourism sector holds a prominent position among service industries and is fundamental to driving economic growth worldwide. It contributed 5.2% to India's GDP and 15.3% to employment in 2019–2020 (Karabulut et al., 2020). According to research commissioned by the Ministry of Tourism, Government of India, tourism was estimated to have contributed directly and indirectly to 5.2% of the country's GDP and 15.3% to its employment in 2019–2020. However, in the fiscal year 2020–2021, while the overall economy experienced a decline of 20.1% in Q1 and 5.1% in Q2, followed by a positive growth rate of 4.3% in Q3, the tourism sector witnessed a much steeper decline of 42.8% in Q1 and 15.5% in Q2. While the overall economy experienced fluctuations, with periods of decline followed by some recovery, the tourism sector faced harsher setbacks. Even as other sectors showed signs of improvement, tourism continued to struggle, recording a 1.1% decline even in Q3 (Puah et al., 2018). The World Travel & Tourism Council (WTTC) noted that travel and tourism, in all its dimensions, represented 10.5% of global employment and 10.4% of GDP in 2019 (Puah et al., 2018). The pandemic has reshaped tourism, highlighting shifts in consumer behaviour towards safety and hygiene (Garcez et al., 2021). It has accelerated the adoption of digital technologies like VR and AI, with travellers increasingly favouring safety-focussed travel packages (Karabulut et al., 2020). Despite these adaptations, the sector continues to grapple with travel restrictions and border closures (Ertaş & Yağci, 2020). The (UNWTO, 2023) reported a staggering 72% drop in international tourism in 2020, a decline not seen in 3 decades (Torres et al., 2021; Yung & Lattimore, 2019). The airline and restaurant industries faced colossal losses, estimated at $118.5 billion and $270 billion, respectively (Beck et al., 2019).

2.2. VR in Tourism

The COVID-19 pandemic severely disrupted tourism, causing a sharp decline in travel and economic challenges. In response, VR and AR have become increasingly significant. VR creates immersive, 360-degree environments that engage users interactively, offering a dynamic and convincing virtual presence (Berg & Vance, 2017). It features three core elements: visualisation – enabling the user to navigate their environment, generally via a head-mounted display, immersion – entailing the suspension of disbelief and the tangible manifestation of objects, and interactivity – signifying the extent of user control over the virtual experience, typically accomplished through the use of sensors and input devices like joysticks or keyboards (Bastug et al., 2017). VR enhances the customer journey by allowing virtual exploration and detailed interaction with destinations, which can also impact on-site travel experiences (Ekmeil et al., 2021; Paliwal et al., 2024). VR and AR are crucial in tourism, where experiences are intangible. They help reduce congestion at popular sites, provide access to remote or inaccessible locations, and offer innovative ways for product design and marketing (Rahman et al., 2021; Yang et al., 2022). AR is used for indoor navigation and enhancing visitor experiences in museums and heritage sites (Huete-Alcocer et al., 2019; Palazzo et al., 2022). During the pandemic, VR surged as a tool for virtual tours and destination marketing, offering a risk-free way for consumers to explore destinations from home (Samaddar et al., 2023). It stimulates interest, enhances engagement, and aids in decision-making by creating emotional connections and positive attitudes towards destinations (Kask, 2018; Oncioiu et al., 2022). VR's role in tourism has been vital for industry recovery, increasing brand loyalty and promoting lesser-known destinations (Sousa et al., 2023; Toubes et al., 2021).

2.3. Sustainable Tourism

Sustainable tourism balances visitor, industry, and host community requirements with resource and biodiversity conservation to address economic, social, and environmental implications today and in the future (Walcott & Campbell, 2018). This notion intersects with responsible tourism and is essential for resource management and environmental protection (Samaddar et al., 2023). Due to travel limitations and economic hardships, the COVID-19 pandemic has boosted sustainable tourism (Rahman et al., 2021). Pollution and landscape deterioration from overtourism are also areas of major concern (Schiopu et al., 2021). VR is gradually paving its way into sustainable tourism. VR lets users experience destinations virtually, decreasing travel and aiding environmental conservation. VR can protect landmarks and improve tourist experiences while supporting sustainable tourism, according to research (Oncioiu et al., 2022; Sousa et al., 2023). Moreover, AR and VR can promote ethical travel and sustainability (UNEP & UNWTO, 2005). Film location virtualisation can also boost tourism (Kask, 2018). Study suggests VR influences destination selections and offers a sustainable post-pandemic tourism approach (Ekmeil et al., 2021; Yasin et al., 2022). AI-driven AR and VR technologies provide immersive environmental education and motivation for travellers. These technologies increase understanding and appreciation of local ecosystems and cultures while reducing carbon footprints by offering virtual tours of natural reserves, historical locations, and sustainable initiatives.

3. Research Methodology

3.1. Research Design

This study adopts a mixed-methods approach to explore the role of VR in promoting sustainable tourism practices during the COVID-19 pandemic. The research design integrates both qualitative and quantitative methods to provide a comprehensive understanding of the phenomenon under investigation. This approach is chosen to capture the multifaceted nature of VR's impact on tourism and sustainability, ensuring a robust analysis of both numerical data and narrative insights.

3.2. Data Collection Methods

- *Literature review*: A thorough literature review forms the basis of this research, covering academic journals, industry reports, and case studies on VR in tourism, sustainable practices, and COVID-19's effects. This review situates the study within the current knowledge, identifies research gaps, and frames the theoretical foundation.
- *Case studies*: Selected case studies of VR implementation in tourism are analysed to assess its practical applications, sourced from secondary data including industry reports and academic sources. These studies illustrate VR's role in enhancing visitor engagement, reducing carbon footprints, and fostering responsible tourism.
- *Surveys*: Quantitative data are gathered via surveys sent to tourists and stakeholders (tour operators, destination managers and tech providers). Based on the insights from the literature, these surveys seek to assess the perceptions and experiences of tourists regarding VR's impact on sustainable tourism, engagement and adoption.

4. Data Analysis

4.1. Qualitative Analysis

Qualitative data from the literature review and case studies are analysed through thematic analysis. Coding involves identifying recurrent themes and patterns in the data as they relate to VR use for tourism, its benefits and challenges, and its potential role in driving sustainability. Discussions on thematic analysis offer a fine-grained perspective of contextual factors and influences related to the implementation of VR in the tourism sector.

4.2. Quantitative Analysis

The quantitative data from the surveys are analysed with statistical methods such as descriptive statistics, correlation analysis and regression analysis. These methods are used to identify the relationships between variables like perceived benefits of VR, impact on sustainable tourism practices, and willingness of stakeholders to adopt VR technologies. The quantitative analysis then seeks to test the findings of the qualitative analysis using an empirical method.

4.3. Limitations

Since the study depends on secondary data, especially for the case studies, it has certain limitations which cannot be avoided, and so it may fail to represent all dimensions of VR application in tourism. Additionally, there may be possibilities of self-reporting biases in the survey responses. The rapidly evolving nature of VR technology and the ongoing impact of the COVID-19 pandemic may also influence the generalisation of the findings.

4.4. Qualitative Analysis

Thematic analysis of case studies:

- *Theme 1: Visitor engagement:*
  - o Case Study 1: Increased engagement in virtual tours at a heritage site (coded as 'high engagement').
  - o Case Study 2: Positive visitor feedback on VR-enhanced museum exhibits (coded as 'positive feedback').

- *Theme 2: Environmental impact:*
  - o Case Study 1: Reduction in physical visits led to decreased carbon footprint (coded as 'reduced footprint').
  - o Case Study 2: VR as an alternative to physical travel to remote locations (coded as 'sustainable travel').

- *Theme 3: Challenges in VR adoption:*
  - o Case Study 1: High cost of VR technology (coded as 'high cost').
  - o Case Study 2: Technical difficulties in implementing VR (coded as 'technical challenges').

4.5. Quantitative Analysis

Survey data collection and analysis:

- *Demographics of survey respondents:*

4.6. Graphs and Charts

The visualisations provide a clear representation of the survey data collected as part of the research on VR in promoting sustainable tourism practices. Here is a detailed explanation of each visualisation:

1. *Pie chart: Age distribution of respondents:* This pie chart delineates the age distribution of survey participants, with a predominant 40% in the 26–35 bracket and 25% in the 18–25 range. This demographic profile suggests a substantial representation of younger individuals, potentially shaping perceptions and the adoption of VR technology (see Fig. 7.1).
2. *Bar chart: Perceived benefits of VR:* The horizontal bar chart reveals respondent perceptions of VR benefits: 70% strongly agree on its enhancement of visitor experience, 60% view it as reducing environmental impact, and 50% view it as cost-effective. This data underscores a favourable reception of VR's impact on visitor experience and sustainability (see Fig. 7.2).
3. *Line graph: Respondent agreement levels on VR benefits:* This line graph illustrates respondent consensus on VR benefits across five categories: strongly agree, agree, neutral, disagree, and strongly disagree. It reveals a predominant endorsement of VR's positive effects on visitor experience, environmental impact, and cost-efficiency, with minimal dissent. These visualisations offer a detailed quantitative and qualitative perspective, laying the groundwork for deeper analysis of VR's role in sustainable tourism (see Fig. 7.3).

4.7. Findings

1. *Demographic profile of respondents:* The demographic profile (see Table 7.1) of respondents is crucial in understanding the diversity and representation in the survey. The breakdown of demographic variables is as follows:

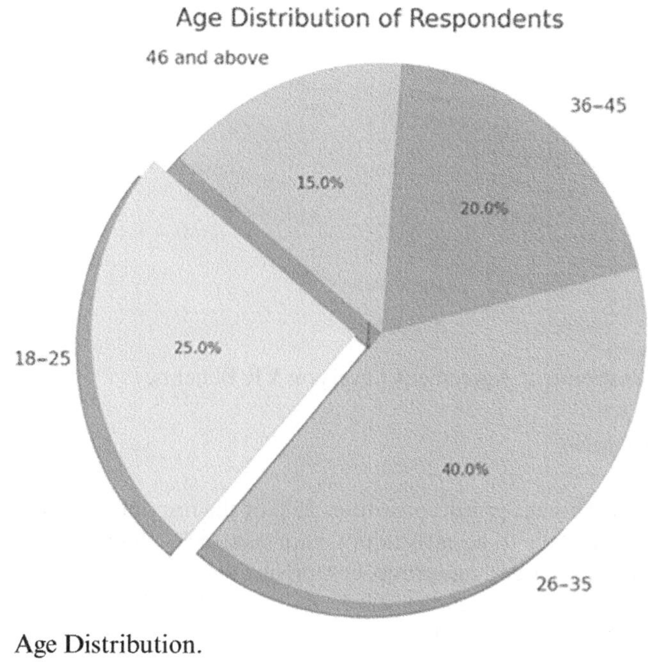

Fig. 7.1. Age Distribution.

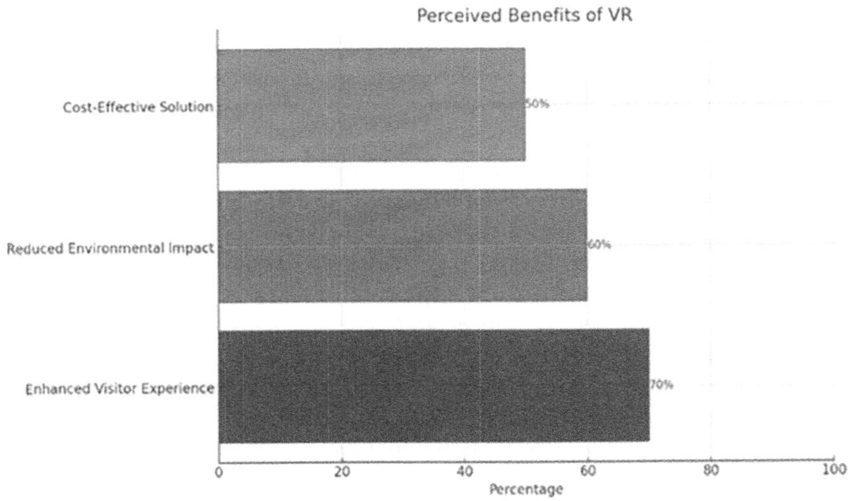

Fig. 7.2. Age Perceived Benefits of VR.

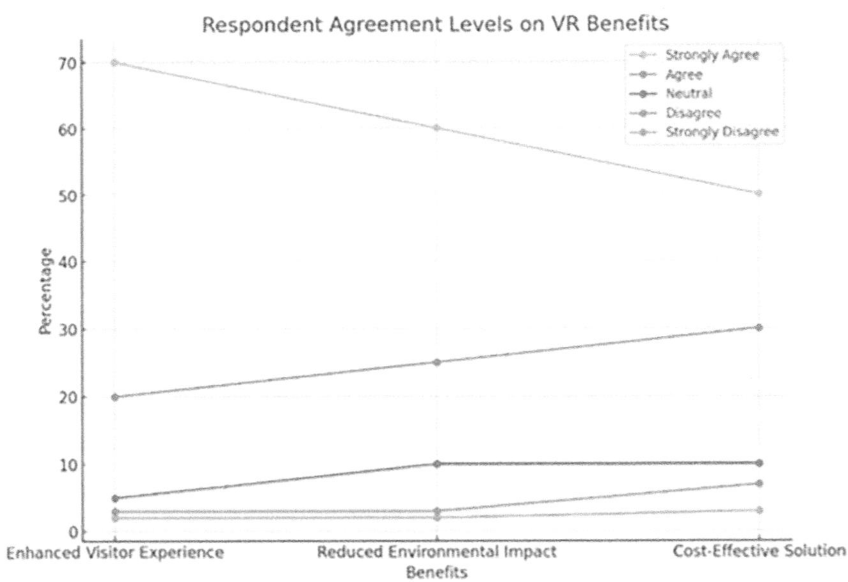

Fig. 7.3. Respondent Agreement Levels on VR Benefits.

Age distribution:

- *18–25 years*: This age group constitutes 25% of the respondents. Being younger, they are more likely to be early adopters of new technologies like VR.
- *26–35 years*: The largest age group, comprising 40% of respondents. This group is typically in their mid-career stages, with a higher likelihood of disposable income and openness to technological innovations in tourism.

Table 7.1. Demographic Profile of Respondents.

Demographic Variable	Frequency	Percentage (%)
Age		
18–25	50	25
26–35	25	40
36–45	40	20
46 and above	30	15
Gender		
Male	100	50
Female	100	50
Occupation		
Tourist	80	40
Tour operator	60	30
Destination manager	40	20
Technology provider	20	10

- *36–45 years*: Representing 20% of the respondents, this group includes individuals who might value VR for family friendly virtual tours and educational purposes.
- *46 and above*: This age group makes up 15% of the respondents, potentially showing less inclination towards technology adoption due to traditional preferences, but still significant for understanding broader perspectives.

Gender distribution:

- *Male*: 50% of the respondents are male. This even distribution of females allows for balanced insights across gender lines.
- *Female*: Similarly, 50% of respondents are female, ensuring that the findings are representative of both genders.

Occupation distribution:

- *Tourist*: 40% of respondents are tourists, providing direct insights into consumer experiences and expectations of VR in tourism.
- *Tour operators*: 30% of respondents are tour operators, offering a professional perspective on the feasibility and impact of VR in their operations.
- *Destination manager*: 20% of respondents are destination managers, who can speak to the strategic and logistical aspects of implementing VR.
- *Technology provider*: 10% of respondents are technology providers, giving technical insights into the development and challenges of VR technology.

Table 7.2. Perceived Benefits of VR.

Benefit	Strongly Agree (%)	Agree (%)	Neutral (%)	Disagree (%)	Strongly Disagree (%)
Enhanced visitor experience	70	20	5	3	2
Reduced environmental impact	60	25	10	3	2
Cost-effective solutions	50	30	10	7	3

2. *Perceived benefits of VR:* The survey respondents' perceptions of VR benefits were measured across five levels of agreement (see Table 7.2): strongly agree, agree, neutral, disagree, and strongly disagree. The key findings are:

Enhanced visitor experience:

- Strongly agree (70%): A significant majority of respondents believe that VR enhances visitor experiences, indicating that immersive technology is highly valued for its ability to provide engaging and interactive tourism experiences.
- Agree (20%): An additional 20% agree with this statement, reinforcing the positive reception of VR.
- Neutral (5%), disagree (3%), and strongly disagree (2%): These minimal percentages suggest that only a small minority are indifferent or sceptical about VR's impact on visitor experience.

Reduced environmental impact:

- Strongly agree (60%): A majority of respondents recognise the environmental benefits of VR, particularly in reducing the need for physical travel, which in turn lowers carbon footprints.
- Agree (25%): A significant portion agrees, supporting the notion that VR can contribute to sustainable tourism practices.
- Neutral (10%), disagree (3%), strongly disagree (2%): Again, these lower percentages indicate general consensus on the positive environmental impact of VR.

Cost-effective solution:

- Strongly agree (50%): Half of the respondents strongly believe that VR is a cost-effective solution, highlighting its potential to offer affordable alternatives to traditional travel.
- Agree (30%): A substantial 30% also agree, further indicating that VR is seen as economically viable.
- Neutral (10%), disagree (7%), and strongly disagree (3%): These findings suggest some level of uncertainty or disagreement, possibly due to the initial high costs of VR technology.

3. *Detailed analysis of agreement levels:* The line graph illustrating the agreement levels across various benefits of VR provides deeper insights:

Strongly agree and agree:

- The high percentages in these categories across all benefits (70% for enhanced experience, 60% for environmental impact, 50% for cost-effectiveness) underscore a strong overall positive perception of VR among the respondents.

Neutral, disagree, and strongly disagree:

- The relatively low percentages in these categories indicate limited scepticism. However, the presence of these responses suggests that while the majority are optimistic, there are still concerns and reservations that need to be addressed, particularly regarding cost and technological barriers.

4.8. Synthesis of Findings

Positive reception of VR: The findings reveal a broadly favourable view of VR technology in tourism, emphasising its efficacy in enriching visitor experiences, minimising environmental impact, and ensuring cost-efficiency. This optimism indicates a strong inclination among stakeholders to embrace VR for advancing sustainable tourism.

Environmental sustainability: Sustainable practices are largely dependent on VR's role in driving the reduction of environmental impact. To mitigate the adverse effects of tourism on inconsistent ecosystems and for supporting adverse effects, VR has an edge over other systems in yielding impactful results.

Economic viability: The underpinning factor of cost-effectiveness has made VR popular; however, the neutral and negative responses show that the initial costs and accessibility remain a matter of concern. These issues need attention for the broader adoption and integration of VR in the tourism industry.

Strategic implications: The importance of investing in VR has been felt by policymakers and tourism operators. The subsidies and incentives for VR adoption, the training programmes for operators, and collaboration with technology providers to enhance affordability and accessibility are all parts of the strategic initiatives.

5. Conclusion

Sustainable tourism has a VR as an emphatic tool that can offer immersive experiences and can reduce the environmental footprint of travel with an array of educational and engaging content. This integration of VR has enhanced the potential of preservation of natural and cultural heritage, along with the promotion of environmental awareness among travellers. This integration has further addressed challenges such as technological, financial and social barriers. For the successful implementation of VR for sustainable tourism, it is imperative to acknowledge the future prospects of VR, offering new opportunities for innovation and sustainability in the tourism industry.

6. Challenges and Future Prospects

The challenges identified, such as high costs and technical difficulties, need to be addressed through collaborative efforts between tourism stakeholders and technology developers. Future research could focus on developing cost-effective VR solutions and exploring innovative applications to overcome these barriers. The data analysis provides compelling evidence of the potential benefits of VR in promoting sustainable tourism practices. The positive reception among diverse respondents underscores the readiness of the tourism sector to embrace innovative technologies. However, addressing the challenges and ensuring accessibility will be key to maximising the impact of VR on sustainable tourism. These findings contribute valuable insights for tourism stakeholders, policymakers, and researchers aiming to leverage VR for a sustainable and resilient future in tourism.

References

Bastug, E., Bennis, M., Médard, M., & Debbah, M. (2017). Toward interconnected virtual reality: Opportunities, challenges, and enablers. *IEEE Communications Magazine*, *55*(6), 110–117.

Beck, J., Rainoldi, M., & Egger, R. (2019). Virtual reality in tourism: A state-of-the-art review. *Tourism Review*, *74*(3), 586–612.

Berg, L. P., & Vance, J. M. (2017). Industry use of virtual reality in product design and manufacturing: A survey. *Virtual Reality*, *21*, 1–17.

Ciotti, M., Ciccozzi, M., Terrinoni, A., Jiang, W. C., Wang, C. B., & Bernardini, S. (2020). The COVID-19 pandemic. *Critical Reviews in Clinical Laboratory Sciences*, *57*(6), 365–388.

Ekmeil, F. A. R., Abumandil, M. S. S., Alkhawaja, M. I., Siam, I. M., & Alaklouk, S. A. A. (2021, March). Augmented reality and virtual reality revolutionize rusiness transformation in digital marketing tech industry analysts and visionaries during Coronavirus (COVID 19). *Journal of Physics: Conference Series*, *1860*(1), 012012.

Ertaş, M., & Yağcı, K. (2020). Understanding the effects of COVID-19 pandemic on the tourism industry. *Turizm Akademik Dergisi*, *7*(2), 327–338.

Garcez, A., Correia, R., & Costa, A. (2021). Understanding the changes in the tourists perceived risk after COVID-19. *Journal of Eastern Europe Research in Business and Economics*, *2021*, 1–10.

Gegung, E. M. (2021). International tourism and the COVID-19 pandemic: The use of virtual reality to increase tourism destination sustainability and how users perceive the authenticity of VR experiences. *Jurnal Kepariwisataan Indonesia: Jurnal Penelitian Dan Pengembangan Kepariwisataan Indonesia*, *15*(1), 9–15.

Gursoy, D., & Chi, C. G. (2020). Effects of COVID-19 pandemic on hospitality industry: Review of the current situations and a research agenda. *Journal of Hospitality Marketing & Management*, *29*(5), 527–529.

Hong, Y., Hu, J., Chen, M., & Tang, S. (2023). Motives and antecedents affecting green purchase intention: Implications for green economic recovery. *Economic Analysis and Policy*, *77*, 523–538.

https://wttc.org/research/economic-impact

Huete-Alcocer, N., López-Ruiz, V. R., & Grigorescu, A. (2019). Measurement of satisfaction in sustainable tourism: A cultural heritage site in Spain. *Sustainability*, *11*(23), 6774.

International Monetary Fund. (2022, October 11). *World economic outlook, October 2022: Countering the cost-of-living crisis*. https://www.imf.org/en/Publications/WEO/Issues/2022/10/11/world-economic-outlook-october-2022.

Karabulut, G., Bilgin, M. H., Demir, E., & Doker, A. C. (2020). How pandemics affect tourism: International evidence. *Annals of Tourism Research, 84*, 102991.

Kask, S. (2018). *Virtual reality in support of sustainable tourism. Experiences from Eastern Europe* [Doctoral dissertation, Eesti Maaülikool].

Khalid, U., Okafor, L. E., & Burzynska, K. (2021). Does the size of the tourism sector influence the economic policy response to the COVID-19 pandemic? *Current Issues in Tourism, 24*(19), 2801–2820.

Lu, J., Xiao, X., Xu, Z., Wang, C., Zhang, M., & Zhou, Y. (2022). The potential of virtual tourism in the recovery of tourism industry during the COVID-19 pandemic. *Current Issues in Tourism, 25*(3), 441–457.

Oncioiu, I., & Priescu, I. (2022). The use of virtual reality in tourism destinations as a tool to develop tourist behavior perspective. *Sustainability, 14*(7), 4191.

Ozbay, G., Sariisik, M., Ceylan, V., & Çakmak, M. (2022). A comparative evaluation between the impact of previous outbreaks and COVID-19 on the tourism industry. *International Hospitality Review, 36*(1), 65–82.

Palazzo, M., Gigauri, I., Panait, M. C., Apostu, S. A., & Siano, A. (2022). Sustainable tourism issues in European countries during the global pandemic crisis. *Sustainability, 14*(7), 3844.

Paliwal, M., Chatradhi, N., Singh, A., & Dikkatwar, R. (2024). Smart tourism: Antecedents to Indian traveller's decision. *European Journal of Innovation Management, 27*(5), 1521–1546.

Puah, C. H., Jong, M. C., Ayob, N., & Ismail, S. (2018). The impact of tourism on the local economy in Malaysia. *International Journal of Business and Management, 13*(12), 151–157.

Rahman, M. K., Gazi, M. A. I., Bhuiyan, M. A., & Rahaman, M. A. (2021). Effect of COVID-19 pandemic on tourist travel risk and management perceptions. *PLoS ONE, 16*(9), e0256486.

Samaddar, K., & Mondal, S. (2024). AR and VR-based travel: A responsible practice towards sustainable tourism. *International Journal of Tourism Cities, 10*(1), 105–128.

Schiopu, A. F., Hornoiu, R. I., Padurean, M. A., & Nica, A. M. (2021). Virus tinged? Exploring the facets of virtual reality use in tourism as a result of the COVID-19 pandemic. *Telematics and Informatics, 60*, 101575.

Sousa, N., Jorge, F., Teixeira, M. S., Losada, N., Melo, M., & Bessa, M. (2023). An exploratory study about the effect of COVID-19 on the intention to adopt virtual reality in the tourism sector. *Sustainability, 15*(11), 8725.

Spenceley, A., McCool, S., Newsome, D., Báez, A., Barborak, J. R., Blye, C.-J., Bricker, K., Sigit Cahyadi, H., Corrigan, K., Halpenny, E., Hvenegaard, G., Malleret King, D., Leung, Y.-F., Mandić, A., Naidoo, R., Rüede, D., Sano, J., Sarhan, M., Santamaria, V., Beraldo Sousa, T., & Zschiegner, A.-K. (2021). Tourism in protected and conserved areas amid the COVID-19 pandemic. *Parks, 27*(Special Issue), 103–118.

Torres, E. N., Ridderstaat, J., & Wei, W. (2021). Negative affectivity and people's return intentions to hospitality and tourism activities: The early stages of COVID-19. *Journal of Hospitality and Tourism Management, 49*, 89–100.

Toubes, D. R., Araújo Vila, N., & Fraiz Brea, J. A. (2021). Changes in consumption patterns and tourist promotion after the COVID-19 pandemic. *Journal of Theoretical and Applied Electronic Commerce Research, 16*(5), 1332–1352.

United Nations Environment Programme (UNEP), Division of Technology, Industry and Economics, & World Tourism Organization (UNWTO). (2005). *Making tourism more sustainable: A guide for policy makers*. UNEP, Division of Technology, Industry and Economics; World Tourism Organization.

Walcott, T. H., & Campbell, C. E. A. (2018). New directions in sustainable tourism research. *Tourism Review, 74*(2), 138–149.

Yang, J., Menhas, R., Dai, J., Younas, T., Anwar, U., Iqbal, W., Laar, R. A., & Muddasar Saeed, M. (2022). Virtual reality fitness (VRF) for behavior management during the COVID-19 pandemic: A mediation analysis approach. *Psychology Research and Behavior Management*, *2022*, 171–182.

Yasin, S. N. S., Majid, H. A. M. A., Ishak, S. N. H., Hamzah, S. S., Bahrin, U. F. M., & Raju, R. (2022, November). A systematic literature review of virtual reality utilization in tourism during COVID-19 pandemic. In *2022 International visualization, informatics and technology conference (IVIT)* (pp. 266–271). IEEE.

Yung, R., & Khoo-Lattimore, C. (2019). New realities: A systematic literature review on virtual reality and augmented reality in tourism research. *Current Issues in Tourism*, *22*(17), 2056–2081.

Chapter 8

Environmental Informatics Promotion Using Artificial Intelligence and Allied Technologies: The Applications, Sustainability and Educational Perspectives

P. K. Paul

Department of Computer & Information Sciences, Raiganj University, Raiganj, West Bengal, India

Abstract

Environment is not only an important facet of the field but also a field of study with various nomenclatures, such as environmental studies, environmental science, environmental systems, environmental engineering, and environmental management. Other subfields and nomenclatures have emerged related to the environment, such as environmental statistics, environmental informatics, ecology, etc. Environmental informatics is the integration of environmental science with informatics, or information technology. Environmental informatics is required for various purposes related to the management, monitoring, and development of the environment supported by various technologies. Different tools and techniques are highly essential in developing a healthy and sophisticated practice of environmental and ecological informatics. Apart from basic information technologies, there are many emerging technologies, such as cloud computing, big data systems, AI and deep learning (DL), Internet of Things (IoT), edge computing, fog computing, cyber-physical systems, blockchain, robotics, GIS, etc. Artificial intelligence (AI), including other emerging technologies, is highly progressing in the development of environmental and ecological systems, including its better and enhanced sustainability. Today, AI and robotics are not only required for the design and development of machines and so-called robots, but also for developing intelligent systems that

Harnessing the Potential of Artificial Intelligence to Promote Environmental Sustainability, 119–142

Published under exclusive licence by Emerald Publishing Limited
doi:10.1108/978-1-83662-996-220251008

support the environment and ecology. Environmental informatics and its development have not only reached this stage as an interdisciplinary research area, but also as a field of study and a practical area. diverse applications, foundations, and educational perspectives of environmental informatics are described in chapter. The chapter also highlighted the emerging applications of AI and allied technologies in the environment and ecology, with benefits and applications that address issues and challenges.

Keywords: Environmental informatics; ecology; environmental systems; artificial intelligence; sustainability; AI & ML

1. Introduction

Informatics is an interdisciplinary field and is also known as information science. *Environmental informatics* is the merger of two important domains for the geo-centric and environmentally focused solutions (Amato et al., 2020; Bogue, 2023; Huang & Chang, 2003). Though basically it is a combination of environmental science and information science for the environmental solutions and has close contact with geo-informatics, and thus it is dedicated to environmental monitoring, management, and solutions, and other aspects of ecological sciences. Additionally, there are other subjects and areas where the impact of environmental informatics is emerging, such as:

- Agriculture, agricultural sciences.
- Oceanography and marine science.
- Climatology and weather technology.
- Forestry and wood sciences.
- Anthropological sciences, etc. (Allen et al., 2003).

In support of healthy environmental informatics practice, various components and sub-sections of information technology are highly useful, such as database systems, web systems, networking systems, communication systems, multimedia systems, and so on. In regard to the promotion of the environment and ecological systems, all such systems and technologies are impactful. The growing role of environmental informatics in diverse fields has become a field of study, and as a result, many universities and higher educational institutions have started offering environmental informatics as a field of study and research. As far as educational and training programs are concerned, some of the levels include certificates, bachelor's, and master's degrees in environmental informatics or other allied fields, internationally. As far as emerging technologies are concerned, a few impactful subjects are included (but not limited to the following):

- Cloud and virtualization systems.
- Virtualization and emerging technologies.

- Data science and analytics.
- HCI and usability systems.
- Edge computing and fog systems.
- AI and ML.
- IoT and allied technology.
- Cyber-physical systems.
- Blockchain technologies, etc.

In such a system, the basic role of *AI* also impacts several environmental activities, including those in space, underwater, high-heat environments, and hazardous materials management, such as radiation management, and so on. As far as AI is concerned, it helps in diverse areas and fields, and among them, monitoring air quality is important (Hoang et al., 2022). It offers real-time air quality information, which is impactful for the health of common people in various respects. As far as the environmental footprint is concerned, AI is considered valuable, and impactful, which leads to the role of the products using supply chain management systems in relation to the environment (Kim & Park, 2009). Regarding agricultural applications, AI is valuable, especially in precision agriculture and systems. In regard to the optimization of renewable energy, AI is also required and gaining popularity, as it has the ability to optimize the renewable energy through its sources and also has the ability to enhance its efficiency. New research findings also indicate that AI supports energy consumption in many ways, particularly by reducing carbon emissions, and applicable in diverse buildings and making in smart building ventures. As far as endangered species are concerned, AI is helpful in their preservation (Dunbabin & Marques, 2012). AI is important in enhancing the quality of the air for diverse reasons, and it is especially helpful when used by AI-based sensor networks. Such support is helpful in human and public health at large. In regard to waste management and its recycling aspects, AI is valuable in the reduction of landfill waste and also in the enhancement of resource efficiency in many contexts. In the environment, we also suffer from the problem of disaster management tricks, and here, AI applications are impactful, worthy, and emerging. In regard to the identification and mapping of the icebergs in the ocean, AI is applicable and has many opportunities to offer complete sustainability. In regard to e-waste management, AI also has a wider role and potentialities for solving environmental issues and challenges in several circumstances (Cinderby, 1999).

There are emerging applications of *robotics*, as an allied technology of AI, in environmental management and smart environmental monitoring. Robotics is simply the conceptualization, designing, and development of the robots and allied devices and mechanisms that help in automated, easy, and effective operation for the betterment of humans as well as individuals. Robots are useful in different sectors and contexts beyond the environment, and this phase is also increasing gradually. In several activities, in general, the process and operation are difficult, and in such systems, robotics is useful, which involves radioactive materials, bomb detection, and manufacturing processes. As far as another allied technology of AI, *ML* is concerned, it also has significance in various areas

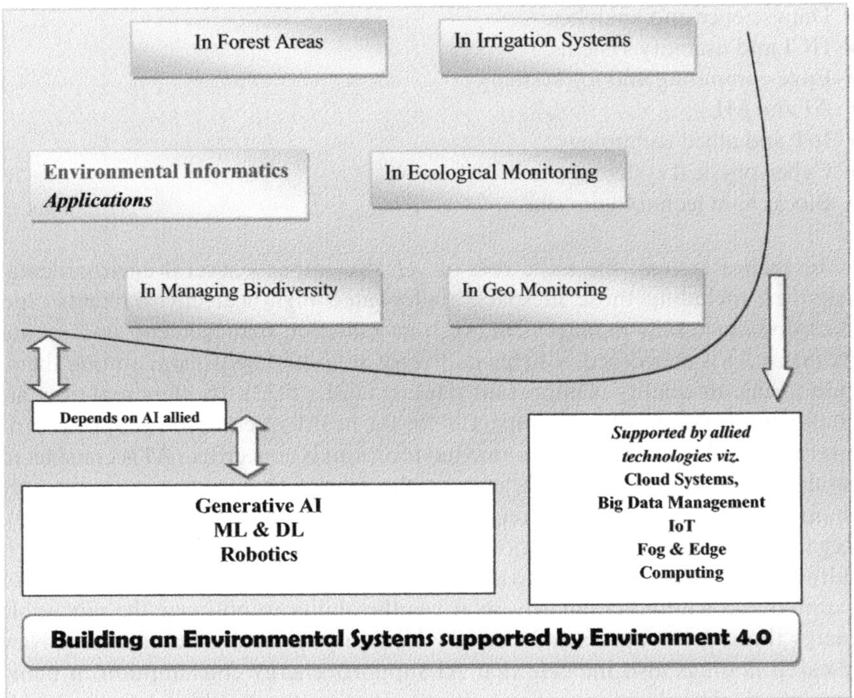

Fig. 8.1. AI and Allied Technologies in Environmental Sustainability.

related to the environment and ecology, such as anomaly identification of the environment, which involves finding environmental hazards and ecologies for better and healthier sustainability. Finding and identifying pattern is another benefit of ML, which empowers ecology and the environment in many ways. It basically works in such a way that it finds complex patterns, seasonal variations, climate trends, and factor identification regarding environmental systems and processes. Regarding finding future patterns using ML, it helps ecology and environmental monitoring in many ways. As far as monitoring ML is concerned, it is useful in finding the quality of lands, water identification, etc. Experts also find suitable ways to support decision-making using ML, which is ultimately helpful in finding and proposing models and enhancing the decision-making process. In regard to automating tasks and operations, ML is helping in environmental management and monitoring, which is ultimately promoting the environment and ecology, in many ways, as depicted in Fig. 8.1. Thus, for reducing time and saving resources, ML is healthy and very important.

2. Objective of the Work

The chapter entitled "Environmental Informatics Promotion Using Artificial Intelligence and Allied Technologies: The Applications, Sustainability and

Educational Perspectives" is intended with the following aim and objective (but not limited to):

- To know about the basics of environmental informatics, including its foundations, features, and characteristics, in brief.
- To learn about the basic advantages and significance of environmental informatics in regard to environmental management and transformation.
- To find out the ways and systems that help in environmental informatics practice for a healthy and effective environmental management and sustainability.
- To get a brief knowledge of AI, ML, DL, robotics, in general.
- To find out the advantages of AI and allied technologies in environmental practices and development, leading to sophisticated environmental informatics practice.
- To learn about the issues, challenges, and concerns in healthy environmental informatics practices using AI and allied technologies.

3. Methods Undertaken

This chapter, entitled "Environmental Informatics Promotion Using Artificial Intelligence and Allied Technologies: The Applications, Sustainability and Educational Perspectives," is a theoretical work and interdisciplinary in nature. For this study, theoretical works that have been previously published have been studied and incorporated into this work. Various companies and organizations are engaged in environmental-related work, and their services have been studied using online resources. Journals, magazines, and news reports have also been studied in relation to the environment with AI, ML, and allied technologies.

4. Environmental Informatics: The Fusion of Environment and Information Science

Environmental informatics is an interdisciplinary subject and a practical area and field merged with the environment and informatics.

The aspects of *Environment* are concerned with environmental science and other allied subjects; on the other hand, *informatics* is very close to ICT, information systems, information technology, and other allied subjects (Henricks et al., 2003; Kistemann et al., 2002). Environmental informatics is initially considered as a concept, research area, and practicing field, and in the recent past, it has been considered as a field of study globally. Internationally, undergraduate, postgraduate, and PhD degrees have been started in many universities in allied areas of environmental informatics, as depicted in Fig. 8.2.

Environmental informatics is broader than the geo-informatics area, and it is very close to other subjects, such as:

- Agricultural informatics.
- Water informatics.
- Forest informatics.
- Irrigation informatics (Paul & Aithal, 2020).

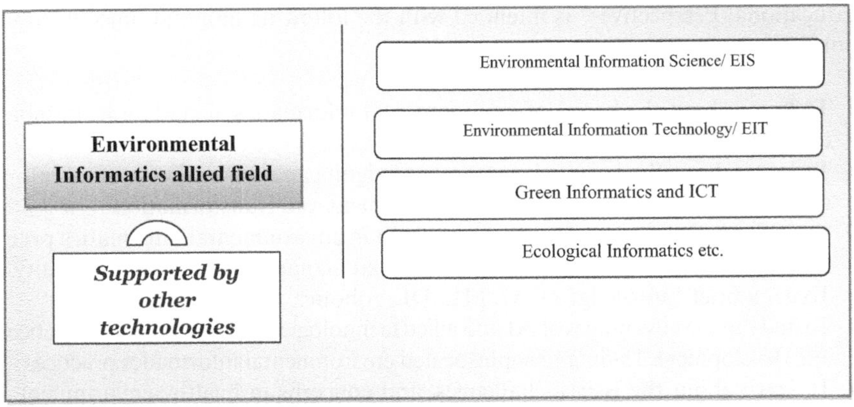

Fig 8.2. AI and Allied Technologies in Environmental Sustainability.

Experts also examined the relationship of environmental informatics with other allied subjects, such as "Social Informatics." Environmental informatics is equipped with various latest technologies for advanced environmental monitoring and digital environmental solutions (Marques et al., 2005; Nikolov, 1987).

5. AI, ML and DL in Environmental Process and Mechanism: An Overview

Environmental informatics is powered by many facets in order to provide its services. Apart from technologies, many other facets are involved in this, as depicted in Fig. 8.3. Among the technologies, AI is emerging, and AI is responsible for building intelligent systems for the products as well as services (Cortès et al., 2000; Kosovic et al., 2020). Machines play a leading role in AI as they perform like humans and mimic their actions. In addition to this, AI has a learning ability with a problem-solving approach (Chen et al., 2021). AI is dedicated to performing desired goals and is utilized in different sectors and industries (Chen et al., 2008). In diverse areas, AI is emerging and growing, including healthcare, administration and governance, commerce and business, transportation, education, etc. (Himeur et al., 2022). Main technologies and systems that interact with AI include automated machines, electronic self-supporting devices, etc. The following are considered valuable features in AI (but not limited to):

- AI is based on simulation to perform like humans, and here, intelligence is considered vital for all connected devices as well as machines.
- Learning, reasoning, and perception; these three are considered valuable in AI and allied technologies (Francisco, 2023).
- Among the variants, two are important: weak AI, which is strong AI, and is dedicated to performing several complex jobs, similar to human abilities.

Weak AI is dedicated to designing particular jobs that are already defined, whereas strong AI, or strong AI, is considered more complex and intelligent than

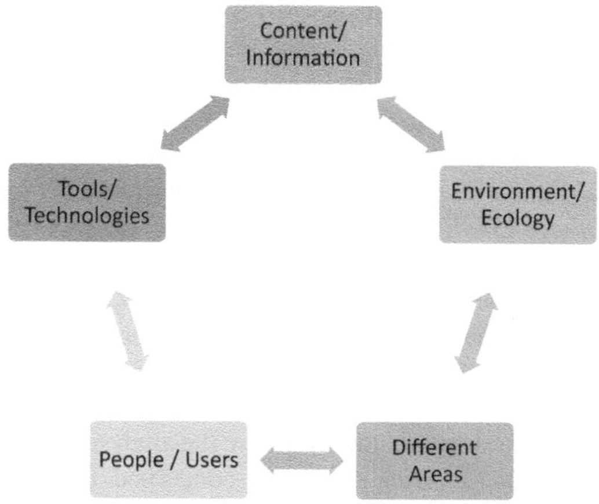

Fig. 8.3. Various Stakeholders and Facets in Developing Environmental Informatics.

humans, and is dedicated to complicated systems. Thus, strong AI is able to solve a problem even without the presence of a person.

ML, and treated as a sub-area and part of AI, is performed using statistical techniques for doing several computational jobs and decision-making processes, etc. (Cui et al., 2023). In 1959, Arthur Samuel first introduced the word to mean "deep involvement," and it is dedicated to the proper development of algorithms supported by the following (Forootan et al., 2022; Gulati & Sharma, 2020).

- Decision and association tree learning.
- Artificial neural networks.
- DL and clustering.
- Inductive logic programming (Lee et al., 2017).

DL is another subset of ML similar to AI (Chen et al., 2020). Among several architectures of DL, a few are important:

- Deep neural networks.
- Deep belief networks.
- Recurrent neural networks, etc. (Christin et al., 2019; Fan et al., 2023).

There are diverse areas where DL in generally is applicable such as computer vision, natural language processing, speech recognition, pattern recognition, image restoration, virtual assistant, face recognition, robotics, fake news detection, autonomous vehicles management, environmental monitoring, neural networks, computer vision, fraud detection, etc. (Kumari & Pandey, 2023; Nishant et al., 2020). As far as environmental management and monitoring are concerned, ML is applicable in diverse activities and areas in order to keep healthy and sustainable environmental systems. As far as *Analysis of the Data*, DL is useful using its algorithms including satellite images, GPS-based systems to identify the status of the water and also as quality, this is also important to get updates about the pattern, scenario as well as correlations of environmental matters in order to boost environmental dynamics (Malakar et al., 2021). In *Remote sensing*-related activities, DL is useful to identify the environmental parameters, predict the environmental data, and provide geo-spatial solutions. *Ecological Monitoring* is another area where DL in regard to ecology can be applicable, especially to determine the type and behavior of the animal and for the identification of biodiversity, etc. As far as the *Conservation of Environment* is concerned, DL may be treated as important for the segregation and classification of the information, and it may be done in a visual, spatial, or acoustic manner.

There is tremendous potential for *Water Protection & Management* using DL, using image processing and segmentation, where the analysis of water images is considered valuable. As far as *Detecting Anomaly* is concerned, DL is useful in managing environmental data for environmental hazards management. In regard to the identification of patterns of various types of data, DL is worthy and emerging, and this is applicable in finding trends of climate, behaviors of species, etc. As far as *Decision Support System* is concerned, DL is considered impactful for simulations, proper predictions, etc., for environmental matters, including environmental hazards. *Automation* is another benefit of DL for several continuous ecological machines and systems for improving processes, mechanisms, and efficiency. In *Climate and Weather Management*, DL is important in several affairs, including the identification of temperature, rainfall probability, and monitoring sea-level rise. Weather-related matters, mainly forecasting or prediction. In regard to finding droughts, floods, as well as predicting heat waves, becomes possible with DL applications as far as the environment is concerned. Air management is another potential benefit of DL in the environment and ecological systems, and it includes predicting pollution status, as well as sources in the air, and proper remedies for the same. In addition to these, DL is important in the environment for the following purposes, viz.

- Monitoring and managing ecosystems and biodiversity management.
- Identification and mapping of the habitat and other invasive species.
- Solar and water energy forecasting and further dealing.
- Assessment of the damage to the natural resources.
- Urgent and quick case-to-case basis response planning and identification.
- Finding and tracking the recovery progress.

All these activities in favor of the environment from the end of DL are positively possible through several sources, including sensor networks, satellite images, existing and future environmental databases, and so on.

6. AI and Allied Technologies in Environmental Systems Mapping and Execution

AI is treated as an important component in computational sciences and technology with diverse applications in environmental solutions, and ecological management, and this trend is growing gradually. Furthermore, many allied fields of environmental informatics may be beneficial in environmental development, as detailed in Fig. 8.4.

The temperature of the Earth is increasing day by day, and this change in weather is also responsible for climate change. The planet is becoming hotter day by day, and this number was 777 in the year 2016, which is 3 times more than the year 1980. Thus, for this activity of warming of the Earth, 20% of species are facing several issues and challenges, and environmental scientists predict this percentage may reach "fifty percent" in the year 2100. As far as pre-industrial timing is concerned, the temperature has increased by 3 °C. In managing such situations, AI and allied technologies are impactful and have wider potentialities for several environmental issues, particularly in climate change management, with their sensor-based results and decision-making process. Here, among the allied technologies, IoT, cloud, and virtualization may be considered meaningful. Some countries, such as Australia, Norway, and England, are playing a greater role in managing the environment using AI.

In the identification of cyclones especially tropical cyclones, several AI-based tools and technologies are considered valuable for prediction. Ultimately, weather forecasting will become effective, with more predictions based on AI. Thus, all these are effective in proper disaster management; however, apart from AI-allied technologies like IoT, robotics, and DL, which are also considered significant, here. Different ICT and environmental organizations are engaged in several activities related to environmental management and sustainability, and among them, important ones are IBM, Google, Dell, and Microsoft. Several natural disasters are ongoing every time, such as a disaster or a cyclone in a forest, which can be managed using AI-based tools. As human eyes may be unable to identify and map the situation, AI-based technologies, along with sensor networks, are considered valuable in identifying results compared to traditional methods. In renewable energy management, including the identification of power fluctuations and improving energy storage, AI and allied technologies are valuable and important. ML-based algorithms are essential in modern environmental protection, especially in energy management, as far as quick decision-making is concerned. Identification of vulnerabilities, grid management, power management,

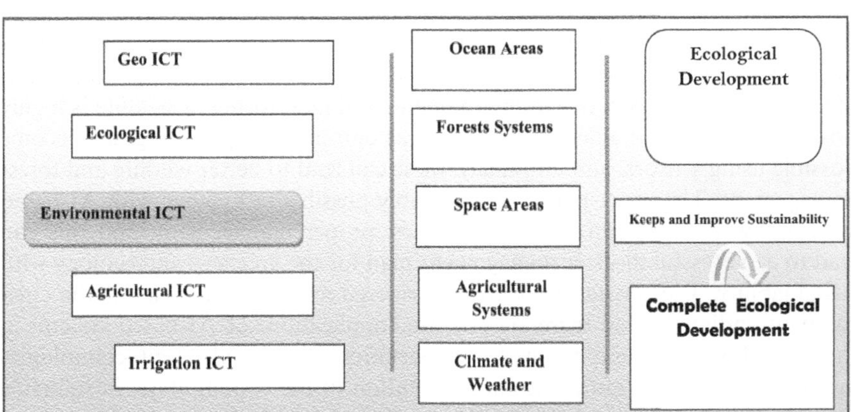

Fig. 8.4. Environment Informatics Allied Areas and Ultimate Beneficials.

and auto-based renewable energy management are all positively possible with AI and allied technologies, and these are supported without direct human involvement. Today, wind-depended energy systems are growing rapidly, and in such a context, AI is essential for cleaning the devices and systems, and to keep systems up-to-date. AI and allied systems are impactful in many environmental issues of urban and rural areas for a sophisticated urbanization using AI with sustainability. Lives become easier with AI in several environmental matters, including floods and air quality management in urban areas. In this context, environmental informatics is closely related to urban informatics.

ML and allied technologies are playing a vital role in tree plantation, cultivation, etc., using intelligent systems and technologies (Jahed Armaghani et al., 2015). Here, several sensors are useful in getting real-time data, which can be fruitful for several cultivation-related matters and healthy agricultural sustainability, viz.

- Crop moisture.
- Crop management.
- Precision agriculture.
- Soil management, etc.

Thus, environmental systems are also protected and prioritized using AL and allied technologies in the enhancement of the efficiency, enhanced yields, and in reducing water, fertilizer, and pesticide uses (Paul, Aithal, Bhuimali, et al., 2020). As far as ocean-based AI applications are concerned, combining with other technologies, it helps in tracking ocean vehicles, mining from the ocean, marine fishing, etc., and all real-time data can be treated as impactful in healthy ocean sustainability. Globally, climate change is considered one of the major problems worldwide, and there are various potential prediction models that are worthy of consideration in the identification of climate situations and model development, leading to future climate solutions with sustainability. In such a prediction-based system, AI and allied technologies are considered valuable. Among the allied technologies, IoT and fog computing are treated as important for prediction model development, as per weather and climate. As far as atmospheric dynamics are concerned, AI-based systems are required for several activities including their sub-fields, such as ML and DL. Regarding data management of such atmospheric dynamics, cloud-based tools are also useful and emerging globally. Wildlife is an important part of the environment, and monitoring of wildlife is highly possible with AI and allied technologies, as current data gathering has become possible using sensors, and ultimately, these can lead to better wildlife and forest management. The water part is also suitably possible to manage with AI-based systems by identification of vulnerabilities, proper management, and this can lead to a successful disaster management plan for the greenery and ecology with sustainability. Transportation is also considered an important part of the environment, indirectly, and there are potential applications of AI-based systems in this area. For building a planned transportation system, AI-based technologies are worthy and need more and more attention in the coming days. Sustainable transportation is the need of the hour as it is shared by common citizens and keeps the environment better, including traffic and future-intelligent transportation systems. In gathering real-time data, sensor-based systems and AI-based mechanisms are essential.

7. Sector-specific Practice of Environmental Informatics Practice

As environmental informatics is about managing information for environmental matters, it is being practiced with several allied technologies and systems. The applications of AI with allied technologies (i.e., ML and DL) are described here, and in later sub-sections, applications and potentialities of robotics have been analyzed.

7.1. AI and Allied Technologies

Environmental informatics offers sustainable and healthy environmental systems with various supportive technologies and systems like AI, ML, DL, etc. And all these technologies are impactful in managing land systems, air systems, and water systems, which are connected with the environment (Paul, Bhuimali, Aithal, et al., 2020). Fig. 8.5 is depicted in allied and basic technologies, which help in environmental management.

7.1.1. Land Management

AI is treated as an important technology in land management, including soil populations and management, which is required not only in agricultural-related matters but also in construction management-related activities. As agriculture lies on soil purely, therefore, in the identification of soil with its quality, AI is considered valuable. As far as land identification is concerned, an AI-based system will be helped by gathering automated data and further storage in databases, which will lead to the decision-making process (Yuan et al., 2020). AI is able to offer

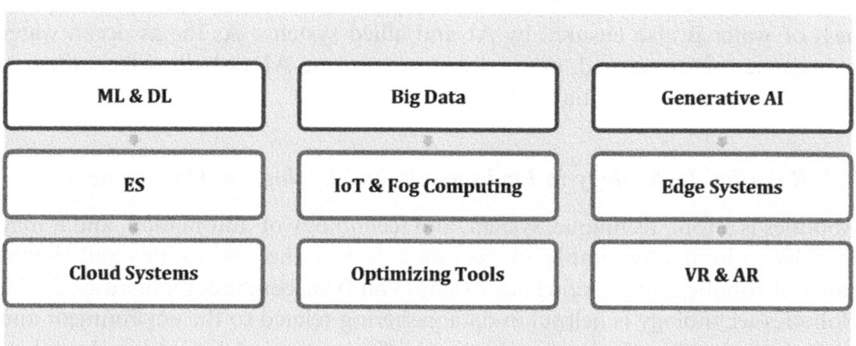

Fig. 8.5. Allied Technologies of AI in Effective and Intelligent Environmental Practice.

land-friendly crops in an efficient manner with a proper ecosystem. AI-supported drones can collect data on land and crops, and thus it becomes easy to perform several activities, viz.

- Soil quality identification.
- Identification of the plant disease.
- Poacher root prediction.
- Managing and monitoring erosion.
- Finding of the species.
- Animal migration, etc.

Here, for all these concerns, AI and its applications are highly essential in order to have healthy land management systems, directly and indirectly promoting agricultural systems (Willard, 2022).

7.1.2. Air-based Applications

In regard to managing "Air," AI is treated as a valuable tool for air monitoring using AI-based technologies. In addition to the identification of air pollution, accurate air pollution identification is another major aim of AI. In some cases, an AI-based system is dedicated to finding gas leakages using modern sensors (may be WSN as well) as a prevention measure. Air pollution is quickly and effectively possible using AI-based systems, thus it will reduce harmful emissions and also help save us from the dangerous global crisis. The World Health Organization (WHO) has its air quality guidelines, and AI technology-based vehicles are dedicated to reducing oil use, as well as greenhouse gas emissions by 2%–4%.

7.1.3. Water-based Applications

AI is a machine-based system, and it is therefore useful in water quality management and monitoring, supported by allied technologies in different parameters. As water is crucial for all of us, and needed for survival, quality, and quantity-wise, water system development and management need AI support. The cleanliness of water is also ensured by AI and allied systems. As far as ocean water management is concerned, especially in monitoring AI and allied technologies, they are considered essential and need of the hour.

7.2. Robotics Technology in Environment and Ecological Management

Robotics is a tool, technique, system, and technology of automation, and it may look like a human or simply an electronic device. The applications and significance of robotics are emerging day by day (Van Wynsberghe & Donhauser, 2018). Robotics technology is helpful in data gathering related to the environment and ecology, and serves the environment in different ways. Advanced and modern robotics-based devices are even able to perform various ecological jobs through integrated devices. In forest management, ocean management, including river monitoring and management, robotics is also considered valuable and impactful. These technologies/devices are able to find destructive, harmful algal blooms. In regard to the identification of the spreading level of populations, this can ultimately lead in monitoring several environmental phenomena, viz., climate variables, monitoring of the drainage, volcanoes, etc. Robots can be employed in the ocean, air monitoring, water management, agricultural management, and so on. In the recent past, robots integrated with the IoT, wireless sensor networks, and cloud-based systems have been considered impactful in large-scale environmental dealing and monitoring. In such a situation, robots or robotics technology can be used. Regarding natural disaster management and artificial disaster management, AI-based robotics can be effective and a good alternative. As far as climate change is concerned, robotics and other AI-based systems are able to study various climate change concerns. The changing scenario of climate change is the reason for the victims of plants as well as animals (Van Wynsberghe & Donhauser, 2018). Robotics and allied technology are rising rapidly in diverse fields in environmental management and monitoring, as depicted in Fig. 8.6.

7.2.1. Automated and Numerous Tree Plantations

AI-based robotics technology is dedicated and emerging as an automated tree plantation, and internationally several ventures have been launched for such an initiative, in regard to moving the trees here, automated cars and vehicles can be used, ultimately uses of such technology may lead 10 times faster plantation and later its management including cutting the trees and also in monitoring.

7.2.2. Farmer-centric Drought Management

AI-based robotics technology is able to provide various farmer-centric solutions. As cultivators always face different kinds of problems and issues in cultivation,

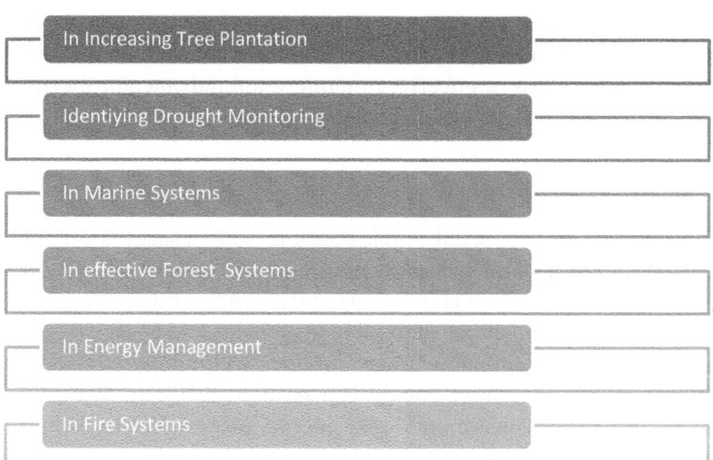

Fig 8.6. Basic Uses of Agricultural Robots for Sustainability.

such as drought. Here, drought is an alarming issue, and here robotics applications can be effective, so that not only farmers but also plants can survive better. Here, a technically AI-based sensor may be inbuilt for proper growth, and plants can grow accordingly. As climate change also affects agricultural production, AI-based robotics technology may be effective.

7.2.3. Marine System Monitoring and Management

As far as ocean and marine system management is concerned, AI-based robotics technology is effective in several ways. Using various devices and electronic devices are worthy in ocean-based systems, including coral reefs in the Red Sea. In addition to coral reefs, there are other plants and life in the ocean, and the same can be properly managed using robotics. The oil and gas industry is growing rapidly, and it is truly depends on the ocean, and there are tremendous applications and opportunities with AI-based robotics technology for more effective operations without human involvement or less human involvement in certain contexts. Scientists also developed a system so that AI-based robotics technology is able to ingest microbes from the ocean and convert them into energy, thus it can manage energy as well. In reducing oil leakages, robotics technology is also important (Taghikhah et al., 2022). There are other ways of robotics technology in oceans, and among these, waste management of the ocean is considered valuable and impactful. As far as sea waste is concerned, robotics technology is useful in collecting, organizing, and monitoring waste, including plastic materials, and thus it reduces direct human involvement. It is a fact that the initial cost of robotics technology is higher, but post-production may be limited.

7.2.4. Ecological Data Management

Robotics technology supported with AI leads to data collection, organization, management, processing, and delivery related to the environment, ecology, and biodiversity. Here, sensors including IoT and fog computing-based systems can be employed to get data from the forest, agriculture, marine sectors, etc. Various multiple small robots can be effective in modern and advanced robotics technology-based environmental data management.

7.2.5. Solar Energy Systems

As far as robotics technological applications in solar energy are concerned, it has wider potentialities and is increasing gradually. Fossil fuel is an important source of energy, and modern engineering systems have gifted various AI-driven technologies in better and effective fossil management and energy from the same. In regard to managing climate change, robotics technology is also considered impactful, and here, renewable energy can be used properly. Wave Gilder is a prime name in regard to wave and solar energy, using robotics technology can simplify solar energy development, and this can lead to the environment and ecology. In developing solar energy, dust management is very important in deserts, and here, AI-driven robotics technology is effective in dust management including cleanliness. With built-in solar panels, robotics technology is useful for energy efficiency.

7.2.6. Management of Water Pollutions

Water pollution is an important concern, and here AI-driven robotic technology can be considered as an effective means for managing water pollution. Many devices have been invented for managing water pollution and all these are connected with sensors powered by IoT with AI-based systems (Poch et al., 2004; Shuford, 2024). In regard to renewal and alternative energy, microbes can be treated as valuable, which can be used for cleanliness and transformed into energy. Thus, environment-wise AI-based robotics is urgent and need of the hour.

7.2.7. Recycling of Technologies

Regarding recycling of the technology, robotics and AI-based systems are treated as important for an easier recycling process, with this, traditional work may be reduced, and here, AMP robots can be an important name. In this approach, robots can find out the materials and then place them into a particular bin (Tien et al., 2022). Thus, recycling technologies are impacting the environment properly and effectively.

7.2.8. Minimizing Carbon Emissions

In respect of the reduction of carbon emissions, robots and robotics technologies can also be worthy. In manual vehicles and trunks, there is a huge amount of energy used and dedicated to emissions every day. In this context, AI and technology-integrated systems vehicles are more widely used for transportation of the systems than worthy and indirectly beneficial for the reduction of carbon, and help in the environment and ecology.

7.2.9. Minimizing Transportation Emissions

Transportation is one of the major causes of pollution, and this is treated as the largest pollution segment to the environment. There are ways to minimize transportation emissions, and among them, the use of an automated car, an AI-based, low-emission car, can be the best alternative in regard to managing the environment and ecological systems. AI-based robots can be effective in the population management of cars, fossil fuel-based devices, and machines.

7.2.10. Waste Monitoring and Management

Robotics-supported AI is effective in waste monitoring and management, and waste management causes environmental pollution, leading to climate change all over the world. Waste management with AI and robotics is able to perform diverse activities, such as in production units, in pollution prevention, etc.

(Trincavelli et al., 2008). AI-based systems are dedicated to minimizing and reducing the manufacturing process, which is environmentally friendly. As humans produce a lot of waste here and there, robotics-based systems are effective in reducing waste, and the problem of a large amount of waste can be solved by vacuuming, cleaning, sorting the waste, and garbage of the household, etc. Here, sensor-based robots can be effective in waste management, and the same can be best in environmental impact. Machines and devices supported by Robotics can also be used in the treatment and recycling of waste, as well as minimizing CO_2 emissions.

7.2.11. Automated Alerts Management Systems

Automated AI-based robotics technology is useful in designing, developing, and managing automated alert management systems, which can be useful in environmental monitoring in the ocean, forests, agricultural sectors, earthquake prediction, and altering systems (Zhong et al., 2021). Apart from these, in any disaster situation, AI-integrated robotics is also useful and impactful, like in urgent weather conditions. In support of automated systems the following technologies are impactful,

- DL.
- ML.
- IoT.
- Fog computing, etc.

7.2.12. Fire Management Systems of Forest

In regard to the protection of the forest from fire, automated AI-based robotics technology is useful and emerging rapidly. In many countries globally, forest fire is an alarming issue and they destroy plants, species of animals, and the health of humans in addition to various properties, thus here robotics-based systems may be employed effectively (Paul, Saavedra, et al., 2020). It has been reported that in a country like the USA, about 100,000 fires happen in the forest yearly, and in this context, AI-based robotics technology may be employed. In prediction, ML can be useful, whereas robots can be used after fire management for quick solutions and control. There are different means of managing forest fires, such as

- Use of extinguishers in fire safety and management.
- Water-propelling devices are used in forest-related monitoring and management.
- GPS-connected AI-based robotics technology for gathering real-time data.
- Sensor-based devices in environmental monitoring, etc.

7.2.13. Developing Sustainability in Agriculture

AI-based robotics technology is dedicated to the development of the agricultural sector, particularly sustainable agriculture, using other allied technologies and systems. In finding the chemical level, identification of fertilizer quality, planting of crops, and watering of plants, AI-based robotics technology is useful (Zhong et al., 2021). As far as harvesting of the crop is concerned, AI-based robotics technology is useful; thus, it helps in finding suitable timing for fruits and vegetable picking, farming, post-production activities, and so on. Therefore, AI-based robotics technology is helpful in developing ecological sustainability, directly and indirectly.

8. Educational Scenario and Potentialities of Environmental Informatics in AI and Allied Technology Context

Initially, the informatics stream was started by the universities as an academic program and subject, and gradually different field-specific informatics have been developed, among which geo-informatics is important (Paul, Aithal, et al., 2020; Paul, Bhuimali, Aithal, Tiwary, et al., 2020). In recent years, internationally, many universities have initiated environmental informatics programs, which have also been considered as a field (Page, 1996; Page et al., 2009) and a subject leading to BS, BSc, and MSc programs, including joint degree programs (Table 8.1). There are potentialities in offering environmental informatics nomenclature in AI and other allied subject contexts as proposed in Tables 8.2–8.8. In regard to offering a new-age program for environmental sustainability, it is also proposed (Tilak, 2008).

Environmental informatics may be offered as an academic program for the creation of environment-friendly systems supported by AI and other allied technologies. There are ways in engineering, science, and management streams to offer environmental informatics as general programs, or as specializations in other relevant programs, there is also potential to offer this subject with AI and other allied technologies (Dayal, 2002). Table 8.2 provides engineering degrees with environmental informatics specializations.

Table 8.3 provides potential degrees of science stream with environmental informatics specialization, and such a science degree is proposed with the subjects of computer science, information science, computer applications, simple environmental sciences, or environmental management.

As many universities worldwide have started environmental informatics/environmental ICT as a subject, it is possible to start AI as a specialization in the said programs, and such degrees may be from BSc, BTech, or BS. Refer to Table 8.4 in this regard.

Data science is increasing day by day, and there are universities that have started academic, research, and training programs on data science. As big data analytics has potential with AI, a specialization program may be started with the nomenclature on "Environmental Data Science," and this is may be with AI concentrated as depicted in Table 8.5.

Computer Application is one of the flagship programs in India and many other countries, and thus, there are opportunities to offer ML and DL concentrated Environmental Informatics programs. Here, Table 8.6 depicts such proposed programs.

Table 8.1. Some of the Universities Started Environmental Informatics as an Academic Program.

Universities	Country	Level of Program Offered	Degree Offered	Subjects
Auburn University	USA	Undergraduate	BS	Geo-spatial Environmental Informatics
Wuhan University	China	Undergraduate	BSc	Geo-environmental Informatics
Northern Arizona University	USA	Undergraduate	BS	Informatics (Environmental Informatics)
Georg August University of Göttingen	Germany	Undergraduate and postgraduate	BSc and MSc	Environmental Informatics Integrated
University of North Carolina at Chapel Hill	USA	Undergraduate and postgraduate	BS and MS	Environmental Science and Information Science Dual Degree
Virginia Polytechnic Institute and State University	USA	Undergraduate	BS	Environmental Informatics
The University of Applied Sciences	Germany	Undergraduate	(BSc	Environmental Informatics and Business Information Systems (Dual Degree)

Table 8.2. Possible Engineering Degrees with Environmental Informatics/EI with AI.

Some of the Possible Engineering Degrees with Environmental Informatics/EI)	
BTech-CSE (EI with AI)	MTech-CSE (EI with AI)
BTech-IT (EI with AI)	MTech-IT (EI with AI)
BTech-ECE (EI with AI)	MTech-ECE (EI with AI)
BTech-Mechanical Engineering (EI with AI)	MTech-Mechanical Engineering (EI with AI)
BTech-Civil Engineering (EI with AI)	MTech-Civil Engineering (EI with AI)

Table 8.3. Possible Science with Environmental Informatics/EI Specializations.

Some of the Possible Science Degrees with Environmental Informatics/EI	
BSc-CS (EI with AI)	MSc-CS (EI with AI)
BSc-IT (EI with AI)	MSc-IT (EI with AI)
BCA (EI with AI)	MCA (EI with AI)
BSc-Environmental Science (EI with AI)	MSc-Environmental Science (EI with AI)
BSc-Environmental Management (EI with AI)	MSc-Environmental Management (EI with AI)

Table 8.4. Possible AI Specialization with Environmental Informatics/EICT.

Some of the Possible Environmental Informatics Degrees with AI Specialization	
BSc-Environmental Informatics (AI)	BSc-Environmental ICT (AI)
BTech-Environmental Informatics (AI)	BTech-Environmental ICT (AI)
MSc-Environmental Informatics (AI)	MSc-Environmental ICT (AI)
MTech-Environmental Informatics (AI)	MTech-Environmental ICT (AI)

Table 8.5. Possible AI Specialization with Environmental Informatics/EICT.

Some of the Possible Data Science Program with AI Specialization	
BSc-Environmental Data Science (AI)	BBA (Environmental Information Systems Management)
BTech-Environmental Data Science (AI)	MBA (Environmental Information Systems Management)
MSc-Environmental Data Science (AI)	
MTech-Environmental Data Science (AI)	

Similar to the previous proposed program to bring an intelligent environmental system, another set of academic programs has been proposed in Table 8.7 on environmental informatics with ML specialization or potentialities; such a degree may be offered with a science or engineering degree.

There are opportunities to offer Environmental Informatics programs as a doctoral program, and the same can be offered as a specialization of AI or allied branches, as depicted in Table 8.8.

Thus, AI and allied technological involvement can be enhanced in a more sophisticated way by introducing new-age academic programs related to environmental informatics and environmental sustainability.

Table 8.6. Possible ML and DL Specialized Environmental Informatics Program in Computer Applications.

Some of the Possible Environmental Informatics Degrees in CA	
BCA/MCA Environmental Informatics (Machine Learning)	BCA/MCA Environmental Informatics (Deep Learning)
BCA/MCA-Environmental Informatics (Artificial Intelligence)	BCA/MCA-Environmental Informatics (Intelligent Systems and Robotics)

Table 8.7. Possible ML Specialized Environmental Informatics Program in Science and Engineering Stream.

Some of the Possible Environmental Informatics at the Doctoral Level	
BSc-Environmental Informatics (Machine Learning)	BTech-Environmental Informatics (Machine Learning)
MSc-Environmental Informatics (Machine Learning)	MTech-Environmental Informatics (Machine Learning)

Table 8.8. Possible Environmental Informatics Program at the Doctoral Level with AI and Allied Areas.

Some of the Possible Environmental Informatics at the Doctoral Level	
PhD-Environmental Informatics (Artificial Intelligence, AI)	PhD-Computer Science (Environmental Informatics with AI)
PhD-Environmental Informatics (Machine Learning)	PhD-Information Science (Environmental Informatics with AI)
PhD-Environmental Informatics (Robotics)	PhD-ICT (Environmental Informatics with AI)

9. Concluding Remarks

Environmental informatics is growing rapidly as a study and practice field, and its technologies are also increasing gradually in diverse areas and sections. Apart from AI, some other technologies are also putting their effort into environmental monitoring, development, management, and complete environmental informatics solutions. Among the allied technologies, cloud and virtualization technology, big data analytics, IoT, fog computing, blockchain technology, and metaverse systems are the need of the hour in environmental systems for proper environmental digital solutions. There are issues and challenges in better and effective environmental informatics practices, and all these need to be addressed properly in order to have effective societal and anthropological development. Environmental informatics practice is needed for natural as well as man-made disaster-related activities. Using AI-based technologies and robotics, it is easy to tackle several environmental problems and concerns, and its effective control can lead to the betterment of the health of the environment and humans, too. Remote sensing, GIS- and GPS-based technologies, automated data management systems, automated devices, sensor-based technologies, and machines, including drones, are effective in achieving better environmental solutions. In vehicle management, transportation, the agricultural sector, as well as applications and significance of the environment, have emerged significantly. As far as better reliability, safety, and real-time approaches are concerned, GIS- and GPS-based systems supported by AI may be more productive in bringing sustainability. Different countries worldwide are putting their effort into introducing environmental-related education and also various environmental informatics nomenclature or allied areas, combined with various technologies. AI and robotics specialized technologies may be offered in concentration with environmental informatics to bring sustainability and societal development. It has been noted that bio-inspired robots are also emerging rapidly globally in order to bring sustainability and societal development.

References

Allen, T. F., Giampietro, M., & Little, A. M. (2003). Distinguishing ecological engineering from environmental engineering. *Ecological Engineering*, *20*(5), 389–407.

Amato, F., Guignard, F., Robert, S., & Kanevski, M. (2020). A novel framework for spatio-temporal prediction of environmental data using deep learning. *Scientific Reports*, *10*(1), 22243.

Bogue, R. (2023). The role of robots in environmental monitoring. *Industrial Robot: The International Journal of Robotics Research and Application*, *50*(3), 369–375.

Chen, J., Huang, S., BalaMurugan, S., & Tamizharasi, G. S. (2021). Artificial intelligence based e-waste management for environmental planning. *Environmental Impact Assessment Review*, *87*, 106498.

Chen, S. H., Jakeman, A. J., & Norton, J. P. (2008). Artificial intelligence techniques: An introduction to their use for modelling environmental systems. *Mathematics and Computers in Simulation*, *78*(2–3), 379–400.

Chen, Z., Jiang, C., Masood, M. K., Soh, Y. C., Wu, M., & Li, X. (2019). Deep learning for building occupancy estimation using environmental sensors. In *Deep learning: Algorithms and applications* (pp. 335–357). Springer International Publishing.

Christin, S., Hervet, É., & Lecomte, N. (2019). Applications for deep learning in ecology. *Methods in Ecology and Evolution, 10*(10), 1632–1644.
Cinderby, S. (1999). Geographic information systems (GIS) for participation: The future of environmental GIS? *International Journal of Environment and Pollution, 11*(3), 304–315.
Cortès, U., Sànchez-Marrè, M., Ceccaroni, L., R-Roda, I., & Poch, M. (2000). Artificial intelligence and environmental decision support systems. *Applied Intelligence, 13*, 77–91.
Cui, S., Gao, Y., Huang, Y., Shen, L., Zhao, Q., Pan, Y., & Zhuang, S. (2023). Advances and applications of machine learning and deep learning in environmental ecology and health. *Environmental Pollution*, 122358.
Dayal, I. (2002). Developing management education in India. *Journal of Management Research, 2*(2), 98.
Dunbabin, M., & Marques, L. (2012). Robots for environmental monitoring: Significant advancements and applications. *IEEE Robotics & Automation Magazine, 19*(1), 24–39.
Fan, Z., Yan, Z., & Wen, S. (2023). Deep learning and artificial intelligence in sustainability: A review of SDGs, renewable energy, and environmental health. *Sustainability, 15*(18), 13493.
Forootan, M. M., Larki, I., Zahedi, R., & Ahmadi, A. (2022). Machine learning and deep learning in energy systems: A review. *Sustainability, 14*(8), 4832.
Francisco, M. (2023). Artificial intelligence for environmental security: National, international, human and ecological perspectives. *Current Opinion in Environmental Sustainability, 61*, 101250.
Gulati, S., & Sharma, S. (2020). Challenges and responses towards sustainable future through machine learning and deep learning. *Data Visualization and Knowledge Engineering: Spotting Data Points with Artificial Intelligence, 32*, 151–169.
Henricks, W. H., Boyer, P. J., Harrison, J. H., Tuthill, J. M., & Healy, J. C. (2003). Informatics training in pathology residency programs: Proposed learning objectives and skill sets for the new millennium. *Archives of Pathology & Laboratory Medicine, 127*(8), 1009–1018.
Himeur, Y., Rimal, B., Tiwary, A., & Amira, A. (2022). Using artificial intelligence and data fusion for environmental monitoring: A review and future perspectives. *Information Fusion, 86*, 44–75.
Hoang, T. D., Ky, N. M., Thuong, N. T. N., Nhan, H. Q., & Ngan, N. V. C. (2022). Artificial intelligence in pollution control and management: Status and future prospects. *Artificial Intelligence and Environmental Sustainability: Challenges and Solutions in the Era of Industry 4.0*, 23–43.
Huang, G. H., & Chang, N. B. (2003). The perspectives of environmental informatics and systems analysis. *Journal of Environmental Informatics, 1*(1), 1–7.
Jahed Armaghani, D., Hajihassani, M., Monjezi, M., Mohamad, E. T., Marto, A., & Moghaddam, M. R. (2015). Application of two intelligent systems in predicting environmental impacts of quarry blasting. *Arabian Journal of Geosciences, 8*, 9647–9665.
Kim, K., & Park, J. (2009). A survey of applications of artificial intelligence algorithms in eco-environmental modelling. *Environmental Engineering Research, 14*(2), 102–110.
Kistemann, T., Dangendorf, F., & Schweikart, J. (2002). New perspectives on the use of geographical information systems (GIS) in environmental health sciences. *International Journal of Hygiene and Environmental Health, 205*(3), 169–181.
Kosovic, I. N., Mastelic, T., & Ivankovic, D. (2020). Using artificial intelligence on environmental data from Internet of Things for estimating solar radiation: Comprehensive analysis. *Journal of Cleaner Production, 266*, 121489.
Kumari, N., & Pandey, S. (2023). Application of artificial intelligence in environmental sustainability and climate change. In *Visualization techniques for climate change with machine learning and artificial intelligence* (pp. 293–316). Elsevier.

Lee, D., Kang, S., & Shin, J. (2017). Using deep learning techniques to forecast environmental consumption level. *Sustainability*, *9*(10), 1894.

Malakar, P., Sarkar, S., Mukherjee, A., Bhanja, S., & Sun, A. Y. (2021). Use of machine learning and deep learning methods in groundwater. In *Global groundwater* (pp. 545–557). Elsevier.

Marques, L., Martins, A., & de Almeida, A. T. (2005). Environmental monitoring with mobile robots. In *2005 IEEE/RSJ international conference on intelligent robots and systems* (pp. 3624–3629). IEEE.

Nikolov, R. (1987). Integrating informatics into the curriculum. *Education and Computing*, *3*(3), 269–274.

Nishant, R., Kennedy, M., & Corbett, J. (2020). Artificial intelligence for sustainability: Challenges, opportunities, and a research agenda. *International Journal of Information Management*, *53*, 102104.

Page, B. (1996, May). Environmental informatics towards a new discipline in applied computer science for environmental protection and research. In *Environmental software systems: Proceedings of the international symposium on environmental software Systems, 1995* (pp. 3–22). Springer US.

Page, B., Wohlgemuth, V., & Kiekheben, U. (2009). Review of environmental informatics education in Germany and selected European universities. *EnviroInfo* (2), 63–69.

Paul, P. K., & Aithal, P. S. (2020). Environmental informatics and its features, functions and stakeholders: A comprehensive overview. *Educational Quest: An International Journal of Education and Applied Social Science*, *11*(1), 01–05.

Paul, P. K., Aithal, P. S., & Bhuimali, A. (2020). Environmental informatics and educational opportunities in post graduate level—Indian potentialities based on international scenario. *IRA-International Journal of Management & Social Sciences*, *16*(2), 45–58.

Paul, P. K., Aithal, P. S., Bhuimali, A., Kalishankar, T., & Saavedra M, R. (2020). Research activities, opportunities & possibilities in environmental informatics: International scenario & Indian potentialities. *SCHOLEDGE International Journal of Management & Development*, *7*(06), 99–106.

Paul, P. K., Bhuimali, A., Aithal, P. S., Kalishankar, T., & Saavedra M. R. (2020). Artificial intelligence & cloud computing in environmental systems – Towards healthy & sustainable development. *International Journal of Inclusive Development*, *6*(1), 01–08.

Paul, P. K., Bhuimali, A., Aithal, P. S., Tiwary, K. S., & Sinha, R. R. (2020). Environmental informatics: Educational opportunities at bachelors level-international context and Indian potentialities. *International Journal of Applied Engineering and Management Letters (IJAEML)*, *4*(1), 243–256.

Paul, P. K., Saavedra, R., Aithal, P. S., Aremu, B., & Baby, P. (2020). Environmental informatics: Potentialities in *iSchools* and information science & technology programs—An analysis. *International Journal of Management, Technology, and Social Sciences (IJMTS)*, *5*(1), 238–250.

Poch, M., Comas, J., Rodríguez-Roda, I., Sanchez-Marre, M., & Cortés, U. (2004). Designing and building real environmental decision support systems. *Environmental Modelling & Software*, *19*(9), 857–873.

Shuford, J. (2024). Interdisciplinary perspectives: Fusing artificial intelligence with environmental science for sustainable solutions. *Journal of Artificial Intelligence General Science (JAIGS)*, *1*(1), 106–123.

Taghikhah, F., Erfani, E., Bakhshayeshi, I., Tayari, S., Karatopouzis, A., & Hanna, B. (2022). Artificial intelligence and sustainability: Solutions to social and environmental challenges. In M. Asadnia, A. Razmjou, & A. Beheshti (Eds.), *Artificial intelligence and data science in environmental sensing* (pp. 93–108). Academic Press.

Tien, P. W., Wei, S., Darkwa, J., Wood, C., & Calautit, J. K. (2022). Machine learning and deep learning methods for enhancing building energy efficiency and indoor environmental quality – A review. *Energy and AI, 10*, 100198.

Tilak, J. B. (2008). Transition from higher education as a public good to higher education as a private good: The saga of Indian experience. *Journal of Asian Public Policy, 1*(2), 220–234.

Trincavelli, M., Reggente, M., Coradeschi, S., Loutfi, A., Ishida, H., & Lilienthal, A. J. (2008, September). Towards environmental monitoring with mobile robots. In *2008 IEEE/RSJ international conference on intelligent robots and systems* (pp. 2210–2215). IEEE.

Van Wynsberghe, A., & Donhauser, J. (2018). The dawning of the ethics of environmental robots. *Science and Engineering Ethics, 24*, 1777–1800.

Willard, J., Jia, X., Xu, S., Steinbach, M., & Kumar, V. (2022). Integrating scientific knowledge with machine learning for engineering and environmental systems. *ACM Computing Surveys, 55*(4), 1–37.

Yuan, Q., Shen, H., Li, T., Li, Z., Li, S., Jiang, Y., Xu, H., Tan, W., Yang, Q., Wang, J., Gao, J., & Zhang, L. (2020). Deep learning in environmental remote sensing: Achievements and challenges. *Remote Sensing of Environment, 241*, 111716.

Zhong, S., Zhang, K., Bagheri, M., Burken, J. G., Gu, A., Li, B., Ma, X., Marrone, B. L., Ren, Z. J., Schrier, J., Shi, W., Tan, H., Wang, T., Wang, X., Wong, B. M., Xiao, X., Yu, X., Zhu, J.-J., & Zhang, H. (2021). Machine learning: New ideas and tools in environmental science and engineering. *Environmental Science & Technology, 55*(19), 12741–12754.

Chapter 9

E-wastes Management in AI Context: The Opportunities and Challenges in Educational and Healthcare Waste – *A Scientific Study*

Ritam Chatterjee[a] *and Abhijit Bandyopadhyay*[b]

[a]*Department of Computer and Information Science, Raiganj University, West Bengal, India*
[b]*Raniganj Institute of Computer and Information Science (RICIS), Raniganj, West Bengal, India*

Abstract

Electronic waste (E-waste) is one of the concerns of the modern era. Different types of educational institutions and healthcare organizations are generating different types of waste. E-waste is one of them. It is a very challenging task for educational institutions and healthcare organizations to properly procure the E-waste. It is necessary to have a proper waste management plan for educational institutions and healthcare organizations. This chapter discusses the concept of E-waste, E-waste generation in educational institutions, and digital healthcare. This chapter discusses different types of E-waste in educational institutions and E-waste management using artificial intelligence (AI). Harmful effects of E-waste on health, remedial measures of E-waste in digital healthcare, and E-waste management guidelines for electrical and electronic equipments (EEE) are also discussed in this chapter. This chapter focuses on the application of AI in digital healthcare and the AI-driven healthcare ecosystem. This chapter discusses the opportunities and challenges of AI in digital healthcare as well as the potential of AI in E-waste management.

Keywords: Waste; waste management; E-waste; E-waste management; artificial intelligence; digital education; digital healthcare

Harnessing the Potential of Artificial Intelligence to Promote Environmental Sustainability, 143–163

doi:10.1108/978-1-83662-996-220251009

1. Introduction

Different types of products that can be thrown into the garbage as useless things are called waste. Unwanted, nonfunctional, unused, or damaged materials that are no longer useful for everyday life can be considered waste. The nonfunctional and damaged equipment and parts of electronic devices that are ready to be discarded can be considered E-waste. E-waste is one of the concerns of the modern era. It is a very challenging task to dispose the E-waste. The manufacturing of electronic devices are increasing day by day. Dependency on electronic devices are increasing also. As a result, the amount of E-waste also increases. According to the World Health Organization (WHO), it is estimated that 62 million tons of E-waste were generated worldwide in the year 2022. Among them, it was documented that only 22.3% of the E-waste formally collected was recycled. To procure the E-waste, it is necessary to adopt a proper E-waste management strategy. It is necessary to build a proper management plan for the complete processing of E-waste. From E-waste generation to collection, from segregation to procurement, from reuse to recycling, and from material extraction to safe disposal, and these are integral parts of E-waste management. Fig. 9.1 shows the storage of E-waste by the E-waste vendor.

Fig. 9.1. Storage of E-waste.

2. Related Works

The previous related works are discussed in this chapter, titled – "E-wastes Management in AI Context: The Opportunities and Challenges in Educational and Healthcare Waste – A Scientific Study." This review of the literature plays a crucial role in exploring the existing and research relevant to the topic. It provides valuable insights into the context of E-waste management, particularly within the realms of education and healthcare, highlighting both the opportunities and challenges in these sectors.

A case study was conducted by Chibunna et al. (2012) to identify various challenges related to E-waste management in different educational institutions. The study was carried out at Universiti Kebangsaan Malaysia, using 500 questionnaires. It aimed to assess the awareness and expression of dissatisfaction regarding E-waste among employees and students. Dayaday and Galleto (2022) worked on E-waste Management, focusing on higher education institutions in South Central Mindanao, Philippines. The study was conducted on 13 higher education institutions. The main objective of the study was to gather useful information that could help in formulating various management plans and programs for E-waste. Ernawati et al. (2024) conducted a literature review on health education in E-waste management in the context of sustainability. The study focused on various global health awareness initiatives and highlighted the concept of green literacy. It discussed the importance of health education in E-waste management, as well as the challenges in implementing green literacy. The review also suggested solutions to these challenges through public–private collaboration.

Gupta (2011) provided several strategies for managing E-waste. The study suggested approaches to reduce, reuse, and recycle products in order to support sustainable development. It discussed the environmental impact of E-waste and emphasized the dangers associated with it. Additionally, the study highlighted the critical need for proper E-waste management and outlined potential strategies for effective management. Hawari and Hassan (2008) addressed the ethical implications of education and research in ensuring the proper management of E-waste. It discussed the need for an appropriate E-waste management plan and reviewed Islamic principles on environmental protection, along with the ethical implications for curriculum development and future research directions. The study also examined the technical aspects and side effects of dumping E-waste, as well as the risks associated with certain toxic substances. It offered suggestions for E-waste management and provided a review of the implications for curriculum development within the Faculty of Engineering at the International Islamic University Malaysia (IIUM). Thangavel (2024) discussed effective smart waste management strategies for maintaining sustainable development using AI and machine learning (ML) techniques. The study focused on higher educational institutions and conducted a case study on Indian higher educational institutions for analysis. It explored the various roles of education in waste management and introduced the concept of transitioning from a linear economy to a circular economy. The study examined the role of AI in supporting a circular economy and highlighted the benefits of AI and ML techniques for this model. Additionally, it discussed current and potential AI applications in a circular economy, emphasizing the advantages of AI and ML tools for effective E-waste management.

Ilankoon et al. (2018) provided a review of trade flows, guidelines, risks, and technologies for value recovery in E-waste management. The study focused on efficient E-waste management strategies, identifying key challenges in the international context and offering suggestions for improving E-waste processing to ensure sustainable development. It also included a flow sheet outlining the recovery of valuable elements from E-waste. Kahhat et al. (2008) analyzed the current situation and various strategies for E-waste management systems in the United States, reviewing the existing recycling systems. The study explored global E-waste collection and recycling systems, emphasizing resource conservation and recycling. It also provided recommendations for E-waste collection, recycling, and reuse procedures in the United States. Additionally, it included a diagram illustrating the E-market for a returned deposit system for a particular product.

Lu et al. (2015) provided an overview of E-waste management in China. The study discussed various sources of E-waste and the process of E-waste generation in relation to the urbanization rate. It examined China's E-waste recycling system and treatment procedures. The study also reviewed the policies and laws governing E-waste management in the country. Furthermore, it highlighted the challenges faced in procuring E-waste and offered futuristic suggestions for improving the system. Shreyas Madhav et al. (2022) proposed a potential solution for household E-waste collection and segregation through the application of AI in the Indian context. The study suggested implementing a mobile robot that identified common E-waste using transfer learning, which could be attached to existing municipal garbage trucks. The goal was to collect E-waste from households with minimal human intervention, enhancing the efficiency of the process.

3. Objectives

E-waste management is a very important task to protect the environment and to maintain sustainable development. It is necessary to consider the potentialities, opportunities, and challenges of E-waste in educational institutions and digital healthcare. The main objectives of this chapter are as follows:

- To give an overview of E-waste and E-waste management using AI.
- To review the previous works related to E-waste.
- To discuss E-waste generation in educational institutions and digital healthcare.
- To know about the harmful effects of E-waste on health, remedial measures of E-waste in digital healthcare, and E-waste management guidelines for EEE.
- To discuss AI in digital healthcare and E-waste in the AI-driven healthcare ecosystem.
- To learn about opportunities and challenges in AI for digital healthcare and the potentialities of AI in E-waste management.

4. Methodology

The work entitled "E-wastes Management in AI Context: The Opportunities and Challenges in Educational and Healthcare Waste – A Scientific Study" is a theoretical chapter, and it is interdisciplinary in nature. Various secondary sources are studied from different areas and subjects, viz. Environmental science, sustainable development, education, digital healthcare, AI, and so on, have been studied to pursue the work.

5. E-waste – An Overview

The waste material generated by the electronic devices is called E-waste. Electronic devices are becoming essential in day-to-day life. One person may use more than one electronic device. According to the Telecom Authority of India, as of February 29, 2024, the total number of telephone subscribers in India is 1,197.75 million, among whom 1,164.64 million are using wireless connections and 33.10 million are using landline connections. The subscribers are continuously increasing. It means the number of users of electronic devices is increasing. The more electronic devices there are responsible for the more E-waste. There are different types of E-waste. The waste can be generated from household appliances that can be small in size like – toaster, griller, roti maker, rice cooker, coffee maker, mixer grinder, juicer, and so on or large like – refrigerator washing machine, and so on, Digital devices and communication devices like – computer, desktop, laptop, mobile, scanner, printer, photocopies, router, hub, bridge, and so on. Entertainment devices include television, radio, tape recorder, headphone, microphone, speaker, and so on. Lighting devices include Compact Fluorescent Lamp (CFL) bulbs, fluorescent bulbs, Light Emitting Diode (LED) lights, and so on. Electrical and electronic tools include drill machines, testers, screwdrivers, electric saws, etc. Toys include robot, remote control cars, different types of electronic games, and other electronic play items. Batteries are one of the key components of waste. By removing toxic components and different acids from the battery, it could be recycled and converted into new batteries. Fig. 9.2 shows different types of E-waste.

6. E-waste Generation in Educational Institutions

Various types of electronic devices are used in different types of educational institutions. It is necessary to use different types of electronic devices for different purposes. Different types of technology are used in educational institutions to serve better to the students. Admission register maintenance, student information maintenance, result calculation, mark sheet generation, record storing and maintenance, teacher and staff pay management, and many more tasks can be done electronically by educational institutions. In the COVID-19 period, e-learning and online learning gained popularity. From the school level to the college level, universities also used digital education to support students during the COVID-19 period (Chatterjee, 2023). Even some popular preschools and nursery schools also adopted online learning during that period. Table 9.1 shows that as of

Fig. 9.2. Different Types of E-waste.

Table 9.1. Total Number of Universities in India.

Sl. No.	Type of University	Number of Universities
1	Central University	57
2	State University	491
3	Deemed to be University	138
4	State Private University	496
Total		1,182

Source: https://www.ugc.gov.in.

November 19, 2024, the total number of universities in India. Fig. 9.3 shows the increase in the number of students in universities in India.

It is clearly visible that the number of students is increasing in Indian universities. The number of students, the university, and educational institutions adopt the digital education to serve the students (Chatterjee, Bandyopadhyay, et al., 2023). Information technology and information and communication technology are used for different purposes in universities and educational institutions (Chatterjee, Chowdhury, et al., 2023).

7. Different Types of E-waste in Educational Institutions

Different types of educational institutions use different types of electronic devices. Kindergarten schools and preschools use audio-visual devices to give the kids something to listen. They use different types of electronic toys to give joyful learning to the students. Nonfunctional televisions, tape recorders, speakers, electronic toys, and batteries are generated as E-waste. Primary schools or

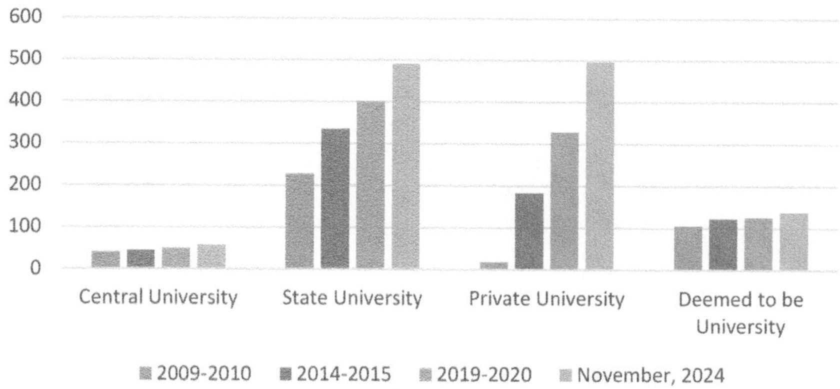

Fig. 9.3. Increase of Students in the Universities in India Year Wise.
Source: https://www.ugc.gov.in.

elementary schools use smartboards, smart pens, tablets, and so on for their learning purpose. Middle schools, junior high schools, secondary schools, high schools, and higher secondary schools use various devices, such as desktops, projectors, printers, digital laboratory equipment, and many more. Various types of schools generate various types of E-waste. The schools generate the E-waste, such as nonfunctional computer parts like monitors, keyboards, mouses, buses, Random Access Memory (RAM), hard disks, cabinets, Printed Circuit Board (PCB), and so on. It also produces E-waste like printers, scanners, ink cartridges, projectors, smartboards, and so on. Digital laboratory equipment used in physics laboratory, chemistry laboratory, biology Laboratory, geography laboratory, and computer laboratory also generates E-waste (Garlapati, 2016). Higher educational institutions like colleges and universities also produce a huge amount of E-waste. The infrastructure of the institutions is comparatively larger than at any school level. The dependence on electronic devices is higher than at any school level. They have used mobile phones, desktops, laptops, televisions, projectors, printers, scanners, smartboards, digital display boards, and many more. The higher educational institutions have advanced laboratory facilities that use digital equipment for hands-on practical examination and for different types of research purposes. Various types of digital laboratory equipment are used in the laboratories. The laboratories have an electronics microscope, a spectrometer, a digital weight machine, a digital thermometer, a data logger, and so on. Different universities offer online mode of learning, massive open online admission, distance mode of learning, blended mode of learning, hybrid learning, e-learning, and other types of learning to the students. To incorporate the digital education parallel with the face-to-face mode campus-based education, it is necessary to use different types of basic and emerging technologies. The technologies are completely dependent on electronic devices. For online education, it needs mobile phones or computers and networking devices. That networking device, like a router, bridge, hub, and so on, also generates E-waste. Higher educational

Fig. 9.4. Different Types of E-waste in Educational Institutions.

institutions also have a digital library with updated library management software and e-textbook facilities. In skill-based educational institutions, vocational institutions, and engineering colleges use different types of electronic devices. They use common electronic devices, like other colleges and universities, as well as some special types of digital devices to train their students. Technical institutions have a laboratory with facilities, such as multi-meter, an oscilloscope, a computer-controlled cutting machine, a 3D printer, a power supply device, different types of ICs, and wires. Medical colleges and nursing colleges also use special types of electronic devices apart from the common electronic devices used in different institutions. The medical institutions use digital, electrocardiograms (ECGs), Magnetic Resonance Imaging (MRI) simulators, diagnostic analyzers, smart watches, patient monitoring devices, virtual learning environment, virtual reality, and augmented reality devices to get that 3D visualization of the human body and surgery simulation, advanced robotics surgery devices, and many more. Fig. 9.4 shows different types of E-waste in educational institutions.

8. E-waste Management Using AI in Educational Institutions

Various types of Institutions are using various types of electronic devices for different purposes. If some of the electronic devices are nonfunctional or malfunction, then erroneous devices generate E-waste for the institutions. It is a very challenging task for educational institutions to procure and manage the devices (Osibanjo & Nnorom, 2007). Different types of E-waste are generated from different types of educational institutions. The educational institutions can be preschools, nursery schools, middle schools, high schools, higher secondary schools, vocational or skill development institutions, engineering colleges, medical colleges, nursing colleges, teacher training institutions, visual and performing arts institutions, online-based virtual institutions, and many more. After the generation of E-waste, it is necessary to collect the E-waste and send it to the vendor who collects the waste. E-waste has different types of products, so it is necessary to categorize the products. Different basic technologies and emerging technologies are used in digital products. AI plays a vital role in categorization. The AI-based automated system will help to identify the products and try to find the faults present in the devices. After that, the AI-based automated engine separates the products according to their types. The AI engine gives some reuse ideas; if reuse is possible, the product can be reused according to its purpose (Kim & Paulos, 2011). If it is not reusable, then it tries to identify whether the electronic devices are repairable or not. If it is repairable, then it could be sent to the mechanic for repair of the product, and after the repair, it is ready to be reused. But if it is not repairable, then E-waste is sent to authorized E-waste collectors. The E-waste collectors use an AI-based system to identify different components of the products. The AI-based system helps to separate different parts of the products. It separates different parts and helps in the expression of electronic parts. It separates Cathode Ray Tube (CRT) monitor screens, various types of electromagnetic elements, magnetic elements, different types of ICs, PCBs, wires, batteries, and so on. It sends the extracted elements to the proper manufacturing factories. The AI engine tries to identify different categories of plastic. Such as acrylonitrile butadiene styrene (ABS) (used in laptops, smart phones, TVs, and remote controls, keyboard keys, power adapters, connectors, and so on), polycarbonate (PC) (used in protective covers for LCDs display screens, compact disks (CDs), digital versatile disks (DVDs), and Blu-ray disks, lenses for cameras, and so on), polyvinyl chloride (PVC) (used in insulation for wires and cables, connector jackets, power cords, and so on), polypropylene (PP) (used in battery holders, circuit boards, and capacitors, and so on), polyethylene terephthalate (PET) (used in capacitors and transformers, and so on), polyamide (nylon) (used in printers, scanners, and so on), polytetrafluoroethylene (PTFE) – Teflon (used in insulation for high-temperature wires, cables, insulation for high-temperature wires, cables, and so on), epoxy resins (used in semiconductors, transistors, and so on), thermoplastic polyurethane (TPU) (used in phone cases, cable jackets), polystyrene (PS) (used in resistors, capacitors, and so on), liquid crystal polymer (LCP) (used in connectors, chips, antennas, and so on), polyetheretherketone (PEEK) (used in connectors in aerospace, medical devices, and so on).

The AI engine identifies the glass materials and sends the glasses to the glass manufacturing factories. The AI-based engine also helps in metal extraction. It identifies different types of metal and segregates category-wise (Bandyopadhyay et al., 2022). It helps in the separation of metals like copper, iron, steel, zinc, brass, silver, gold, and so on. After the extraction of different categories of things and sending them to the proper factory is also a challenge in the task. Various types of collecting vendors collect appropriate material for reuse. The vendors try to recycle the product after procurement and generate some new products. At the end of the processing, the waste material should be disposed of properly with proper

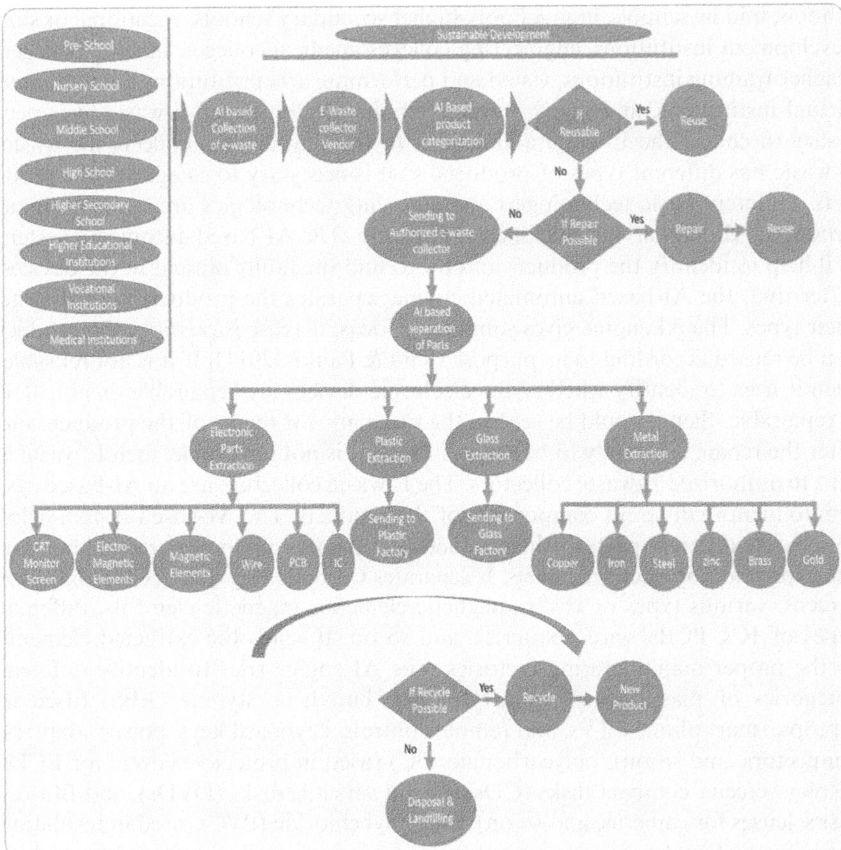

Fig. 9.5. Conceptual Diagram on E-waste Management Using AI in Educational Institutions.

measures, and some of the waste is utilized for land farming. Fig. 9.5 shows the conceptual diagram of E-waste management using AI in educational institutions.

9. E-waste Generation in Digital Healthcare

E-waste generated by medical devices includes hazardous materials like lead (Pb), mercury (Hg), cadmium (Cd), and chemical flame retardants, and if these are not disposed of properly, they can contaminate our soil and water, posing a serious risk to our overall health and environment. Lead is used in electronic devices like cathode-ray tubes, circuit boards, batteries, and solder because it is durable, corrosion-resistant, and has a high melting point. But lead as E-waste can cause irreversible neurological diseases, anemia, damage to nerves, learning and cognition problems, behavioral changes, and even death (Bhaskar & Singh, 2021). Mercury is a toxic chemical that is present in many types of EEE, like fluorescent lights, switches, desktop PC, batteries, mobile phones, laptops, and computer screens, and approximately 50 tons of mercury are annually found in E-waste globally, causing severe health damage to children and pregnant women making them exceptionally vulnerable (Dahl, 2002). Cadmium, found in a variety of electronic components like rechargeable nickel-cadmium (NiCd) batteries, circuit boards, monitors, printers, switches, solder joints and PVC cables, is a toxic carcinogenic metal that can damage kidneys and bones, and can also trigger respiratory system diseases (Baldé et al., 2020). Apart from these, all electrical and electronic devices are mostly made up of plastics and bakelite used for insulation purposes, and we know that plastic materials are nonbiodegradable; hence, these wastes can remain inside earth for many years and damage soil and crops, pollute water bodies and damage aquatic plants and animals (Esmaeilian et al., 2020).

9.1. Harmful Effects of E-waste on Health

There are many harmful effects of E-waste, broadly categorized into the following five types:

1. *Health effects*: Toxic substances like brominated flame retardants, and toxic metals like lead, mercury, nickel, and cadmium can disrupt the central nervous system (CNS), damage lungs, cause obesity, asthma, and neurological disorders and even cancer, and may result in miscarriages, neurological damage and diminished cognitive ability (Frazzol et al., 2010).
2. *Environmental effects*: E-waste can pollute air, soil, and water, and harm living beings by releasing pollutants like heavy metals, organic pollutants, airborne particulate matter, and polycyclic aromatic hydrocarbons into the environment (Jain & Lal, 2022).
3. *Carbon footprint issues*: Large amounts of carbon footprint arise out of data centers that are increasingly being used for data storage and computation, hence in this era of big data in healthcare, large data centers release enormous amounts of carbon footprint that affects our environment and consequently, it affects public health very adversely (Han et al., 2022).
4. *Incineration problems*: Burning out toxic E-waste causes major problems for the environment by releasing toxic and environmentally harmful gases and particles into the air.
5. *Residue hazards*: Slow collection of E-wastes lead to residue problems over time and destroys the environment, and slowly damages human health (Perkins et al., 2014).

9.2. Remedial Measures of E-waste in Digital Healthcare

The remedial measures of the E-waste problem in digital healthcare include the following:

1. Before discarding electronic devices, the stored data needs to be wiped out as a measure of safe disposal so that data security and privacy issues are resolved beforehand.

2. Disposal of E-waste should be done with an R2-certified recycling facility (Forti et al., 2018).
3. All stakeholders should behave responsibly in the safe disposal of E-waste; hence, the users of E-waste and producers of electrical and electronic devices used in digital healthcare are equally responsible for solving the E-waste problem and their safe disposal (Dasgupta et al., 2017).
4. Capacity building for diagnosis, monitoring, and preventing toxic exposures of E-waste must be prioritized in digital healthcare policymaking (Ali & Shirazi, 2022).
5. Health-based assessment for assessing E-waste policies and regulations for children's health, in particular, must be done periodically to benefit from the revolution in technologies.
6. Raising awareness about E-waste and the health risks associated with its recycling must be spread to encourage authorities to opt for responsible recycling options (Pandve, 2007).
7. Sustainable disposal methods must be opted for, such as dismantling, recycling, and recovering valuable materials from medical electronic devices that form a large part of E-waste generated in the digital healthcare sector (Debnath et al., 2018).
8. E-waste management principles must be adhered to properly while disposing of E-wastes (Wath et al., 2010).

9.3. E-waste Management Guidelines for EEE

Guidelines have been issued by the Central Pollution Control Board (CPCB) of the Government of India for producers, recyclers, refurbishers, manufacturers, and any other non-registered entities involved in collection and storage, transportation, sale, processing, and recycling of E-waste (Milovantseva & Fitzpatrick, 2015). It has also calculated the environmental compensation (EC), if any of the above said entities cause damage to the environment or bring adverse environmental impact due to violation or noncompliance of E-waste Management Rules-2022 and amendments made in 2023 and 2024 and upon paying requisite monetary penalties, extended producer responsibility (EPR) certificate can be issued to the said entities by government to compensate for the damage caused due to violation of rules of E-waste management as enshrined in E-waste portal of Government of India. Table 9.2 shows EC for EEE categories, and Fig. 9.6 shows EEE category-wise EC charged for E-waste offenders. The formula for calculating EC for issuing an EPR certificate to the violators of E-waste management rules is as follows:

Formula: EPR Certificate Price = $0.3 \times$ EC item code (Rs. Per kg.)

It can be easily observed that compensation for E-waste offenders is highest in the digital healthcare category, namely, medical devices and laboratory instruments which shows the government's laws and punitive measures and regulatory willingness to restrict the growing environmental degradation due to rising adoption and use of medical devices, IoT and wearable gadgets in digital healthcare.

Table 9.2. Environmental Compensation for EEE Categories.

Types of E-waste	EEE Category	EC Item Code	EPR Certificate Price (Rs. per kg)
IT and telecom equipment	ITEW	112	34
consumer electrical and electronics, and photovoltaic panels	CEEW	74	22
Large and small electrical and electronic equipment	LSEEW	76	23
Electrical and electronic tools (with the exception of large-scale stationary industrial tools)	EETW	82	25
Toys, leisure, and sports equipment	TLSEW	34	10
Medical devices (with the exception of all implanted and infected products)	MDW	135	41
Laboratory instruments	LIW	136	41

The data above are presented in Fig. 9.6 in the form of comparative statistics.

Source: https://climeto.com/environmental-compensation-under-e-waste-management-rules-2022.

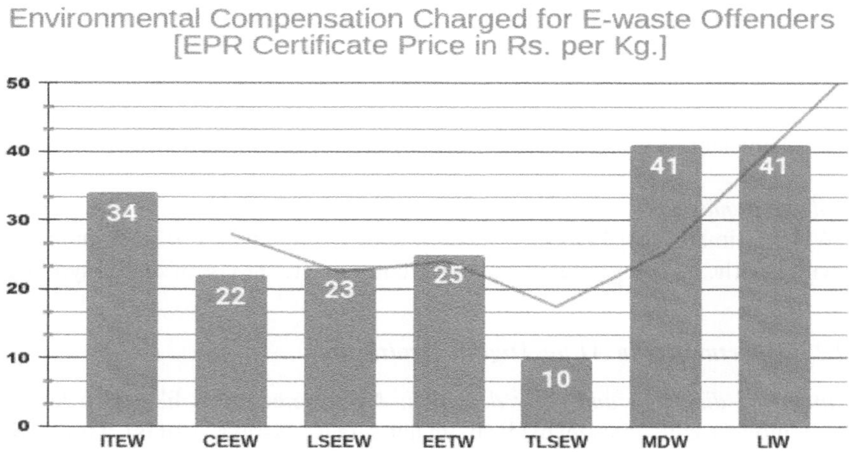

Fig. 9.6. EEE Category-wise Environmental Compensation Charged for E-waste Offenders. *Source*: https://climeto.com/environmental-compensation-under-e-waste-management-rules-2022.

10. AI in Digital Healthcare

The digital revolution in healthcare, powered by AI, has led to remarkable breakthroughs, from predictive analytics to AI-enabled imaging systems. However, this technological leap comes at a cost: the accumulation of E-waste. E-waste, defined as discarded electronic devices and components, poses environmental and health risks due to toxic substances like lead, cadmium, and mercury. The rapid obsolescence of AI-integrated devices exacerbates the problem. This chapter examines the lifecycle of AI-driven healthcare devices, their contribution to E-waste, and potential solutions for mitigating environmental impacts.

AI has enabled a paradigm shift in healthcare through applications such as:

- *Diagnostics*: AI-powered imaging devices, such as CT and MRI scanners with advanced algorithms, provide precise results.
- *Wearable technology*: Smart watches and health trackers embedded with AI monitor patients' vitals in real time.
- *Telemedicine*: AI systems support remote diagnosis and patient monitoring through advanced communication devices.
- *Robotic surgery*: Sophisticated AI-driven robots perform minimally invasive surgeries with high precision.

10.1. E-waste in the AI-driven Healthcare Ecosystem

- *Sources of E-waste*:
    - o *Hardware replacement*: The constant upgrading of AI systems necessitates newer hardware.
    - o *Wearable devices*: Short life spans and limited recyclability of health trackers and smart watches.
    - o *Medical imaging equipment*: Complex devices are often discarded without proper recycling.

- *Environmental impacts*:
    - o Toxic chemicals in E-waste can contaminate soil and water.
    - o Inefficient recycling processes release harmful emissions.

- *Global trends*:
- WHO estimates that E-waste is increasing by approximately 3%–5% annually, with healthcare being a significant contributor due to the rise of digital systems.

10.2. Opportunities in AI for Digital Healthcare

- *Improved diagnosis and early detection*: AI-powered tools like deep learning models can analyze medical imaging (e.g., X-rays, MRIs) with high accuracy, enabling early detection of diseases such as cancer and heart conditions. Algorithms can detect patterns in patient data that may not be visible to clinicians.

- *Personalized medicine*: AI enables tailored treatment plans based on genetic profiles, lifestyle, and medical history, optimizing outcomes.
- *Operational efficiency*: AI automates administrative tasks like patient scheduling, billing, and documentation, reducing costs and time.
- *Telemedicine and remote monitoring*: AI-driven wearable devices and telehealth platforms provide continuous monitoring of patients, making healthcare accessible, especially in remote areas.
- *Drug discovery and development*: AI accelerates drug discovery by identifying potential compounds, analyzing drug interactions, and predicting outcomes, reducing time and cost.
- *Predictive analytics*: Predictive models help anticipate patient deterioration, hospital readmissions, and outbreaks of infectious diseases, enabling proactive measures.
- *Enhanced patient engagement*: Chatbots and virtual health assistants offer 24/7 support, answering queries and reminding patients about medications or appointments.
- *Reduction in medical errors*: Decision-support systems help reduce errors by suggesting evidence-based recommendations to clinicians.

10.3. Challenges in AI for Digital Healthcare

- *Data privacy and security*: Healthcare data are highly sensitive, and breaches can lead to severe consequences. Ensuring compliance with regulations like General Data Protection Regulation (GDPR) and Health Insurance Portability and Accountability (HIPAA) is essential.
- *Bias in AI algorithms*: If trained on biased datasets, AI models may produce inequitable outcomes, adversely affecting certain patient groups.
- *Integration with existing systems*: Many healthcare organizations use legacy systems, making it challenging to integrate AI solutions seamlessly.
- *Regulatory and ethical concerns*: Approving AI tools for clinical use involves difficult validation and certification processes, which can be time-consuming. Ethical issues, like the explainability of AI decisions, also arise (Hawari & Hassan, 2008).
- *High costs of implementation*: Developing and deploying AI solutions requires significant investment in technology, infrastructure, and training.
- *Skill gap:* Healthcare professionals may lack the expertise to work with AI tools, necessitating training and upskilling.
- *Dependence on high-quality data*: AI systems require vast amounts of accurate and labeled data. Poor data quality or incomplete records can hinder effectiveness.
- *Resistance to change*: Some healthcare providers and institutions may be reluctant to adopt AI due to fear of job displacement or skepticism about its accuracy.
- *Legal liability*: Determining accountability in cases of misdiagnosis or treatment errors caused by AI systems is a complex issue.
- *Interoperability challenges*: Ensuring that AI tools work across different platforms and electronic health record (EHR) systems is essential for widespread adoption.

11. The Potentialities of AI in E-waste Management

AI has huge potential to manage the E-waste in a safe manner. With the application of AI in E-waste Management, from collection to recycling, the whole process will be automated (Kalambura et al., 2015). It will maximize the outcome from E-waste processing and minimize the risk of environmental threats. It is possible to use AI in the complete waste management process. Fig. 9.7 shows the concept of resource reduction.

AI could be used in the collection process of the E-waste. The AI-powered smart bins will be able to collect the E-waste more efficiently (Sinthiya et al., 2022). At the time of collection, it will be able to detect the biodegradable and nonbiodegradable waste. It will automatically detect the E-waste. The computer vision technology will help in the efficient identification of the E-waste. The data analytics and data mining technology will be able to create the E-waste generation pattern for a particular area. It could predict the amount of waste generated in any educational institution or in any healthcare organization. The AI-based system will be able to detect the condition of the E-waste and the age of the E-waste. On the basis of the characteristics and condition of the E-waste system, a proper E-waste handling plan will be suggested. Difference sensors will help to detect the level of E-waste in the smart bins. When the bins are full, it will generate an alarm for the proper disposal (Sivaramanan, 2013).

Sorting of E-waste is one of the challenging tasks. AI will help in the automated sorting and segregation process of waste (Abou Baker et al., 2021). E-waste has different types of materials. It may have plastic, metal, glass, or any hazardous chemical (Pinto, 2008). It may generate health challenges for workers who are working in E-waste procurement. The AI-powered robots will help in sorting elements. Different technologies will help in product sorting. ML, deep learning, computer vision, IoT, cloud computing, big data analytics, and other emerging

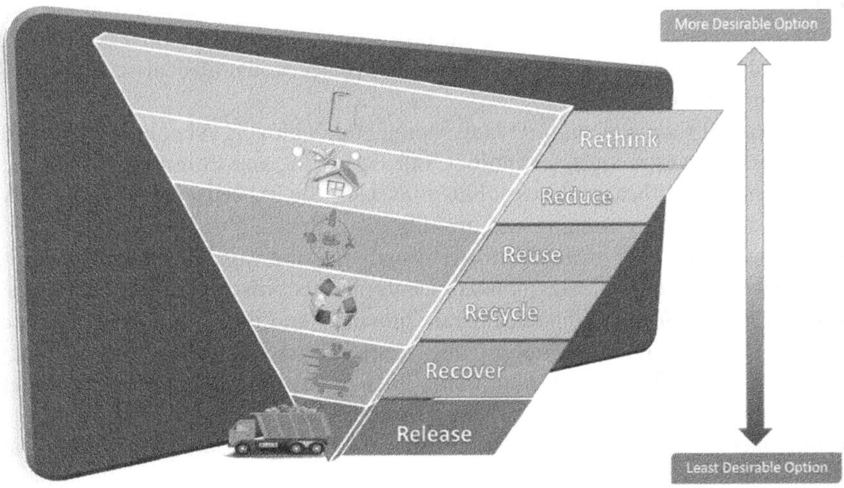

Fig. 9.7. The Concept of Resource Reduction.

technologies will work collectively in sorting the products (Paul, Aithal, et al., 2020). The robotic arm will protect against human intervention. The AI-based automated system will help in maximizing the metal collection from any product. It will be able to extract the maximum possible outcome from the E-waste processing.

AI-powered system will be able to tackle and manage the E-waste in the best possible way (Kiddee et al., 2013). It will help in the automatic collection of bins by the smart waste collection trucks. It will suggest an optimized way of carrying E-waste. It will improve the E-waste supply chain (Shevchenko, 2021). Different E-waste processing centers need a continuous supply of E-waste to execute their system efficiently. The AI-enabled data analysis will manage the E-waste supply chain effectively.

The circular economy concept is an effective waste management strategy to maintain sustainable development (Paul & Aithal, 2020). Instead of throwing the nonfunctional products into the garbage, it should try to rethink repair. If repair is possible, then it should be reused. By following proper measurement, it should recycle the E-waste (Zhang & Kim, 2019). The next level is material extraction. By extracting the maximum possible metals, the metals should be sent for the creation of new products, and then the products to the consumers (Mohamad et al., 2022). Official intelligence will help at all levels of circular economy concepts and help to maintain the product life cycle efficiently with low cost (Srivastav, 2023). Fig. 9.8 shows a conceptual diagram of the circular economy.

AI-based advanced data analytics will help in predictive maintenance of the recycled products (Paul, Bhimali, et al., 2020). It will adjust the proper maintenance

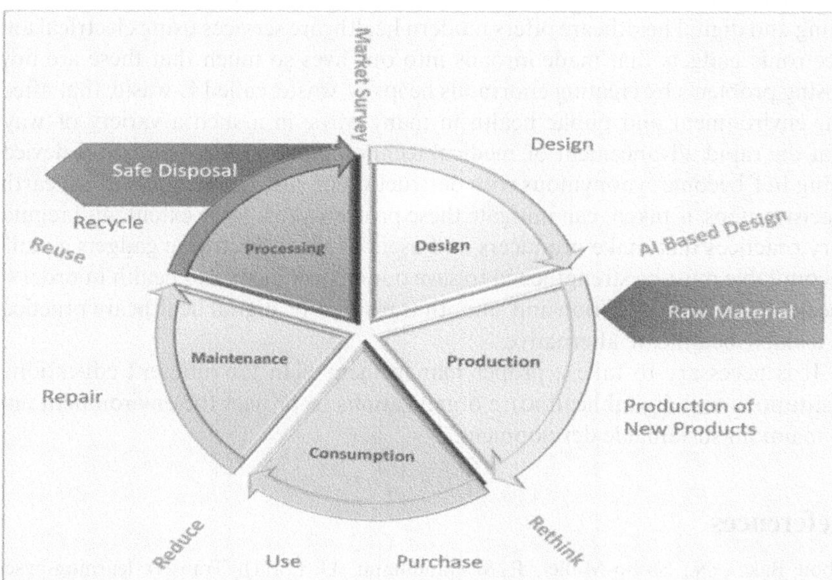

Fig. 9.8. Conceptual Diagram of Circular Economy.

alarm for the user. If any error occurs, then it will help to detect the actual location of the error. It will help in the life assessment of any product (Simaei, 2022). It also helps in the redesign of the new product that could be created using the extracted elements and metals from the E-waste (Simaei & Rahimifard, 2024). Various types of AI-based applications will take an active role in redesigning the product. It will suggest the best product that can be made from recycled materials. AI-based engine plays a vital role in generating awareness among the people (Subhaprada & Kalyani, 2017). It will generate awareness among the students, teachers, staff, guardians, administrators of the educational institutions, and the patients, doctors, nurses, hospital staff, relatives of the patients, and so on of the healthcare sectors (Nanath & Ajit Kumar, 2021). By proper E-waste processing and reuse and recycling of the E-waste, we will be able to create a healthy environment and maintain sustainable development (Mor et al., 2021).

12. Conclusion

The management of E-waste is one of the concerns from an environmental perspective. To protect the environment, it is necessary to take the proper measures to reduce the use of E-waste, rethink before throwing any E-waste, try to repair the E-waste, make it ready to reuse the E-waste, send it for recycling, recover different types of material, and recreate new products. It is necessary to build awareness among different levels of people in society. For the proper management of E-waste, educational institutions should take appropriate measures and implement a proper E-waste management plan. Educational institutions should allocate a budget for the management of E-waste and for the safe disposal of E-waste.

The healthcare industry plays a vital role in safeguarding our life and well-being and digital healthcare offers modern healthcare services using electrical and electronic gadgets that made inroads into our lives so much that these are now posing problems by creating enormous heaps of waste, called E-waste, that affect our environment and public health in many ways, in a such a variety of ways that the rapid advancement of medical technologies and use of medical devices using IoT become synonymous with destruction of sustainability of life on earth. Decisive steps, if taken, can mitigate these problems to a large extent, and regulatory practices that make producers and users of these electronic gadgets equally accountable must be strengthened to save our environment and health in order to accelerate the safe adoption and smooth transition of digital healthcare practices as a viable healthcare alternative.

It is necessary to take a proper management plan for different educational institutions and digital healthcare organizations to protect the environment and to maintain sustainable development.

References

Abou Baker, N., Szabo-Müller, P., & Handmann, U. (2021). Transfer learning-based method for automated e-waste recycling in smart cities. *EAI Endorsed Transactions on Smart Cities*, *5*(16), e1.

Ali, S., & Shirazi, F. (2022). A transformer-based machine learning approach for sustainable e-waste management: A comparative policy analysis between the Swiss and Canadian systems. *Sustainability*, *14*(20), 13220.

Baldé, C. P., Forti, V., Gray, V., Kuehr, R., & Stegmann, P. (2020). *The global e-waste monitor 2020*. United Nations University.

Bandyopadhyay, A., Chatterjee, R., & Das, N. (2022). E-waste management in digital healthcare system and sustainability paradigm. In P. K. Paul, A. Choudhury, A. Biswas, & B. K. Singh (Eds.), *Environmental informatics: Challenges and solutions* (pp. 157–166). Springer Nature Singapore.

Bhaskar, H., & Singh, S. (2021). AI in healthcare: Opportunities and challenges. *Journal of Healthcare Informatics Research*, *5*(2), 101–115.

Chatterjee, R. (2023). Digital educational industry vis-à-vis education analytics and big data analytics: A conceptual study. In P. K. Paul, S. Sharma, & E. Roy Krishnan (Eds.), *Advances in business informatics empowered by AI & intelligent systems* (pp. 173–186). CSMFL Publications. https://dx.doi.org/10.46679/978819573220312

Chatterjee, R., Bandyopadhyay, A., Chakraborty, S., & Dutta, S. (2023). Digital education: The basics with slant to digital pedagogy – An overview. In A. Choudhury, A. Biswas, & S. Chakraborti (Eds), *Digital Learning Based Education: Transcending Physical Barriers* (pp., 63–80).

Chatterjee, R., Chowdhury, S., Das, N., Bandyopadhyay, A., & Hoque, M. (2023). Private EdTech companies in India: The techno-financial aspects. *Economic Affairs*, *68*(04), 2131–2144.

Chibunna, J. B., Siwar, C., Begum, R. A., & Mohamed, A. F. (2012). The challenges of e-waste management among institutions: A case study of UKM. *Procedia-Social and Behavioral Sciences*, *59*, 644–649.

Dahl, R. (2002). Who pays for e-junk? *Environmental Health Perspectives*, 110(4), 196–199.

Dasgupta, D., Debsarkar, A., Hazra, T., Bala, B. K., Gangopadhyay, A., & Chatterjee, D. (2017). Scenario of future e-waste generation and recycle-reuse-landfill-based disposal pattern in India: A system dynamics approach. *Environment, Development and Sustainability*, *19*, 1473–1487.

Dayaday, M. G., & Galleto, F. A., Jr. (2022). Electronic waste (E-waste) management of higher education institutions in South Central Mindanao, Philippines. *Environment and Natural Resources Journal*, *20*(5), 534–542. https://doi.org/10.32526/ennrj/20/202200053

Debnath, B., Chowdhury, R., & Ghosh, S. K. (2018). Sustainability of metal recovery from E-waste. *Frontiers of Environmental Science & Engineering*, *12*, 1–12.

Ernawati, K., Burhan, A., Albar, A. S., Al-Khaliel, A. T., & Al-Fatich, A. S. F. (2024). Health education for sustainable E-waste management. *International Journal of Engineering, Science and Information Technology*, *4*(3), 128–131.

Esmaeilian, B., Wang, B., Lewis, K., & Duarte, F. (2020). The future of waste management in smart and sustainable cities: A review and concept paper. *Waste Management*, *81*, 177–195.

Forti, V., Baldé, C. P., & Kuehr, R. (2018). *E-waste statistics: Guidelines on classification, reporting, and indicators*. United Nations University.

Frazzol, C., Orisakwe, O. E., Dragone, R., & Mantovani, A. (2010). Diagnostic health risk assessment of electronic waste on the general population in developing countries scenarios. *Environmental Impact Assessment Review*, *30*(6), 388–399.

Garlapati, V. K. (2016). E-waste in India and developed countries: Management, recycling, business, and biotechnological initiatives. *Renewable and Sustainable Energy Reviews*, *54*, 874–881.

Gupta, S. (2011). E-waste management: Teaching how to reduce, reuse and recycle for sustainable development-need of some educational strategies. *Journal of Education and Practice*, *2*(3), 74–87.

Han, Y., Shevchenko, T., Qu, D., & Li, G. (2022, July). Smart e-waste management in China: a review. In *Congress on Intelligent Systems: Proceedings of CIS 2021, Volume 2* (pp. 515–533). Springer Nature Singapore.

Hawari, M., & Hassan, M. H. (2008). E-waste: Ethical implications for education and research. *IIUM Engineering Journal*, *9*(2), 11–26.

Ilankoon, I. M. S. K., Ghorbani, Y., Chong, M. N., Herath, G., Moyo, T., & Petersen, J. (2018). E-waste in the international context – A review of trade flows, regulations, hazards, waste management strategies and technologies for value recovery. *Waste Management*, *82*, 258–275.

Jain, A., & Lal, N. (2022). Role of AI in managing E-waste from healthcare devices. *Environmental Science and Pollution Research*, *29*(11), 15234–15246.

Kahhat, R., Kim, J., Xu, M., Allenby, B., Williams, E., & Zhang, P. (2008). Exploring E-waste management systems in the United States. *Resources, Conservation and Recycling*, *52*(7), 955–964.

Kalambura, S., Racz, A., & Kalambura, D. (2015, February). Education in waste management. In M. Alamgir, K. A. B. M. Mohiuddin, S. M. T. Islam, & M. H. Hasan (Eds.), *Proceedings of the WasteSafe 2015 – 4th international conference on solid waste management in the developing countries* (pp. 1–9).

Kiddee, P., Naidu, R., & Wong, M. H. (2013). Electronic waste management approaches: An overview. *Waste Management*, *33*(5), 1237–1250.

Kim, S., & Paulos, E. (2011, May). Practices in the creative reuse of e-waste. In *Proceedings of the SIGCHI conference on human factors in computing systems* (pp. 2395–2404).

Lu, C., Zhang, L., Zhong, Y., Ren, W., Tobias, M., Mu, Z., Ma, Z., Geng, Y., & Xue, B. (2015). An overview of e-waste management in China. *Journal of Material Cycles and Waste Management*, *17*, 1–12.

Milovantseva, N., & Fitzpatrick, C. (2015). Barriers to electronics reuse of transboundary e-waste shipment regulations: An evaluation based on industry experiences. *Resources, Conservation and Recycling*, *102*, 170–177.

Mohamad, N. S., Thoo, A. C., & Huam, H. T. (2022). The determinants of consumers' E-waste recycling behavior through the lens of extended theory of planned behavior. *Sustainability*, *14*(15), 9031.

Mor, R. S., Sangwan, K. S., Singh, S., Singh, A., & Kharub, M. (2021). E-waste management for environmental sustainability: An exploratory study. *Procedia CIRP*, *98*, 193–198.

Nanath, K., & Ajit Kumar, S. (2021). The role of communication medium in increasing e-waste recycling awareness among higher educational institutions. *International Journal of Sustainability in Higher Education*, *22*(4), 833–853.

Osibanjo, O., & Nnorom, I. C. (2007). The challenge of electronic waste (e-waste) management in developing countries. *Waste Management & Research*, *25*(6), 489–501.

Pandve, H. T. (2007). E-waste management in India: An emerging environmental and health issue. *Indian Journal of Occupational and Environmental Medicine*, *11*(3), 116–117.

Paul, P. K., & Aithal, P. S. (2020). Environmental informatics: Aspects in society, economy and development—A study. In P. K. Paul (Ed.), *Applied arts science in IT age* (pp. 73–83). New Delhi Publishers.

Paul, P. K., Aithal, P. S., Bhuimali, A., Tiwary, K. S., & Deka, G. C. (2020). Environmental informatics vis-à-vis big data analytics: The geo-spatial & sustainable solutions. *International Journal of Applied Engineering and Management Letters (IJAEML)*, *4*(2), 31–40.

Paul, P. K., Bhimali, A., Aithal, P. S., Kalishankar, T., & Saavedra, M. R. (2020). Artificial intelligence & cloud computing in environmental systems-towards healthy & sustainable development. *International Journal of Inclusive Development*, *6*(1), 01–08.

Perkins, D. N., Drisse, M. N. B., Nxele, T., & Sly, P. D. (2014). E-waste: A global hazard. *Annals of Global Health*, *80*(4), 286–295.

Pinto, V. N. (2008). E-waste hazard: The impending challenge. *Indian Journal of Occupational and Environmental Medicine*, *12*(2), 65–70.

Shevchenko, T., Saidani, M., Danko, Y., Golysheva, I., Chovancová, J., & Vavrek, R. (2021). Towards a smart E-waste system utilizing supply chain participants and interactive online maps. *Recycling*, *6*(1), 8.

Shreyas Madhav, A. V., Rajaraman, R., Harini, S., & Kiliroor, C. C. (2022). Application of artificial intelligence to enhance collection of E-waste: A potential solution for household WEEE collection and segregation in India. *Waste Management & Research*, *40*(7), 1047–1053.

Simaei, E. (2022). *Intelligent e-wastes processing for effective end-of-life management* [Doctoral dissertation, Loughborough University].

Simaei, E., & Rahimifard, S. (2024). AI-based decision support system for enhancing end-of-life value recovery from e-wastes. *International Journal of Sustainable Engineering*, *17*(1), 1–17.

Sinthiya, N. J., Chowdhury, T. A., & Haque, A. K. M. B. (2022). Artificial intelligence based smart waste management—A systematic review. In M. Lahby, A. Al-Fuqaha, & Y. Maleh (Eds.), *Computational intelligence techniques for green smart cities. Green energy and technology* (pp. 67–92). Springer. https://doi.org/10.1007/978-3-030-96429-0_3

Sivaramanan, S. (2013). E-waste management, disposal and its impacts on the environment. *Universal Journal of Environmental Research & Technology*, *3*(5), 531–537.

Srivastav, A. L., Markandeya, Patel, N., Pandey, M., Pandey, A. K., Dubey, A. K., Kumar, A., Bhardwaj, A. K., & Chaudhary, V. K. (2023). Concepts of circular economy for sustainable management of electronic wastes: Challenges and management options. *Environmental Science and Pollution Research*, *30*(17), 48654–48675.

Subhaprada, C. S., & Kalyani, P. (2017). Study on awareness of e-waste management among medical students. *International Journal of Community Medicine and Public Health*, *4*(2), 506–510.

Thangavel, V. (2024) Sustainable development of effective smart waste management practices by AI&ML techniques in higher educational Institutions. *International Journal of Advances in Engineering and Management (IJAEM)*, *6*(11), 563–581.

Wath, S. B., Vaidya, A. N., Dutt, P. S., & Chakrabarti, T. (2010). A roadmap for development of sustainable E-waste management system in India. *Science of the Total Environment*, *409*(1), 19–32.

Zhang, X., & Kim, J. (2019). Circular economy strategies for e-waste management in healthcare. *Journal of Environmental Management*, *248*, 109236.

Chapter 10

Artificial Intelligence and Sustainability in the Context of Smart City and Urban Development: An Overview

Nilanjan Das

Department of Computer Application, Siliguri Institute of Technology, Siliguri, West Bengal, India

Abstract

Urban areas are expanding as the population grows uninterruptedly. Developing urban areas with proper planning and initiatives provides sustainable and healthy accommodation for the inhabitants. Proper policies and strategies are required to drive urban development. Proper initiatives need to be taken for developing an adequate living environment. Emerging technologies are playing leading roles in urban development. Artificial intelligence (AI) is able to make changes and develop automated decision-making solutions in every domain. The addition of AI provides robust solutions for urbanization. Smart city is the ultimate solution for progressive and advanced urban development. A healthy environment offers a healthy place for living. As the population in a smart city is growing continuously, a smart city offers a better, sustainable environment for an excellent living ambience. This study gives views about AI and its impact on sustainability concerns in the context of smart cities and urban development. Many issues regarding sustainability, in addition to environmental impact on urban development, are explored in this study.

Keywords: Sustainability; urbanization; smart city; artificial intelligence; environment; AI; machine learning; ML

Harnessing the Potential of Artificial Intelligence to Promote Environmental Sustainability, 165–183

doi:10.1108/978-1-83662-996-220251010

1. Introduction

As per the observation 3% land allotted to the cites in all over the world (UNEP-UN Environment Programme, 2024). According to the statistics 60%–80% energy utilized and 75% carbon emitted (UNEP-UN Environment Programme, 2024). Sustainability issues are the major concern in urbanization due to the various environmental causes. Pollution and global warming are the major environmental concerns in urbanization. State of art technology addition in progress of environment leads major role. Aid of AI in environmental sustainable solutions builds robust application. As for example AI associated in agriculture increases productivity that leads to favor food safety. On the other hand AI solutions mitigate pollutions which are one of the prime environmental concerns in urban areas (Akter, 2024). Strategies and policies are required to make sustainable environment in development of urbanization. Modern cities are developing due to the progress of urbanization. There are some barriers in evolution of cities as advance urbanization (Paul & Hidalgo, 2023). Environmental enhancement required to improve the environment in cities. Strong renewable energy resources, green infrastructure, alternative energy, alternative energy resources, water quality improvement, green procurement, energy preservations are the strategies and planning for advancement or development of cities (Rasoolimanesh et al., 2012). As the eco-friendly environment becomes essential part of cities it is required to develop cities like environment friendly cities. Smarter technologies are included to develop solutions for the eco-friendly environment in the cities. AI and Internet of Things (IoT) are the recent smart eco-friendly technologies to develop smarter applications for the smart cities and in urbanization. Nowadays, environment friendly smart eco-cities build up using AI and AIoT solutions (Bibri et al., 2024). AI play significant role in environmental sustainability in the urbanization. Addition of AI in environmental solutions including climate changes, weather forecaster, disaster management, protection of natural resources, agricultural issues make significant transformation in sustainable environment (Paul & Aithal, 2020; Yadav & Singh, 2023). Environmental barriers are resolved using AI solutions in terms of the biodiversity, transportations, energy, and water management related concerns (Raihan et al., 2024). The demand of urbanization extensively enhancing in this 21st century. Due to the advancement of technologies and potentialities urbanization is transforming as smart urbanization (Bandari, 2022). Smart city is the outcome of sustainable and advance urbanization. In developing countries, urbanization is extending and cities are transformed according to the innovative planning and strategies. Small cities are developing as smart cities in accordance with development strategies of governance, mobility, quality of life, economy, and environment using advance technologies addition (Ortega-Fernández et al., 2020).

2. Objectives

Following are the objectives of this chapter entitled "Artificial Intelligence and Sustainability in the Context of Smart City and Urban Development: An Overview":

- To study about different solutions of technologies in development of urbanization.
- To study about technology evolution in solutions of environmental challenges.
- To analyze the impact of emerging technology in development of eco-friendly environment in urban development.
- To study AI and it's significant for the environmental sustainability in urban development.
- To study about smart cities sustainable environment and the benefits obtained with the solutions of AI in environment of smart cities.

3. Methodology

This study, entitled "Artificial Intelligence and Sustainability in the Context of Smart City and Urban Development: An Overview," is based on the different facts and views on AI solutions in environmental sustainability to develop sustainable smart cities. Various research papers, articles, website contents, and reports are surveyed as secondary sources in this work. Information with valid facts and findings regarding AI in sustainable urban development is analyzed and emphasized in this study after gathering the secondary sources. This work is divided into four sections according to the following research questions:

Question1: What is the development scenario of a smart city in the context of urbanization advancement?

Question 2: What are the challenges and barriers to environmental sustainability in urban development?

Question 3: What are the roles and responsibilities of AI in a clean and sustainable environment of the smart cities?

Question 4: What are the AI technology-based solutions in connection with the sustainable development of smart cities?

Four sections in this study depict the outcomes of the following questions. Four sections of this work are "foundation of smart city and urbanization," "sustainable issues and challenges in development of urbanization," "fundamental aspects of Artificial Intelligence and its role in sustainable environment," and "Artificial intelligence and sustainability in context of smart city and urban development." The first section describes the foundation of the smart city and the progress of urbanization. The second section focuses on the issues and challenges in terms of environmental sustainability for urban development. The third section defines AI with various perspectives and the roles of AI in connection with the environmental sustainability of the expansion of smart cities. The fourth section describes the smart cities' sustainable development with AI-based solutions.

4. Foundation of Smart City and Urbanization

Advancement of the cities and modern urbanization are the emerging trends in terms of transformed living standards, transformation of society, and economic growth. This section emphasizes the foundation of urbanization with cities' advancement in terms of smart or intelligent cities.

Urban development has been started for many years. Nowadays, urbanization stands at an advanced stage in accordance with the technology revolution (Sikora-Fernandez & Stawasz, 2016; Solly et al., 2021). As per the statistics, the urban population incremented extensively, which causes difficulties in habitation (Shahidehpour & Ganji, 2018). Therefore, urban areas are required to be extended or transformed in order to provide residences for extensive population growth (Newman, 2016). Smart cities of this generation fulfill the demand and need of the inhabitants in terms of the quality of life standard, employability, and economic ability. As per the development and scenario of urbanization across the world, cities are developing in different directions. Intelligent cities, megacities, eco-cities, sustainable cities, green cities, digital cities, and smart cities are different shapes of urbanization (Hajduk, 2016). The main objective of the cities is to control and manage the growth of population, weather changes, quality of environment, economic development, and enhance safety and security (Eremia et al., 2017). There are many barriers to building advanced cities like smart cities. Barriers are financial limitations are one of the major challenges to developing cities, according to the urban development plan. Different limitations exist according to the different fields of the cities. Unemployability, governance flexibility, energy saving issues, sustainability in transportation and mobility, traffic congestion, multimodal transportation, cyber security concerns, security and safety, lack of ICT infrastructure in mobility, health issues, poverty issues, social issues, urban sprawl, and economic limitations. Therefore, enormous limitations impacted the development of smart cities (Monzon, 2015). Smart cities development facilitates and provides various solutions regarding issues in improving living standards (Wolniak & Stecuła, 2024).

Smart city generates many opportunities and scopes for the improvement of quality of life. There are various features of smart cities as per the evolution of smart cities. The features of smart cities are as follows:

- Smart city is an advanced urban development planning that gives information-centric services to the residents. Information-centric services are delivered to the residents using ICT infrastructures (Pellicer, 2013).
- The goal of the smart city development is to build and moderate residential places that provide a clean and eco-friendly environment.
- Smart city provides safety and security to the residents who belong to the smart cities.
- A smart city fulfills the economic and social requirements of the citizens who reside in it.
- Technology builds the information-centric infrastructure to develop a smart city. Therefore, technology is directly associated with the advancement of smart cities.

Efficient transportation and mobility are the benefits of smart cities. Therefore, smart sustainable mobility is built into smart cities for an effective transportation system. Connected and autonomous vehicles are the smart mobility solution for sustainable transportation in smart cities. Connected autonomous vehicle helps to reduce the emission of carbon footprint, which prevents air pollution (Campisi et al., 2021; Seuwou et al., 2020). Intelligent transportation and logistics are part of the smart transportation of smart cities. City logistics enhances the transportation system in smart cities. In a sustainable or green city, an efficient sustainable transportation and logistics system is required to make a green city (Reyes-Rubiano et al., 2021; Voda & Radu, 2018). Recent technological additions, such as AI, with other integrated technologies connected with the development of urbanization and advancement of the cities (Ortega-Fernández et al., 2020). AI and machine learning (ML) implications in smart cities are to enhance smart and intelligent transportation, sustainable energy management, smart waste management, smart urbanization, public safety and security, smart governance, and smart healthcare (Deep & Verma, 2023). Moreover, the smart city developed toward advance smart city from the infancy stage. Nowadays, the smart city has obtained significance due to the immense potentialities and opportunities generated for the inhabitants of the smart cities. Smart city begins its journey in the early 1990s. The popularity of the smart city is rising day by day in the 21st century, as per the observations of recent research and development trends (Singh et al., 2022).

5. Sustainability Issues and Challenges in Development of Urbanization

In this part of this study, various issues and barriers of environmental impacts in the development of smart cities are depicted precisely. Enhanced carbon footprint, weather changes are the barriers to the development of cities. Major challenges in the environmental impacts of the cities are described here.

Environmental issues are the barriers in urban development and smart cities (Raharjana, 2019). Environmental changes have impacted urbanization and the progress of urban development. Due to the incremental population growth in the cities, various environmental issues are arising and increasing day by day. Environmental impacts are mostly observed in transportation and mobility, industries, and energy sectors of the cities. Sustainable cities and smart cities are possibly focusing on environmental sustainability (Toli & Murtagh, 2020). There are various environmental factors effects in cities development, including air pollution enhancing continuously in cities, water pollution, waste management, enhanced greenhouse gas emissions, huge energy consumptions, and increasing heats (Wu et al., 2022). Therefore, cities are developing with a proper sustainability plan. Advanced sustainable technologies will be used for the development of cities in the future (Riffat et al., 2016). In transportation and mobility, mobility as a service (MaaS), smart parking, and self-service cars are the smart applications in the sustainable development of cities. In cities, energy consumption and utilization are increasing as per the increasing demand. To minimize the energy consumption, proper planning, policies, and strategies are required. Emerging technologies, including ICT, Big Data, AI, IoT, sensors, and wireless networks, build strong intelligent applications with robust communication systems to enhance sustainability in different fields of smart cities, including transportation, energy, and industrial sectors (Razmjoo et al., 2022). Smart cities' development growth relies on technology. Smart cities are enhancing as per the technological growth and by balancing with societal development (Kopackova & Libalova, 2017). The following are the challenges in the environment for urban development:

- *Air pollution:* Air pollution is the major concern in the cities. Fuel-based vehicles are increasing day by day in the cities due to the increase of large number of populations in the cities. Industries are developing in cities areas and it has been observed that various industries are growing in the cities. Industries also directly involved in the air pollution due to the emissions of chemicals, harmful gases, waste materials. Day-by-day pollution is enhancing very fast due to the lack of planning to mitigate the air pollution (McGranahan & Satterthwaite, 2022).
- *Water pollution:* Pollution is the main issue according to the incremental progress of urbanization. There is a lack of purified water in the urban areas due to the impact of pollution. Water is polluted due to various reasons, in terms of households, industrial waste materials and garbage spread into the water, harmful chemical resources from industries and transportation are poured into the water. Therefore, water pollution affects the environment of urban areas (McGranahan & Satterthwaite, 2022).
- *Large volume of waste materials:* The management of a large volume of waste materials is one of the major challenges in cities. Due to the huge population growth and city lifestyle, huge waste materials are produced in the cities. It is difficult to clean and dispose of huge amounts of waste materials in the cities due to the lack of planning and strategies. Therefore, a huge volume of waste materials and their enhancement directly affected the environment (McGranahan & Satterthwaite, 2022).
- *High energy consumption:* In the city areas, energy consumption is very high due to the giant industries, advanced transportation and mobility, advanced healthcare, and daily requirements of large populations. Therefore, a huge amount of fossils and fuels are required to be burned to fulfill the demand and requirement for energy. High energy consumption also increases the heat, which is related to the global warming effect. The burning of fossils and fuels increases pollution in the cities. Therefore, high energy requirements and enhanced consumption implied to global warming.
- *Environmental impact on urban biodiversity:* Urban biodiversity might be affected by the environment. Increasing pollution and greenhouse gas impacts are the causes of species losses. Environmental impact directly destroys the ecosystem and biodiversity in the cities. A clean and pollution-free environment needs to be built up for biodiversity.
- *Industrial waste:* In smart cities, industries are growing regularly as economic development increases in the cities. Therefore, the expansion of industries in the smart cities directly affects the environment. Industrial waste materials contain harmful chemicals and gases that might be emitted into the air and mixed with the water. The emission of greenhouse gases into the air causes air pollution. Harmful chemical materials mixed in the water increase water pollution. Therefore, industrial growth affects environmental sustainability, which increases the threats to the environment.

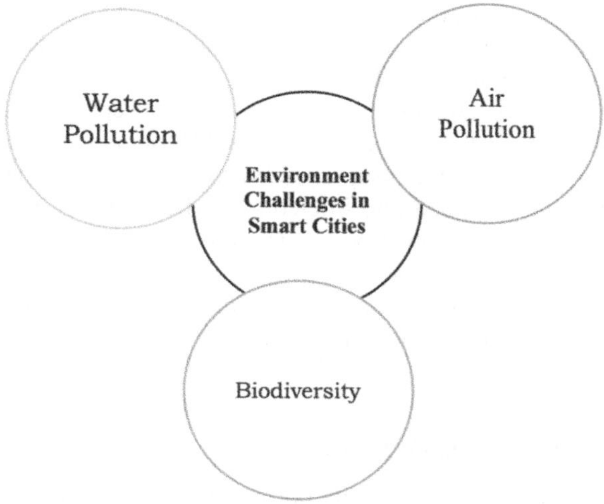

Fig. 10.1. Environment Challenges in Smart City.

Therefore various environmental challenges impede the development growth of urbanization. In this regard, accurate planning and policies are required to minimize environmental impacts in urban progress. According to these possible environmental issues green infrastructure in the urban development play vital role. Green infrastructure needs to be built up in the cities' sustainable development. Green building, renewable energy resources, efficient water management, sustainable transportation system are the green infrastructures facilities make clean environment in urbanization (Bandari, 2022). Cities are suffering from air pollution and environmental impacts. Smart applications need to incorporate to monitor the environmental condition and provide information of environment status. Mobile- and sensor-based applications build in this regard to send real time information about weather condition to the inhabitant of the smart cities (Bacco, 2017). Industries environmental impact shows how the industries directly affected environment in the smart cities enhancement. Due to the different waste materials of industries increase carbon foot print and pollute environment (Ragab, 2023). Fig. 10.1 highlights the environmental issues in smart cities.

6. Fundamental Aspects of AI and Its Role in Sustainable Environment

In this section, various fundamental aspects of AI and its aspects regarding environmental sustainability are emphasized. AI has many contributions in connection with societal, economic, and environmental developments. This section defines the AI significance and its role in the environment.

AI and ML are recent state-of-the-art technology trends that have made many contributions in various areas. In this era, as per technological progress, AI is rising in terms of demand and its significant role in every sector. ML and deep learning are revolutionary and innovative approaches in AI (Paul et al., 2023). As the AI expanded in every domain in terms of intelligent solutions and systematic applications, AI mostly integrated with other technologies to develop smart and intelligent autonomous systems (Paul, 2022). The concept of ML is based on critical decision-making and predictive analysis. ML offers many algorithms and models in terms of supervised, unsupervised, semi-supervised, and reinforcement learning. AI is widely applied and interconnected with many fields to analyze large volumes of datasets and produce decision-making prediction models to solve various problems. AI aggregated with Big Data and IoT to make a system for the protection of the environment of sustainable smart cities (Herath et al., 2022; Jha et al., 2021). These integrated technologies solution helps to make the cities more intelligent (Bibri et al., 2023).

6.1. Role of AI in Sustainable Environment

- Monitoring of air pollution and its prevention using AI solutions. AI-based applications make smart systems that detect air pollution as well as prevent it (Akter, 2024).
- Development of an energy-efficient intelligent system to reduce energy consumption. AI used to control power generation and distribution efficiently, which mitigates energy consumption (Akter, 2024; Stecuła et al., 2023).
- Intelligent waste management system to prevent environmental pollution. Management of a large volume of waste is challenging work. AI provides a solution to efficiently manage a huge amount of waste (Akter, 2024).
- Water flow management, control of water consumption, and water quality control using AI technological applications. AI application used to improve the quality of water to prevent pollution (Akter, 2024).
- AI also plays an extensive role in biodiversity. AI is used to build intelligent systems in biodiversity to predict ecosystem services, observation, and conservation (Akter, 2024).
- AI in agricultural fields enhances productivity by reducing environmental impact. AI is associated with the agricultural system to make sustainable agriculture (Akter, 2024).
- AI is also connected with natural disaster management. AI has the capability to mitigate the impact of environmental disasters. Climate changes, including drought, wildfire, water logging, flood, and rising sea level, are monitored and detected using AI very efficiently (Akter, 2024).

6.2. Case Studies on AI Application in Terms of Sustainability Issues

The following are the various AI implementations with valuable solutions to monitor and prevent environmental impact:

In a coal-fired plant, emissions of NO_2, SO_2, TSP, and other gases contribute to environmental pollution. Environmental depletion is a major issue in industrial areas. Therefore, the right pollution control mechanism is required for the protection of the environment. AI enables a system with an AI model developed to identify and control the emission of gases in the air in a coal-fired plant (Lim et al., 2023).

Different ML algorithms are used to detect pollution. Random forest, extreme gradient boosting (XG Boost), artificial neural network (ANN), convolutional neural network (CNN), K-nearest neighbors (KNN), and support vector machine (SVM) are some ML algorithms applied in weather data analysis to monitor environmental pollution. Various sensor-based technologies, including ground-based monitoring sensors, infrared sensors, and gas sensors, are used to detect air pollution. Aerial image capture with aerial vehicles monitors the waste materials. All these sensors gathered information related to chemical particles, harmful gases, and waste hazards are analyzed using a ML-based model to identify the intensity and impact on the environment (Popescu et al., 2024).

River pollution is an environmental concern due to the industrial waste discharged into the river water. Industrial waste contains dangerous waste particles and harmful chemicals, which cause water pollution. A decision support system was implemented to control and reduce the river pollution. Decision support system used with AI-based analytical tools to detect water pollutants in the river (Sulistyaningsih & Oktaviari, 2021).

AI-equipped water management gives support to reduce waste materials in municipalities. In the cities, sensors embedded in waste bins provide real-time information in connection with the filling of waste materials in the bins. AI is used to predict the waste bins' status and inform municipal administrations of the cities. Therefore, AI is used to manage the large volume of waste materials in the cities (Singagerda et al., 2025).

Biodiversity protection is a challenging task today due to the environmental impacts. AI has the prospects to save biodiversity from environmental hazards. In association with ML algorithms, there are possibilities to resolve biodiversity sustainability issues. According to the observation, a reinforcement-based framework model is applied to monitor the loss of the species as per the environmental effects (Silvestro et al., 2022). Table 10.1 shows the different applications of AI in environmental sustainability in terms of different areas.

7. AI and Sustainability in Context of Smart City and Urban Development

This section describes the implications of AI for the sustainable development of smart and advanced cities. This section also highlights the AI-integrated solutions in environmental sustainability in terms case study of different smart cities.

AI has a significant contribution in terms of intelligent and autonomous solutions in every domain. In this decade, environmental concerns and the impact of climate change are linked to the development of urbanization and its sustainability. Therefore, the development of smart and sustainable cities, AI and other technologies is indirectly related to the making of smart and intelligent solutions for a sustainable atmosphere (Kirimtat et al., 2020; Ligozat et al.,

Table 10.1. Artificial Intelligent Solutions in Environment Sustainability.

Artificial Intelligent Applications	Environmental Issues	Environmental Sustainable Solutions	Areas
Weather monitoring (Bolla et al., 2022; Dewitte et al., 2021)	Climate change	IoT and AI integrated solution to monitor weather status	Environment
Water quality (Bolla et al., 2022; Ighalo et al., 2021)	Water pollution	ML algorithms and models are used for water quality measurement as a smart technology solution	
Greenhouse gas monitoring (Bolla et al., 2022; Soheli et al., 2022)	Greenhouse gas emissions	Intelligent AI-based system detects greenhouse gas emissions	
Air quality monitoring (Bolla et al., 2022; Neo et al., 2023)	Air pollution	Smart air quality monitoring using an AI-based system	
Noise pollution monitoring (Shah et al., 2020)	Noise pollution	Noise pollution is monitored using AI-equipped sensors	
Intelligent traffic system car (Musa et al., 2023)	Fossils and fuel burning, which produce a high-carbon footprint	Reduce indefinite waiting time in traffic and efficient traffic management to minimize fossil fuel burning	Transportation and mobility
Autonomous vehicles (Singh, 2024; Seuwou et al., 2020)		Minimize the emission of CO_2 and other harmful gases, automatic route optimization, and minimize travel time, which are the causes to reduce the carbon footprint	
Intelligent parking (Singh, 2024)		Reduce un definite waiting time to detect parking spaces and efficient traffic management to minimize fossils and fuel burning	

Monitoring of energy efficiency (Nurhaeni et al., 2024)	High energy consumption impact on the environment	Energy efficiency is measured using an AI-based smart solution	Energy
Smart grid (Ali & Choi, 2020)		Energy-efficient power distribution using an AI system	
Smart metering (Nuthakki et al., 2022)		efficient distribution of power to the households and minimizing the waste of energy utilization using AI-based metering	
Industries smart sustainable development (Perera et al., 2023)	Environmental pollution, high energy consumption	Reduce waste materials, eco-efficiency, efficient resource management, and efficient material management are the environment sustainable industries manufacturing system using AI	Industry
Intelligent waste monitoring system (Raihan et al., 2024; Vasudevan, 2024; Venkatesh et al., 2022)	Environmental pollution	Real-time waste monitoring and detection of waste from waste bins. Bins provides present status to inform and make decision about bins are full or empty using connected sensing devices. AI solutions to inform real time information regarding waste in the waste bins	Waste management
Biodiversity conservation (Raihan et al., 2024; Shivaprakash et al., 2022)	Biodiversity issues, including deforestation, wildfire, and ecosystem affected in environment	AI smart system for biodiversity conservation. Prevention of deforestation, minimize wildfires are the biodiversity prevention and conservation using AI	Biodiversity

2022; Szpilko et al., 2023). How the AI offers intelligent applications in environmental sustainability to build smart and environment-friendly cities is featured in this study.

AI solutions are implemented in smart transportation systems in smart cities. Therefore, AI and green AI play a main role in mitigating the pollution in transportation and mobility to make sustainable smart cities (Yigitcanlar et al., 2021). Autonomous vehicles are enabled with AI to automatic speed control, automatic parking allotment without wasting time, and control fuel consumption. A large number of autonomous vehicles is a major issue in transportation in smart cities, which affects the urban environment. Therefore, to improve and make a clean environment, autonomous smart AI-enabled vehicles reduce the pollution and emissions of greenhouse gases (Singh, 2024).

AI in traffic management reduces the environmental impact of urban development. AI in traffic management gives support to minimize air pollution by providing an optimal route dynamically while maintaining the continuation of the traffic flow. In the US cities, AI-based traffic system mitigates environmental pollution by minimizing traffic congestion, and emissions of gases (Karmakar et al., 2024).

As per the excessive increasing demand, electric power consumption increases in the cities unprecedentedly. Smart energy is the outcome of an AI technology solution where energy is efficiently managed and controlled. Smart grid is an AI-equipped thermal grid in which electricity is supplied very efficiently. Power consumption is controlled with an AI-based smart energy consumption system. Smart homes and smart vehicles are innovative AI-based applications in smart cities to minimize energy consumption. In a smart home, every electronic appliance is controlled and operated with an AI-based solution that controls the energy utilization effectively (Uriarte-Gallastegi et al., 2024).

Smart grids enhance the power distribution efficiency and automatically manage the power supply and uses. Therefore, power grids are transformed into the smart grids and are widely implemented in the smart cities to connect all the areas of the smart cities with smart electric power grids (Masera et al., 2018). Smart AI enables system used to efficiently manages the energy consumption and energy flows.

In the smart city water logging and flooding is the major issues due to the congestion in the drainage system, lack of waste management, and lack of maintenance of sewerage system. Therefore, to overcome this circumstances proper intelligent system is required to build up in the cities. Explainable AI enabled smart system build up to monitor the flooding and the reasons behind the flooding and water logging in the municipality areas. This intelligent system developed using ML algorithm based on convolution neural network (CNN). Drainage system blockage monitored by processing the images using ML algorithm to identify the expected vulnerable flooding areas. This system useful in prevention of flood in the smart cities. This intelligent flood identification system using Explainable AI is the effective environmental solution in the smart city (Thakker et al., 2020). Fig. 10.2 shows AI-based sustainable solution in smart cities.

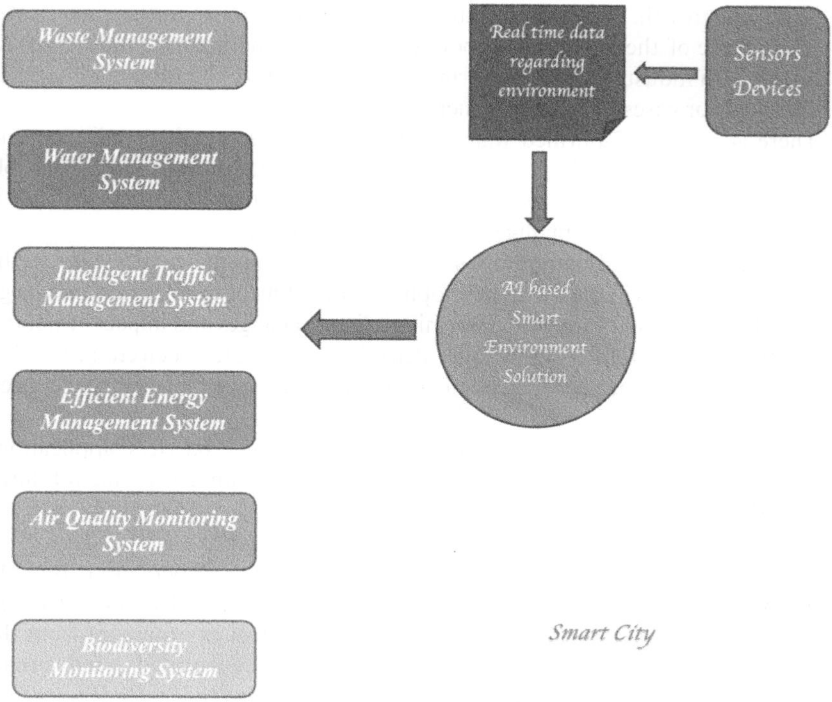

Fig. 10.2. AI Smart Sustainable Solution in Smart City.

8. Findings and Suggestions

AI in association with smart cities sustainable development is fruitful according to the smart technologies intelligent solutions in environment protection. After reviewing all the matters of sustainability issues, environmental barriers prevent progress of smart cities. It has been shown that smart cities are progressing in view of sustainability issues. As per the findings, there are effective solutions of AI in smart cities environment. AI-based solutions in connection with environmental protection for the sustainable smart cities are as follows:

- Autonomous vehicles, smart electric vehicles, intelligent traffic systems, smart or intelligent parking allotments are the solutions of AI to minimize the pollution and sustainable issues in transportation and mobility of the smart cities.
- In the cities, energy consumption is high for enhanced energy utilization. Industrial growth, transportation growth, and population growth are the major reasons for increasing pollution. Smart grids, smart electric vehicles, smart AI equipped electronic home appliances, smart electric meters are some solutions of AI to reduce power consumption.
- Industrial growth in the smart cities may lead to increased pollution in the cities. AI in smart industries in smart cities helps to prevent the industrial

pollution growth. Emission of harmful chemicals or gases in the air or water is the cause of the environment pollution by the manufacturing industries. AI linked with industrial manufacturing units to minimize the spread of harmful chemicals or gases in the atmosphere.
- There is a crisis of purified water in the cities. Water quality prediction and measurements required to enhance the quality of water in the cities. AI enable system monitor the quality of the water in smart cities. Pollution of water is also monitored by the intelligence solutions using AI.
- Climate changes and natural disasters have impacts in smart cities. Due to the lack of greeneries in the urban development environment of the smart and mega cities highly effected with global warming, climate changes and impact of natural disaster. Flood monitoring, wildfire detection, temperature detection, weather fore caste, sea surface heat detection are the AI-based smart intelligence services.

In viewing of all the perspectives as per the challenges, barriers, applications of intelligent solutions in sustainable environment of urban development following are the suggestions describes in this section:

- AI is useful in detection and prevention of environment depletion. But, AI is not sufficient to prevent climate changes, pollution, and natural disaster. Therefore, alternative solutions are required to protect environment from the following issues. Sustainable and green technologies are required to reduce carbon foot print and overcome challenges of environment.
- Nowadays, urban development is rapidly accelerating due to the increased population in the cities. Accommodation and environment friendly space are required for living in the cities. But, most of the cities are overcrowded due to the expanded population. For this causes cities' living accommodation space needs to be expanded as per environmental balance.
- Deforestation is the major barrier in cities development. Most of the cities are developing by destroying forest and natural resources of environment. Therefore, proper urban planning is required to build cities without destroying the environmental ecosystem and resources. Thus, AI or emerging technologies are useless in this context and without forestation and environment conservations technologies are useless.
- Proper environmental awareness is required to develop the cities as sustainable cities. Aside utilization of green and sustainable technologies preservation of forests and trees is highly recommended in development environment friendly smart cities.
- Green AI technologies are efficient and sustainable technologies. Therefore, Green AI is recommended in terms of green energies utilization in urban development.

9. Conclusion

This work light up the views on AI connection with sustainability issues of urbanization and development of the cities as smartest cities. This study incorporates four section with the perspectives of advancing of urbanization with foundations of smart city, issues and challenges of environment in urbanization, AI and roles of AI in environment, AI in sustainability of smart city and urban development. Moreover, AI is everywhere and useful in environmental monitoring and sustainability issues. AI is highly recommended in the prevention of environmental concerns in the cities enhancements toward smarter and intelligent cities. Smart environment in smart cities is the AI-based outcome. AI technologies highly associated with environment friendly cities development. This study useful to the find the future scenario of the AI for the responsibilities of sustainable development of the cities and urbanization.

References

Akter, M. S. (2024). Harnessing technology for environmental sustainability: Utilizing AI to tackle global ecological challenge. *Journal of Artificial Intelligence General Science (JAIGS)*, *2*(1), 61–70.

Ali, S. S., & Choi, B. J. (2020). State-of-the-art artificial intelligence techniques for distributed smart grids: A review. *Electronics*, *9*(6), 1030.

Bacco, M., Delmastro, F., Ferro, E., & Gotta, A. (2017). Environmental monitoring for smart cities. *IEEE Sensors Journal*, *17*(23), 7767–7774.

Bandari, V. (2022). Beyond technology: A holistic framework for smart urbanization in developing countries. *Tensorgate Journal of Sustainable Technology and Infrastructure for Developing Countries*, *5*(1), 1–13.

Bibri, S. E., Alexandre, A., Sharifi, A., & Krogstie, J. (2023). Environmentally sustainable smart cities and their converging AI, IoT, and Big Data technologies and solutions: An integrated approach to an extensive literature review. *Energy Informatics*, *6*(1), 9.

Bibri, S. E., Krogstie, J., Kaboli, A., & Alahi, A. (2024). Smarter eco-cities and their leading-edge artificial intelligence of things solutions for environmental sustainability: A comprehensive systematic review. *Environmental Science and Ecotechnology*, *19*, 100330.

Bolla, S., Anandan, R., & Thanappan, S. (2022). Weather forecasting method from sensor transmitted data for smart cities using IoT. *Scientific Programming*, *2022*(1), 1426575.

Campisi, T., Severino, A., Al-Rashid, M. A., & Pau, G. (2021). The development of the smart cities in the connected and autonomous vehicles (CAVs) era: From mobility patterns to scaling in cities. *Infrastructures*, *6*(7), 100.

Deep, G., & Verma, J. (2023). Embracing the future: AI and ML transforming urban environments in smart cities. *Journal of Artificial Intelligence*, *5*, 57–73.

Dewitte, S., Cornelis, J. P., Müller, R., & Munteanu, A. (2021). Artificial intelligence revolutionises weather forecast, climate monitoring and decadal prediction. *Remote Sensing*, *13*(16), 3209.

Diran, D., Van Veenstra, A. F., Timan, T., Testa, P., & Kirova, M. (2021). Artificial intelligence in smart cities and urban mobility. *Policy Department for Economic, Scientific and Quality of Life Policies*.

Eremia, M., Toma, L., & Sanduleac, M. (2017). The smart city concept in the 21st century. *Procedia Engineering*, *181*, 12–19.

Hajduk, S. (2016). The concept of a smart city in urban management. *Business, Management and Education*, *14*(1), 34–49.

Herath, H. M. K. K. M. B., & Mittal, M. (2022). Adoption of artificial intelligence in smart cities: A comprehensive review. *International Journal of Information Management Data Insights*, *2*(1), 100076.

Ighalo, J. O., Adeniyi, A. G., & Marques, G. (2021). Artificial intelligence for surface water quality monitoring and assessment: A systematic literature analysis. *Modeling Earth Systems and Environment*, *7*(2), 669–681.

Jha, A. K., Ghimire, A., Thapa, S., Jha, A. M., & Raj, R. (2021). A review of AI for urban planning: Towards building sustainable smart cities. In Y. Xin-She et al. (Eds.), *Proceedings of the sixth international conference on inventive computation technologies (ICICT 2021)* (pp. 937–944). IEEE.

Karmakar, M., Debnath, P., & Khan, M. A. (2024). AI-powered solutions for traffic management in US cities: Reducing congestion and emissions. *International Journal of Advanced Engineering Technologies and Innovations*, *2*(1), 194–222.

Kirimtat, A., Krejcar, O., Kertesz, A., & Tasgetiren, M. F. (2020). Future trends and current state of smart city concepts: A survey. *IEEE Access*, *8*, 86448–86467.

Kopackova, H., & Libalova, P. (2017). Smart city concept as socio-technical system. In J. Kostolny (Ed.), *2017 international conference on information and digital technologies (IDT)* (pp. 198–205). IEEE.

Ligozat, A. L., Lefevre, J., Bugeau, A., & Combaz, J. (2022). Unraveling the hidden environmental impacts of AI solutions for environment life cycle assessment of AI solutions. *Sustainability*, *14*(9), 5172.

Lim, J. Y., Teng, S. Y., How, B. S., Loy, A. C. M., Heo, S., Jansen, J., Show, P. L., & Yoo, C. K. (2023). Smart solutions for clean air: An AI-guided approach to sustainable industrial pollution control in coal-fired power plant. *Environmental Pollution*, *335*, 122335.

Masera, M., Bompard, E. F., Profumo, F., & Hadjsaid, N. (2018). Smart (electricity) grids for smart cities: Assessing roles and societal impacts. *Proceedings of the IEEE*, *106*(4), 613–625.

McGranahan, G., & Satterthwaite, D. (2002). The environmental dimensions of sustainable development for cities. *Geography*, *87*(3) 213–226.

Monzon, A. (2015). Smart cities concept and challenges: Bases for the assessment of smart city projects. In H. Markus et al. (Eds.), *2015 international conference on smart cities and green ICT systems (SMARTGREENS)* (pp. 1–11). IEEE.

Musa, A. A., Malami, S. I., Alanazi, F., Ounaies, W., Alshammari, M., & Haruna, S. I. (2023). Sustainable traffic management for smart cities using Internet-of-Things-oriented intelligent transportation systems (ITS): Challenges and recommendations. *Sustainability*, *15*(13), 9859.

Neo, E. X., Hasikin, K., Lai, K. W., Mokhtar, M. I., Azizan, M. M., Hizaddin, H. F., & Razak, S. A. (2023). Artificial intelligence-assisted air quality monitoring for smart city management. *PeerJ Computer Science*, *9*, e1306.

Newman, P. (2016). Sustainable urbanization: Four stages of infrastructure planning and progress. *Journal of Sustainable Urbanization, Planning and Progress*, *1*(1), 3–10.

Nurhaeni, H., Delhi, A., Daeli, O. P. M., Anjani, S. A., & Yusuf, N. A. (2024). Optimizing electrical energy use through AI: An integrated approach for efficiency and sustainability. *International Transactions on Artificial Intelligence*, *2*(2), 106–113.

Nuthakki, S., Kumar, S., Kulkarni, C. S., & Nuthakki, Y. (2022). Role of AI enabled smart meters to enhance customer satisfaction. *International Journal of Computer Science and Mobile Computing*, *11*(12), 99–107.

Ortega-Fernández, A., Martín-Rojas, R., & García-Morales, V. J. (2020). Artificial intelligence in the urban environment: Smart cities as models for developing innovation and sustainability. *Sustainability*, *12*(19), 7860.

Paul, P. K. (2022). Aspects of biosensors with refers to emerging implications of artificial intelligence, big data and analytics: The changing healthcare – A general review. In G. Dutta & A. Biswas (Eds.), *Next generation smart nano-bio-devices* (pp. 1–18)

Paul, P. K., & Aithal, P. S. (2020). Environmental informatics: Aspects in society, economy and development—A study. In P. K. Paul (Ed.), *Applied arts science in IT age* (pp. 73–83). New Delhi Publishers.

Paul, P. K., & Hidalgo, R. S. (2023). An editorial: Enhanced environmental systems using advanced data analytics. *International Journal of Applied Science and Engineering, 11*(1), 1–2.

Paul, P. K., Kayyali, M., Das, M., Chatterjee, R., & Saavedra, R. (2023). Artificial intelligence and smart society: Educational applications, emergences and issues—A scientific review. *International Journal of Applied Science and Engineering, 11*(1), 1–14.

Pellicer, S., Santa, G., Bleda, A. L., Maestre, R., Jara, A. J., & Skarmeta, A. G. (2013). A global perspective of smart cities: A survey. In *2013 seventh international conference on innovative mobile and internet services in ubiquitous computing* (pp. 439–444). IEEE.

Perera, Y. S., Ratnaweera, D. A. A. C., Dasanayaka, C. H., & Abeykoon, C. (2023). The role of artificial intelligence-driven soft sensors in advanced sustainable process industries: A critical review. *Engineering Applications of Artificial Intelligence, 121*, 105988.

Popescu, S. M., Mansoor, S., Wani, O. A., Kumar, S. S., Sharma, V., Sharma, A., Arya, V. M., Kirkham, M. B., Hou, D., Bolan, N., & Chung, Y. S. (2024). Artificial intelligence and IoT driven technologies for environmental pollution monitoring and management. *Frontiers in Environmental Science, 12*, 1336088.

Ragab, A., Osama, A., & Ramzy, A. (2023). Simulation of the environmental impact of industries in smart cities. *Ain Shams Engineering Journal, 14*(6), 102103.

Raharjana, I. K. (2019). A systematic literature review of environmental concerns in smart-cities. In *IOP conference series: Earth and environmental science* (Vol. 245, No. 1, p. 012031). IOP Publishing.

Raihan, A., Paul, A., Rahman, M. S., Islam, S., Paul, P., & Karmakar, S. (2024). Artificial intelligence (AI) for environmental sustainability: A concise review of technology innovations in energy, transportation, biodiversity, and water management. *Journal of Technology Innovations and Energy, 3*(2), 64–73.

Rasoolimanesh, S. M., Badarulzaman, N., & Jaafar, M. (2012). City development strategies (CDS) and sustainable urbanization in developing world. *Procedia-Social and Behavioral Sciences, 36*, 623–631.

Razmjoo, A., Gandomi, A. H., Pazhoohesh, M., Mirjalili, S., & Rezaei, M. (2022). The key role of clean energy and technology in smart cities development. *Energy Strategy Reviews, 44*, 100943.

Reyes-Rubiano, L., Serrano-Hernandez, A., Montoya-Torres, J. R., & Faulin, J. (2021). The sustainability dimensions in intelligent urban transportation: A paradigm for smart cities. *Sustainability, 13*(19), 10653.

Riffat, S., Powell, R., & Aydin, D. (2016). Future cities and environmental sustainability. *Future Cities and Environment, 2*, 1–23.

Seuwou, P., Banissi, E., & Ubakanma, G. (2020). The future of mobility with connected and autonomous vehicles in smart cities. In M. Farsi et al. (Eds.), *Digital twin technologies and smart cities* (pp. 37–52).

Shah, S. K., Tariq, Z., Lee, J., & Lee, Y. (2020, December). Real-time machine learning for air quality and environmental noise detection. In C. Lee (Ed.), *2020 IEEE international conference on big data (big data)* (pp. 3506–3515). IEEE.

Shahidehpour, M., Li, Z., & Ganji, M. (2018). Smart cities for a sustainable urbanization: Illuminating the need for establishing smart urban infrastructures. *IEEE Electrification Magazine, 6*(2), 16–33.

Shivaprakash, K. N., Swami, N., Mysorekar, S., Arora, R., Gangadharan, A., Vohra, K., Jadeyegowda, M., & Kiesecker, J. M. (2022). Potential for artificial intelligence (AI) and machine learning (ML) applications in biodiversity conservation, managing forests, and related services in India. *Sustainability*, *14*(12), 7154.

Sikora-Fernandez, D., & Stawasz, D. (2016). The concept of smart city in the theory and practice of urban development management. *Romanian Journal of Regional Science*, *10*(1), 86–99.

Silvestro, D., Goria, S., Sterner, T., & Antonelli, A. (2022). Improving biodiversity protection through artificial intelligence. *Nature Sustainability*, *5*(5), 415–424.

Singagerda, F. S., Dewi, D. A., Trisnawati, S., Septarina, L., & Dhika, M. R. (2025). Towards a circular economy: Integration of AI in waste management for sustainable urban growth. *Journal of Lifestyle and SDGs Review*, *5*(1), e02642.

Singh, J. (2024). Autonomous vehicles and smart cities: Integrating AI to improve traffic flow, parking, and environmental impact. *Journal of AI-Assisted Scientific Discovery*, *4*(2), 65–105.

Singh, T., Solanki, A., Sharma, S. K., Nayyar, A., & Paul, A. (2022). A decade review on smart cities: Paradigms, challenges and opportunities. *IEEE Access*, *10*, 68319–68364.

Soheli, S. J., Jahan, N., Hossain, M. B., Adhikary, A., Khan, A. R., & Wahiduzzaman, M. (2022). Smart greenhouse monitoring system using internet of things and artificial intelligence. *Wireless Personal Communications*, *124*(4), 3603–3634.

Solly, A., Berisha, E., & Cotella, G. (2021). Towards sustainable urbanization. Learning from what's out there. *Land*, *10*(4), 356.

Stecuła, K., Wolniak, R., & Grebski, W. W. (2023). AI-Driven urban energy solutions—From individuals to society: A review. *Energies*, *16*(24), 7988.

Sulistyaningsih, T., & Oktaviari, V. (2021, March). Artificial intelligence and decision support system to determine policies for controlling river pollution from industrial sectors. In *IOP conference series: Earth and environmental science* (Vol. 717, No. 1, p. 012026). IOP Publishing.

Szpilko, D., Naharro, F. J., Lăzăroiu, G., Nica, E., & de la Torre Gallegos, A. (2023). Artificial intelligence in the smart city—A literature review. *Engineering Management in Production and Services*, *15*(4), 53–75.

Thakker, D., Mishra, B. K., Abdullatif, A., Mazumdar, S., & Simpson, S. (2020). Explainable artificial intelligence for developing smart cities solutions. *Smart Cities*, *3*(4), 1353–1382.

Toli, A. M., & Murtagh, N. (2020). The concept of sustainability in smart city definitions. *Frontiers in Built Environment*, *6*, 77.

UNEP-UN Environment Programme. (2024). *GOAL 11: Sustainable cities and communities*. https://www.unep.org/topics/sustainable-development-goals/why-do-sustainable-development-goals-matter/goal-11

Uriarte-Gallastegi, N., Arana-Landín, G., Landeta-Manzano, B., & Laskurain-Iturbe, I. (2024). The role of AI in improving environmental sustainability: A focus on energy management. *Energies*, *17*(3), 649.

Vasudevan, K. (2024). AI-driven solutions for real-time waste monitoring and management. *Journal of Recent Trends in Computer Science and Engineering (JRTCSE)*, *12*(2), 11–20.

Venkatesh, A. N., Naved, M., Fakih, A. H., Kshirsagar, P. R., & Vijayakumar, P. (2022). An approach for smart city applications using artificial intelligence. In K. S. R. R. Senthil et al. (Eds.), *International conference on research advances in engineering and technology (ICRAET-2021)* (Vol. 2393, No. 1). AIP Publishing.

Voda, A. I., & Radu, L. D. (2018). Artificial intelligence and the future of smart cities. *BRAIN. Broad Research in Artificial Intelligence and Neuroscience*, *9*(2), 110–127.

Wolniak, R., & Stecuła, K. (2024). Artificial intelligence in smart cities—Applications, barriers, and future directions: A review. *Smart Cities*, *7*(3), 1346–1389.

Wu, C. J., Raghavendra, R., Gupta, U., Acun, B., Ardalani, N., Maeng, K., … & Hazelwood, K. (2022). Sustainable AI: Environmental implications, challenges and opportunities. In D. Marculescu et al. (Eds.), *Proceedings of machine learning and systems* (Vol. 4, pp. 795–813).

Yadav, M., & Singh, G. (2023). Environmental sustainability with artificial intelligence. *EPRA International Journal of Multidisciplinary Research (IJMR)*, *9*(5), 213–217.

Yigitcanlar, T., Mehmood, R., & Corchado, J. M. (2021). Green artificial intelligence: Towards an efficient, sustainable and equitable technology for smart cities and futures. *Sustainability*, *13*(16), 8952.

Chapter 11

Developing AI-friendly Environmental Policies Addressing Regulatory Challenges and Opportunities, AI and Global Environmental Governance and Funding, Incentives for AI Driven Environmental Initiatives

Tathagata Roy Chowdhury[a,b] *and Aniruddha Nag*[c]

[a]*Department of Computer Science and Engineering, NIT Silchar, Assam, India*
[b]*Department of Computer Science and Engineering, Techno Engineering College Banipur, West Bengal, India*
[c]*Departtment of Business Administration, Techno India Group, Kolkata, India*

Abstract

The complex and pressing environmental challenges of our time, including climate change, deforestation, biodiversity loss, and water scarcity, demand innovative approaches and collaborative solutions. This chapter explores how emerging technologies can enhance environmental governance by enabling real-time monitoring, improving decision-making processes, and optimizing resource allocation. It examines the significant barriers to technology integration, such as fragmented regulatory frameworks, concerns over data privacy, and global disparities in technological adoption, and offers practical pathways to overcome these challenges. The chapter highlights the potential of technology-driven initiatives, supported by well-structured regulatory frameworks and global cooperation, to foster sustainable development. Drawing on examples such as the European Union's Green Deal, India's environmental policies, and collaborative programs between governments and private sectors, the chapter demonstrates how technology can support early warning systems, emission monitoring, and biodiversity conservation.

Harnessing the Potential of Artificial Intelligence to Promote Environmental Sustainability, 185–197

doi:10.1108/978-1-83662-996-220251011

Recommendations include fostering partnerships across sectors, providing financial incentives to underfunded regions, and ensuring that ethical principles, such as transparency, inclusivity, and sustainability, underpin technological implementation. By aligning innovation with policy and ethical considerations, this chapter envisions a global effort to address environmental crises through shared responsibility and collective action.

Keywords: Environmental governance; sustainable development; regulatory frameworks; technology integration; ethical policy-making; global collaboration

1. Introduction

The escalating environmental crises of the 21st century, including climate change, deforestation, biodiversity loss, and water scarcity, demand innovative and scalable solutions. Artificial intelligence (AI) has emerged as a transformative technology with immense potential to address these challenges. By leveraging its capabilities in data analytics, machine learning, and predictive modeling, AI offers tools to optimize resource allocation, forecast environmental risks, and enhance the efficiency of sustainability programs. However, realizing the full potential of AI in environmental applications requires supportive policies that balance innovation with ethical considerations and inclusivity (Vinuesa et al., 2020).

AI's ability to process vast amounts of data and derive actionable insights is a game-changer in environmental governance. It can aid in real-time monitoring of ecosystems, prediction of extreme weather events, and efficient energy management. Yet, the integration of AI into environmental policy-making faces significant hurdles. Issues such as algorithmic bias, data privacy, regulatory fragmentation, and insufficient funding pose challenges to its widespread adoption. Without an enabling policy framework, these barriers can undermine AI's effectiveness in promoting environmental sustainability (Rolnick et al., 2019).

The need for AI-friendly policies has never been more urgent. Such policies must address key challenges while creating opportunities for collaboration between governments, industries, and academic institutions. For example, regulations that incentivize the development and deployment of AI technologies in climate monitoring or waste management can accelerate innovation and adoption. At the same time, policies must ensure that AI applications are transparent, accountable, and inclusive, avoiding the perpetuation of inequalities or environmental injustices (Goodman & Flaxman, 2017).

The regulatory landscape for AI in environmental governance is still evolving. Globally, there is a lack of standardization in the rules governing AI applications, particularly in environmental sectors. This creates inconsistencies and hinders cross-border collaborations essential for addressing global environmental issues. Ethical concerns, such as the potential misuse of AI and its energy-intensive nature, further complicate the regulatory framework. Policymakers face the dual challenge of fostering innovation while mitigating these risks (European Commission, 2021).

Despite these challenges, the opportunities for integrating AI into environmental policy-making are immense. AI technologies can transform how data is utilized in decision-making, making policies more adaptive and evidence-driven. For instance, AI can assist in creating early warning systems for natural disasters, improving water management, or reducing industrial emissions. These applications highlight the potential for AI to not only address environmental issues but also enhance the governance mechanisms that underpin sustainability efforts (Dwivedi et al., 2021).

This chapter explores the intersection of AI and environmental governance, emphasizing the need for AI-friendly policies that address regulatory challenges and capitalize on emerging opportunities. It delves into the ethical, technical, and financial aspects of integrating AI into environmental sustainability initiatives while providing actionable recommendations for policymakers.

2. Regulatory Challenges in Developing AI for Environmental Policies

The deployment of AI in environmental governance has tremendous potential to revolutionize sustainability initiatives. However, its integration into environmental policies faces significant regulatory challenges that must be addressed to ensure effective, ethical, and equitable outcomes. These challenges, which range from the lack of global standards to concerns over data privacy, algorithmic biases, and transparency, underscore the complexity of balancing innovation with ethical and legal responsibilities.

2.1. Lack of Global Standards for AI Deployment

One of the primary barriers to deploying AI in environmental sectors is the absence of globally harmonized standards and regulations. Environmental issues such as climate change, deforestation, and pollution are inherently transnational, requiring collaborative efforts that transcend national borders. However, the lack of unified guidelines for AI technologies hinders cross-border cooperation and scalability. For example, data collected by AI systems in one country may not adhere to the privacy or security regulations of another, complicating the exchange of critical environmental information (Vinuesa et al., 2020). This regulatory fragmentation limits the global applicability of AI-driven solutions and undermines their effectiveness in addressing large-scale environmental challenges.

2.2. Data Privacy Concerns and Algorithmic Biases

AI systems rely heavily on large datasets to function effectively, but this dependency raises concerns about data privacy and security. Environmental monitoring often involves the collection of sensitive data, such as geospatial information, community activities, or proprietary industrial data. If not managed securely, this data could be misused, leading to privacy violations or breaches of confidentiality. Additionally, biases embedded in AI algorithms pose significant risks. Algorithms trained on unrepresentative or biased datasets may produce skewed results, leading to decisions that disproportionately impact vulnerable communities or prioritize certain environmental objectives over others (Goodman & Flaxman, 2017). For instance, AI tools used to optimize industrial energy consumption might inadvertently overlook the needs of smaller, resource-poor communities.

2.3. Transparency and Accountability

The opacity of many AI systems presents another challenge in developing regulatory frameworks. Known as the "black box" problem, the inability to explain how AI algorithms reach specific decisions can erode trust and hinder their adoption in policy-making. Transparency is particularly critical in environmental governance, where decisions often affect diverse stakeholders, including governments, corporations, and local communities. For example, AI models used for climate predictions or disaster management must be interpretable and verifiable to gain public confidence and ensure accountability in case of errors (Rolnick et al., 2019). Without clear guidelines to ensure algorithmic transparency, AI applications in environmental policies risk being dismissed as unreliable or biased.

2.4. Balancing Innovation with Ethical and Legal Responsibilities

Policymakers face the daunting task of fostering AI innovation while ensuring that its deployment adheres to ethical and legal standards. Striking this balance is especially challenging in rapidly evolving fields like AI and environmental science. Over-regulation may stifle innovation and discourage investment, while under-regulation could lead to unethical practices or environmental harm. For instance, while AI-driven logging and mining operations could optimize resource extraction, they may also accelerate environmental degradation if not properly regulated (Dwivedi et al., 2021).

2.5. Examples of Regional Challenges

Regional disparities further complicate the regulatory landscape. In developing countries, limited access to AI infrastructure and expertise exacerbates existing inequalities, making it difficult to implement sophisticated AI systems for environmental governance. In contrast, developed nations often focus on fine-tuning regulatory frameworks for advanced AI systems, overlooking the global need for inclusive policies. For instance, while Europe has implemented stringent AI regulations as part of its General Data Protection Regulation (GDPR), other regions lag behind in adopting even basic AI governance structures (European Commission, 2021). This uneven progress highlights the need for collaborative efforts to address global environmental issues effectively.

3. Opportunities in Regulatory Frameworks

The development of effective regulatory frameworks presents a significant opportunity to harness AI in addressing global environmental challenges. With the right regulations in place, AI has the potential to transform how policies are formulated and implemented, driving efficiency, sustainability, and innovation. From real-time data utilization to fostering adoption in conservation and sustainability efforts, the possibilities are vast. Moreover, successful case studies highlight how proactive regulations can facilitate the seamless integration of AI technologies into environmental governance.

3.1. Streamlining Policy-making with AI

AI's capacity for processing large datasets and generating actionable insights offers unparalleled opportunities for streamlining policy-making. Traditional policy development often relies on retrospective data and lengthy deliberations, which can limit its adaptability to dynamic environmental challenges. AI, on the other hand, enables real-time data collection and predictive analytics that can provide policymakers with up-to-date information on issues such as deforestation, carbon emissions, or water scarcity (Dwivedi et al., 2021). For example, satellite imagery analyzed by AI can detect illegal logging activities in real-time, enabling faster intervention and reducing environmental damage.

Furthermore, predictive analytics powered by AI can model future scenarios, helping policymakers anticipate environmental risks and plan accordingly. For instance, AI-driven climate models can predict extreme weather events with greater accuracy, allowing governments to allocate resources for disaster preparedness more effectively. Regulatory frameworks that encourage the use of such tools can ensure that environmental policies are not only reactive but also anticipatory, addressing challenges before they escalate (Rolnick et al., 2019).

3.2. Promoting AI Adoption Through Regulations

Regulations play a crucial role in promoting the adoption of AI technologies in environmental conservation and sustainability. By creating incentives for industries and organizations to invest in AI, governments can accelerate the integration into environmental initiatives. For example, tax benefits or subsidies for companies deploying AI in renewable energy optimization or waste management can lower barriers to adoption and encourage innovation.

Moreover, regulations can mandate the use of AI in critical sectors to enhance environmental outcomes. For instance, policies requiring industries to use AI for monitoring their carbon footprint or optimizing energy use can drive significant sustainability improvements. Such regulatory measures not only ensure compliance with environmental goals but also foster a culture of innovation and responsibility among stakeholders (European Commission, 2021).

3.3. Case Studies: Successful Integration of AI and Policy

Several case studies demonstrate how well-designed regulatory frameworks can enable the successful integration of AI into environmental governance:

1. *EU green deal initiatives*:

The European Union (EU) has been a global leader in integrating AI into environmental policies through its Green Deal initiatives. The EU's Climate Action framework leverages AI for monitoring emissions, optimizing energy grids, and enhancing biodiversity protection. Additionally, the GDPR ensures that AI applications adhere to stringent data privacy standards, balancing innovation with ethical considerations (European Commission, 2021).

2. *India's AI policy framework*:
India has also made strides in adopting AI for environmental sustainability under its National AI Strategy, which emphasizes the use of AI in agriculture, water management, and renewable energy. AI-powered platforms like Digital India are utilized for crop monitoring and resource optimization, directly addressing environmental challenges. Regulatory measures supporting these initiatives, such as the Digital India Act, have facilitated the deployment of AI while ensuring its ethical and transparent use (NITI Aayog, 2018).

3. *AI4Earth program*:
Initiatives like Microsoft's AI4Earth showcase how collaboration between private entities and governments can accelerate AI adoption in environmental conservation. The program provides grants and tools for AI-based projects focusing on biodiversity, agriculture, climate change, and water management. Governments can leverage similar public–private partnerships (PPPs) to expand the reach and impact of AI-driven environmental initiatives (Vinuesa et al., 2020).

4. AI and Global Environmental Governance

The integration of AI into environmental governance has the potential to address pressing global challenges, but achieving this requires coordinated efforts on an international scale. Global environmental issues, such as climate change, deforestation, and pollution, transcend national borders, making multilateral cooperation essential. AI can play a pivotal role in these efforts by enabling predictive analytics, optimizing resource use, and improving decision-making. International bodies, cross-border collaborations, and global partnerships are instrumental in fostering AI-driven sustainability initiatives.

4.1. Role of International Bodies in Promoting AI for Sustainability

Organizations such as the United Nations (UN) have been at the forefront of promoting the adoption of AI for achieving environmental sustainability. Through initiatives like the UN Environment Programme (UNEP), the UN has advocated for the use of AI technologies to monitor and combat environmental degradation. UNEP's AI-powered platforms, such as Earth Observations for Sustainable Development Goals (EO4SDG), utilize satellite imagery and machine learning to track deforestation, greenhouse gas emissions, and water pollution in real time (UNEP, 2022).

Additionally, the UN's Global Partnership on Artificial Intelligence (GPAI) serves as a collaborative platform to advance AI applications in climate action and biodiversity protection. By providing technical expertise and facilitating knowledge-sharing among member states, the UN encourages the integration of AI into national and regional environmental strategies. These efforts underscore the critical role international bodies play in fostering a unified approach to AI governance for sustainability (Vinuesa et al., 2020).

4.2. Importance of Multilateral Agreements and Cross-border Collaborations

Environmental governance increasingly requires multilateral agreements that align AI policies across nations. Collaborative frameworks like the Paris Agreement emphasize collective action to combat climate change, creating opportunities for AI integration. For instance, AI can be used to monitor compliance with emission targets, track progress, and forecast climate risks. Cross-border data-sharing agreements are also vital for enabling AI to function effectively at a global scale, as environmental data often originates from multiple regions (Dwivedi et al., 2021).

The success of cross-border collaborations hinges on establishing common standards for data governance, ethical AI practices, and technology transfer. For example, the European Union's Horizon Europe program promotes cross-border research and innovation in AI, focusing on sustainability and climate solutions. These initiatives highlight the importance of international cooperation in leveraging AI's potential for environmental governance while ensuring equity and inclusivity (European Commission, 2021).

4.3. Addressing Funding Gaps Through Global Partnerships and Incentives

The adoption of AI in environmental governance often faces financial barriers, particularly in developing countries. Addressing these funding gaps requires innovative global partnerships and incentive mechanisms. PPPs have proven effective in mobilizing resources for AI-driven sustainability initiatives. For instance, Microsoft's AI for Earth program collaborates with governments and non-governmental organizations to fund projects focusing on biodiversity, climate change, and agriculture (Vinuesa et al., 2020).

International financial institutions, such as the World Bank, also play a crucial role in funding AI adoption in environmental governance. The World Bank's Climate Change Action Plan includes provisions for financing AI-based projects in renewable energy and climate resilience. Additionally, global incentives, such as carbon credits and grants, can encourage industries to adopt AI technologies that reduce emissions and promote sustainability (Rolnick et al., 2019).

4.4. Examples of Global AI Governance Initiatives

Several global initiatives demonstrate the potential of AI in environmental governance when supported by robust policies and international cooperation:

1. *AI for the planet alliance*:

This initiative brings together governments, academia, and the private sector to advance AI solutions for sustainability. It focuses on creating scalable AI models for biodiversity conservation, waste management, and climate adaptation. By fostering international collaboration, the alliance ensures that AI innovations reach underfunded and resource-constrained regions.

2. *United nations AI for good summit*:

Organized by the International Telecommunication Union (ITU), this annual summit explores how AI can address global challenges, including environmental degradation. The summit facilitates dialogue among policymakers, technologists, and environmentalists, driving the development of ethical and effective AI solutions (ITU, 2021).

3. *Google's environmental insights explorer*:

In collaboration with international cities, Google uses AI to provide actionable insights into urban emissions and energy consumption. This initiative exemplifies how private-sector innovation, supported by international collaboration, can contribute to global sustainability efforts (Google, 2021).

5. Funding and Incentives for AI-driven Environmental Initiatives

The adoption of AI for environmental sustainability faces significant financial barriers, particularly in scaling up projects and ensuring equitable access to technology. To overcome these challenges, innovative funding mechanisms and incentives are essential. Governments, private sectors, and international organizations have begun adopting various approaches, including PPPs, grants, and subsidies, to foster the development and implementation of AI-driven environmental initiatives. These strategies, complemented by targeted tax benefits for AI startups, have paved the way for transformative projects addressing global sustainability goals.

5.1. Mechanisms to Fund AI-driven Projects

One of the most effective approaches to funding AI-driven environmental initiatives is through PPPs. These collaborations leverage the resources, expertise, and networks of both government entities and private organizations. Governments often provide initial seed funding or infrastructure support, while private companies contribute technical expertise and innovation. For example, the European Commission's Horizon Europe program encourages PPPs to advance AI technologies in climate resilience and biodiversity conservation. Such partnerships enable the sharing of risks and rewards, fostering innovation that may not emerge in isolated public or private efforts (European Commission, 2021).

In addition to PPPs, grants and funding programs play a critical role in supporting AI-driven projects, particularly for startups and research institutions. Initiatives like Microsoft's AI4Earth provide grants to organizations working on AI solutions for agriculture, water management, and biodiversity protection. These grants enable recipients to access cloud computing resources, machine learning tools, and technical support, accelerating the development and deployment of impactful solutions (Vinuesa et al., 2020). Similarly, the Google AI Impact Challenge has allocated millions of dollars in funding to AI projects addressing environmental and social issues, demonstrating the power of targeted funding to drive innovation (Google, 2021).

5.2. Tax Benefits and Subsidies for AI Startups

Tax incentives and subsidies are another effective way to promote AI adoption in environmental initiatives. Governments can offer tax breaks to startups and companies that develop AI technologies aimed at addressing sustainability challenges. For example, tax deductions for research and development (R&D) expenses can reduce the financial burden on AI innovators, encouraging investment in cutting-edge technologies. In countries like the United States and Canada, R&D tax credits have been instrumental in fostering innovation across various sectors, including AI-driven environmental projects (Dwivedi et al., 2021).

Subsidies can also target specific applications of AI, such as renewable energy optimization or waste management. For instance, subsidies for AI-powered energy management systems can help industries and municipalities adopt technologies that reduce energy consumption and carbon emissions. These incentives not only promote sustainability but also create economic opportunities by fostering a thriving AI ecosystem focused on environmental innovation.

5.3. Case Studies of Successful Funding Models

1. *AI4Earth by Microsoft*:
Microsoft's AI4Earth program exemplifies how strategic funding can drive environmental innovation. By providing grants, cloud computing resources, and AI tools, the program has supported over 700 projects across 100 countries. These projects include AI models for species identification, water quality monitoring, and climate prediction, demonstrating the transformative potential of well-funded initiatives (Vinuesa et al., 2020).
2. *Google AI impact challenge*:
The Google AI impact challenge highlights the role of competitive grants in fostering innovation. In 2019, Google awarded $25 million to 20 organizations using AI to address societal and environmental challenges. Projects funded by this initiative include AI-driven forest fire detection systems and waste management platforms, showcasing the diverse applications of AI in sustainability efforts (Google, 2021).
3. *The World Bank's climate innovation centers*:
The World Bank's Climate Innovation Centers provide funding and technical support to startups developing climate-focused AI technologies. These centers operate in regions like Africa and South Asia, addressing local challenges such as agricultural productivity and disaster management. By combining grants, mentorship, and market access, these centers enable startups to scale their solutions while contributing to regional sustainability goals (World Bank, 2020).

6. Recommendations for Developing AI-friendly Environmental Policies

To harness the transformative potential of AI in addressing global environmental challenges, it is imperative to develop policies that address existing regulatory barriers while fostering innovation. Such policies must prioritize ethical considerations, promote inclusivity, and encourage the adoption of AI in underfunded regions. By integrating sustainability and resilience into AI-driven environmental programs, policymakers can ensure long-term success and equitable benefits.

6.1. Policies to Address Regulatory Challenges While Promoting Innovation

Regulatory challenges, such as the lack of global standards, data privacy concerns, and fragmented governance structures, often hinder AI adoption in environmental sectors. Policies must be designed to mitigate these barriers while encouraging innovation. For instance, creating harmonized international standards for data sharing and AI applications can facilitate cross-border collaboration. Organizations like the United Nations and the European Commission can lead the way by establishing frameworks that align national policies with global sustainability goals (Vinuesa et al., 2020).

Additionally, governments can adopt flexible regulatory sandboxes that allow AI innovators to test new technologies in controlled environments. This approach reduces the risks associated with deploying experimental AI systems while providing valuable insights for scaling solutions. Such sandboxes can be particularly beneficial for startups working on environmental AI applications, enabling them to refine their technologies without the fear of regulatory penalties (Dwivedi et al., 2021).

6.2. Ethical Considerations in AI-driven Environmental Programs

Ethical considerations must be at the forefront of AI-driven environmental policies to ensure fairness, accountability, and inclusivity. Policies should require transparency in AI algorithms, enabling stakeholders to understand how decisions are made. For example, explainable AI models in climate prediction or resource allocation can build trust among governments, industries, and local communities.

Furthermore, policymakers must address the risks of algorithmic bias, which can disproportionately impact vulnerable populations. AI systems trained on biased datasets may prioritize resource allocation to affluent regions while neglecting underprivileged areas. To combat this, regulations should mandate the use of diverse and representative datasets for training AI models (Goodman & Flaxman, 2017).

Ethical policies should also emphasize the responsible use of AI in energy-intensive applications. For example, AI technologies deployed for environmental monitoring or industrial optimization should align with sustainability principles, minimizing their carbon footprint through energy-efficient computing practices (Rolnick et al., 2019).

6.3. Frameworks for Incentivizing AI Adoption in Underfunded Areas

In many underfunded regions, the lack of financial resources and technical infrastructure limits the adoption of AI technologies. To address this disparity, policies should incentivize investment in these areas through tax breaks, subsidies, and PPPs. For example, governments can offer grants to local innovators developing AI solutions tailored to regional environmental challenges, such as water scarcity or deforestation.

Additionally, international organizations and development banks can play a pivotal role by funding AI-driven sustainability projects in low-income countries. Programs like the World Bank's Climate Innovation Centers demonstrate how targeted investments can empower local communities to adopt and benefit from AI technologies (World Bank, 2020).

Encouraging private sector involvement is also critical. Companies engaged in global AI initiatives, such as Microsoft's AI4Earth or Google's AI Impact Challenge, can extend their support to underfunded regions through collaborative projects and knowledge-sharing initiatives.

6.4. Building Resilience Through Sustainable AI Practices

AI-driven environmental programs must prioritize resilience to ensure long-term sustainability. Policies should encourage the development of adaptive AI systems capable of responding to dynamic environmental conditions, such as changing climate patterns or resource availability. For instance, predictive models used for disaster management should incorporate real-time data to adjust forecasts and recommendations as situations evolve.

Sustainability can also be promoted through circular AI practices, where AI systems are designed to minimize waste and maximize resource efficiency. For example, reusing hardware components and optimizing software algorithms can reduce the environmental impact of AI technologies (Dwivedi et al., 2021).

Moreover, policies should integrate community participation into AI-driven programs. Empowering local stakeholders to contribute to data collection, model training, and decision-making processes ensures that AI solutions are both contextually relevant and socially accepted. Such participatory approaches enhance the resilience and scalability of AI systems by aligning them with local needs and values.

7. Conclusion

AI has demonstrated immense potential in addressing global environmental challenges, from climate change to biodiversity loss. However, unlocking its full capacity requires robust, inclusive, and forward-looking policies. Throughout this discussion, we explored the regulatory challenges, funding mechanisms, ethical considerations, and opportunities for AI-driven environmental governance. These insights highlight the importance of harmonized global standards, ethical frameworks, and targeted incentives to foster AI adoption while safeguarding transparency, equity, and sustainability.

A critical takeaway is the dual role of regulatory frameworks: they must mitigate risks such as algorithmic bias and data privacy concerns while actively promoting innovation. Policies that encourage PPPs, provide grants and subsidies, and incentivize AI adoption in underfunded regions can play a transformative role in enabling equitable access to AI technologies. Case studies like the EU Green Deal, India's AI policy framework, and initiatives such as Microsoft's AI4Earth exemplify how funding and governance can drive impactful outcomes. Additionally, ethical considerations, such as explainability and energy efficiency, must be integral to AI deployment, ensuring that advancements in technology align with broader sustainability goals.

Looking forward, the vision for AI-driven environmental policies must prioritize adaptability, inclusivity, and collaboration. The dynamic nature of environmental challenges demands flexible and anticipatory governance models that leverage AI for real-time decision-making. International cooperation will be essential in addressing cross-border issues such as climate change and pollution, fostering a shared commitment to sustainable development. Furthermore, integrating local communities into AI-driven programs will ensure contextually relevant and socially acceptable solutions, amplifying their impact and scalability.

As policymakers, industries, and global organizations come together to shape the future of AI in environmental governance, the focus must remain on creating an ecosystem where technology, ethics, and sustainability coexist. By addressing existing challenges and seizing emerging opportunities, AI can evolve into a cornerstone of global efforts to protect the planet and secure a sustainable future for generations to come. This vision not only underscores the transformative potential of AI but also highlights the shared responsibility of stakeholders in achieving it.

References

Dwivedi, Y. K., Hughes, L., Ismagilova, E., Aarts, G., Coombs, C., Crick, T., Duan, Y., Dwivedi, R., Edwards, J., Eirug, A., Galanos, V., Ilavarasan, P. V., Janssen, M., Jones, P., Kar, A. K., Kizgin, H., Kronemann, B., Lal, B., Lucini, B., Medaglia, R., Le Meunier-FitzHugh, K., Le Meunier-FitzHugh, L. C., Misra, S., Mogaji, E., Sharma, S. K., Singh, J. B., Raghavan, V., Raman, R., Rana, N. P., Samothrakis, S., Spencer, J., Tamilmani, K., Tubadji, A., Walton, P., & Williams, M. D. (2021). Artificial Intelligence (AI): Multidisciplinary perspectives on emerging challenges, opportunities, and agenda for research, practice, and policy. *International Journal of Information Management*, *57*, 101994. https://doi.org/10.1016/j.ijinfomgt.2019.101994

European Commission. (2021). *Coordinated plan on artificial intelligence 2021 review*. https://digital-strategy.ec.europa.eu/

Goodman, B., & Flaxman, S. (2017). European Union regulations on algorithmic decision-making and a "right to explanation." *AI Magazine*, *38*(3), 50–57. https://doi.org/10.1609/aimag.v38i3.2741

Google. (2021). *AI impact challenge*. https://ai.google/social-good/impact-challenge/

ITU. (2021). *AI for good global summit*. https://aiforgood.itu.int/

NITI Aayog. (2018). *National strategy for artificial intelligence*. https://www.niti.gov.in/

Rolnick, D., Donti, P. L., Kaack, L. H., Kochanski, K., Lacoste, A., Sankaran, K., … & Bengio, Y. (2019). *Tackling climate change with machine learning*. ArXiv:1906.05433

UNEP. (2022). *Earth observations for sustainable development goals*. https://www.unep.org/

Vinuesa, R., Azizpour, H., Leite, I., Balaam, M., Dignum, V., Domisch, S., … & Nerini, F. F. (2020). The role of artificial intelligence in achieving the sustainable development goals. *Nature Communications*, *11*(1), 1–10. https://doi.org/10.1038/s41467-019-14108-y

World Bank. (2020). *Climate innovation centers: Catalyzing green growth*. https://www.worldbank.org/

Chapter 12

A Survey on SQL Injection Attack Detection Using Machine Learning

Silambarasan Elkana Ebinazer[a], *Harish Vishwa S. M.*[b], *Harsh Raj*[b], *Harsh Gupta*[b] *and Likhitha S.*[b]

[a]*Department of Computer Science and Engineering-Cybersecurity, IIIT Kottayam, Kerala, India*
[b]*Department of Computer Science and Engineering, IIIT Kottayam, Kerala, India*

Abstract

In today's digital world, sharing data across web platforms is common. However, this exposes sensitive user information to cyber threats like cross-site scripting (XSS), denial of service attacks (DoS), and structured query language (SQL) injection, a top vulnerability for web apps. SQL injection can lead to severe consequences such as financial loss or data leaks. This chapter investigates and compares previous research while attempting to replicate and enhance existing methods for SQL injection attack detection. Various machine learning (ML) models, such as artificial neural networks (ANN), logistic regression and support vector machines (SVM), have been trained and tested with large datasets to maximise accuracy and other parameters to find the best-suited model to detect SQL injection attacks. The chapter also highlights limitations in current techniques and explores their implications on practicality and effectiveness while trying to overcome the same.

Keywords: SQL injection attack; machine learning; LSTM; SVM; ANN

Harnessing the Potential of Artificial Intelligence to Promote Environmental Sustainability, 199–211

doi:10.1108/978-1-83662-996-220251012

1. Introduction

1.1. Background and Motivation

Web-based applications have experienced unprecedented popularity, facilitated by their versatile deployment on diverse execution platforms, such as web servers, web browsers, and network connections. This proliferation has resulted in significant time savings and enhanced user convenience in their daily activities. The web design industry has flourished, reaching a remarkable market value of 11 billion dollars (Garg & Jain, 2018), underscoring the burgeoning demand for online services. No table, mobile devices account for 53.74% of web visits, with desktops comprising the remaining 46.26% (Bhatia & Sharma, 2018).

Despite the manifold advantages offered by web applications, the exponential surge in data generation has raised profound concerns regarding data privacy and security. SQL is a fundamental tool for extracting information from databases; however, its misuse can pose a grave threat to organisational data assets. Malicious actors exploit SQL injection attacks to illicitly obtain sensitive information, including Internet banking and mobile banking passwords, ATM PINs, and user credentials from online applications. Moreover, they can execute commands to manipulate or delete entire database tables. OWASP research highlights SQL-based attacks as not only among the most lethal but also one of the most prevalent forms of cyber threats globally (Gupta & Kumar, 2018).

1.2. Problem Statement

The pervasive nature of SQL injection attacks underscores the critical need for robust detection mechanisms to safeguard against potential breaches and data compromise. Traditional detection methods often fall short in effectively identifying and mitigating these threats, necessitating innovative approaches to enhance the resilience of web applications. ML has emerged as a promising avenue for bolstering SQL injection attack detection capabilities, leveraging advanced algorithms to discern patterns indicative of malicious activities.

1.3. Objectives

This chapter aims to explore and evaluate the efficacy of ML techniques in detecting SQL injection attacks within web-based applications. By conducting a comprehensive literature review and comparative analysis of existing methodologies, we seek to: Assess the strengths and limitations of traditional detection methods vis-a-vis ML-based approaches. Investigate the performance of various ML models, including SVM, logistic regression and ANN in detecting SQL injection attacks. Identify current challenges and limitations in SQL injection detection and propose avenues for future research and development.

1.4. Contribution of the Chapter

This chapter contributes to the existing body of knowledge by offering insights into the application of ML for SQL injection attack detection within web-based environments. By synthesising and analysing relevant literature, we provide an extensive overview of modern detection methods, highlight key findings and trends, and offer recommendations for enhancing the efficacy and robustness of SQL injection detection mechanisms.

2. SQL Injections

2.1. Overview of SQL Injection Attacks

The security of web applications is constantly at risk from SQL injection attacks, which use flaws in input validation systems to run malicious SQL queries. These attacks pose significant risks to the confidentiality, integrity, and availability of sensitive data stored in databases underlying web applications. SQL injection attacks are characterised by their ability to bypass authentication mechanisms, manipulate database queries, and extract sensitive information without proper authorisation. SQL injection attacks typically occur when web applications fail to validate and sanitise user inputs, which allows the injection of malicious SQL code into input fields such as login forms, search bars, or URL parameters. Once injected, this malicious code can alter the intended behaviour of SQL queries, enabling attackers to retrieve, modify, or delete data stored in the database. For example, consider a login form that fails to sanitise user inputs, allowing an attacker to inject a malicious SQL query such as:

```
SELECT * FROM users WHERE username = 'admin' OR
      '2'='2'--' AND password = 'admin';
```

The inserted SQL code (`'2'='2'`) in the sample above always evaluates to true, evading the authentication check and giving the attacker access to the application without authorisation (Smith & Johnson, 2017a, 2017b).

2.2. Common Techniques Used in SQL Injection Attacks

SQL injection attacks employ a diverse array of techniques meticulously crafted to exploit vulnerabilities prevalent in web applications. Among the most prevalent tactics are the injection of malicious SQL payloads into input fields, manipulation of URL parameters, and exploitation of inadequately sanitised user inputs. Notable among these techniques are union-based injection, blind injection, and error-based injection methods, each designed to evade conventional input validation mechanisms and execute arbitrary SQL commands surreptitiously.

2.2.1. Union-based SQL Injection

This is one of the frequent attacks in which unauthorised access is obtained by combining a malicious query with a benign query. As a result, there are more results than are necessary, which exposes sensitive data. In the example provided, the union keyword is used to combine a malicious query with a legitimate one to successfully log in.

```
'UNION SELECT user || '~' || password FROM users list—
```

2.2.2. Error-based SQL Injection

Error-based attacks expose errors that, indirectly, provide insights into the database structure. Vulnerability to error-based injection arises when web applications are developed on a live or online site rather than on an offline platform. Unintentional vulnerabilities to error-based SQL injections can result in technical issues such as command injections and illegal access to data. Developers may see system error messages such as buffer overruns, catching exceptions, and format strings if error-based command injections take place.
https://project.com/main.php?val=456
https://project.com/main.php?val=455'

```
Error in SQL syntax; check the manual for the right
syntax to use near "VALUE".
```

2.2.3. Blind SQL Injection

In this type of attack, true or false questions are posed to the database, and the answer is determined by the application's response. This method is frequently used when the web application has not resolved the SQL injection code vulnerability and is configured to display generic error messages.

```
SELECT heading, detail, content FROM items
WHERE id = 3

SELECT heading, detail, content FROM items WHERE
id = 3 and 1=3

SELECT heading, detail, content FROM items
WHERE id = 3 and 2=2
```

2.2.4. Piggy-backed Injections

This type of attack is one of the most lethal attacks. In this attack, more than one query is appended at the end of the real query, which manipulates the data in a defined way. In the given example, delimiters are used to insert more than one query (Garcia & Martinez, 2019).

```
SELECT * FROM customers list; TRUNCATE TABLE
customers list;
```

2.3. Impact and Consequences of SQL Injection Attacks

The impact of SQL injection attacks extends beyond individual web applications, posing significant risks to organisations and individuals alike. These attacks can lead to:

2.3.1. Unauthorised Access to Sensitive Data

Attackers can exploit SQL injection vulnerabilities to access sensitive information stored in databases, including proof of identity, financial records, and authentication credentials.

2.3.2. Data Breaches and Exposure of Confidential Information

SQL injection attacks can result in data breaches and the unauthorised exposure of confidential information, leading to reputational damage, legal liabilities, and regulatory non-compliance for affected organisations.

2.3.3. Disruption of Services and Financial Losses

The exploitation of SQL injection vulnerabilities can disrupt the functionality and availability of web-based applications, resulting in downtime, financial losses, and remediation costs for affected organisations.

The ramifications of SQL injection attacks highlight how crucial it is to put strong security measures in place, such as parameterised queries, input validation, and web application firewalls, to reduce the chance of exploitation and protect private information from unauthorised access (Choi & Kim, 2020).

3. SQL Injection Attack Detection

SQL injection attack remains a critical concern in the realm of cybersecurity, necessitating robust and effective detection mechanisms to mitigate the risks posed by these insidious threats. In this section, we deep dive into the intricacies of both traditional and ML-based detection methods, providing a comprehensive overview of their principles, methodologies, and performance characteristics.

3.1. Traditional Detection Methods

Traditional detection methods for SQL injection attacks have long been the cornerstone of cybersecurity practices, offering heuristic-based approaches to identify and mitigate potential threats. This subsection explores three prominent traditional detection methods.

3.1.1. Signature-based Detection

Signature-based detection relies on predefined patterns or signatures to identify known SQL injection attack strings within incoming requests or queries. These signatures are meticulously crafted based on known attack patterns and are deployed within intrusion detection systems or web application firewalls to intercept and block malicious traffic. While signature-based detection is effective in identifying known attack vectors, it is inherently limited by its reliance on predefined signatures, rendering it vulnerable to zero-day attacks and variations in attack patterns.

3.1.2. Syntax Analysis

Syntax analysis involves scrutinising the syntax of incoming SQL queries to detect anomalous or suspicious patterns indicative of SQL injection attacks. By analysing the structure and grammar of SQL queries, this method aims to identify deviations from expected syntax and flag potentially malicious queries for further investigation. However, syntax analysis may be prone to false positives and may not effectively detect obfuscated or polymorphic attacks (Brown & Wilson, 2019).

3.1.3. Input Validation and Sanitisation

Input validation and sanitisation entail validating and sanitising user inputs to ensure adherence to predefined criteria and eliminate potential SQL injection vulnerabilities. This method relies on strict input validation rules and data sanitisation techniques to neutralise potential SQL injection attacks before they reach the database. While effective, input validation and sanitisation require meticulous implementation and may be susceptible to bypass techniques employed by sophisticated attackers (Gracia & Martinez, 2018).

3.2. ML Methods for SQL Injection Detection

ML methods offer a promising alternative to traditional detection techniques, leveraging advanced algorithms to discern patterns indicative of malicious activities. This subsection explores various ML-based approaches for SQL injection detection.

3.2.1. Feature-based Models

Feature-based models utilise a set of features extracted from SQL queries to train ML algorithms to distinguish between benign and malicious queries. These features may include syntactic, semantic, or structural attributes of SQL queries, enabling the model to learn to recognise patterns indicative of SQL injection attacks. Feature-based models are versatile and can accommodate a wide range of input features, making them suitable for detecting both known and novel attack patterns (Lee & Park, 2018).

3.2.2. Anomaly Detection Approaches

The goal of anomaly detection techniques is to spot SQL query patterns that deviate from typical behaviour, signalling potential SQL injection attacks. These approaches use ML algorithms to learn the typical patterns of benign SQL queries and flag deviations from these patterns as anomalies. By training on a dataset comprising both malicious and benign queries, anomaly detection models can learn to discern subtle differences indicative of SQL injection attacks (Wang & Zhang, 2019).

3.2.3. Ensemble Methods

Ensemble methods combine multiple ML algorithms to improve the robustness and accuracy of SQL injection detection systems. By aggregating the predictions of diverse ML models, ensemble methods can mitigate the limitations of individual algorithms and enhance overall detection performance. Common ensemble techniques include bagging, boosting, and stacking, each offering unique advantages in terms of model diversity and predictive power (Kim & Lee, 2020).

3.2.4. Deep Learning Techniques

Deep learning techniques, particularly deep neural networks (DNNs), have garnered considerable attention for their capacity to recognise hierarchical representations of data and discern complex patterns automatically. In the context of SQL injection detection, DNNs can leverage the hierarchical structure of SQL queries to automatically extract relevant features and identify subtle indicators of SQL injection attacks. However, deep learning techniques may require large amounts of labelled data and computational resources for training.

4. Experiment Result and Comparative Analysis

SQL injection remains an important threat to the security of web applications, necessitating the development and deployment of effective detection methods. We did a comprehensive and comparative analysis of various detection approaches, considering their performance evaluation metrics, strengths, weaknesses, and real-world applicability in this section.

4.1. Performance Evaluation Metrics

The assessment of performance metrics is crucial for quantifying the effectiveness and efficiency of SQL injection detection methods. Various metrics are commonly employed to evaluate the performance of detection algorithms, encompassing accuracy, precision, recall, $F1$-score, and false positive rate. These metrics serve as quantitative measures to gauge the ability of detection algorithms to accurately identify SQL injection attacks while minimising false positives.

4.1.1. Accuracy (Acc)

It measures the overall correctness of the detection method and is derived as the ratio of correctly classified instances to the total number of instances examined:

$$Acc = \frac{TP + TN}{TP + TN + FP + FN} \tag{1}$$

where TP represents true positives (correctly detected SQL injection attacks). TN represents true negatives (correctly identified benign queries). FP represents false positives (benign queries incorrectly classified as attacks). *FN* represents false negatives (attacks incorrectly classified as benign queries). It is expressed in Equation 1.

4.1.2. Precision (PR)

Precision measures the reliability of positive predictions made by the detection method and is calculated as Equation 2.

$$PR = \frac{TP}{TP + FP} \tag{2}$$

4.1.3. Recall (Sensitivity) (REC)

Recall quantifies the completeness of the detection method in capturing positive instances and is determined as the ratio of true positives to the total of actual positive instances:

$$REC = \frac{TP}{TP + FN}. \tag{3}$$

4.1.4. F1-score (F1)

It is the harmonic mean of recall and precision, giving a fair assessment of the effectiveness of the detection technique:

$$F1 = 2 \times \frac{PR \times REC}{PR + REC}. \tag{4}$$

4.1.5. False Positive Rate (FPR)

The false positive rate measures the proportion of negative instances incorrectly classified as positive (Smith & Johnson, 2017a, 2017b) and is determined as:

$$FPR = \frac{FP}{TN + FP}. \tag{5}$$

4.2. Strengths and Weaknesses of Different Approaches

4.2.1. Signature-based Detection

4.2.1.1. Strengths. High precision: Signature-based detection relies on already defined signatures and patterns of known SQL injection attacks, resulting in high precision in identifying known attack patterns.

Low false positive rate: By matching incoming requests against a database of known attack signatures, signature-based detection methods can effectively reduce false positive alarms.

4.2.1.2. Weaknesses. Vulnerability to zero-day attacks: Signature-based detection methods are susceptible to zero-day attacks, where attackers utilise previously unseen attack patterns that are not covered by existing signatures

Maintenance overhead: Continuous updates and maintenance of signature databases are required to keep pace with evolving attack techniques, posing a logistical challenge for organisations.

4.2.2. Anomaly-based Detection

4.2.2.1. Strengths. Adaptability to new attack patterns: Anomaly-based detection methods can adapt to new and unseen attack patterns by learning the normal behaviour of SQL queries and flagging deviations as anomalies.

Resilience to polymorphic attacks: Unlike signature-based methods, anomaly-based detection techniques can detect polymorphic attacks that dynamically alter their syntax and structure to evade detection.

4.2.2.2. Weaknesses. Higher computational overhead: Anomaly-based detection methods often require more computational resources and processing time to analyse SQL query patterns and identify anomalies, leading to potential performance overhead.

Potential false positive alarms: The reliance on statistical models and behavioural analysis may result in false positive alarms, particularly in complex and dynamic environments where legitimate queries exhibit unusual patterns.

4.2.3. Input Validation and Sanitisation

4.2.3.1. Strengths. Simplicity and effectiveness: Input validation and sanitisation techniques provide a straightforward and effective means of preventing SQL injection attacks by validating and sanitising user inputs before processing them.

Developer control: Developers have direct control over the implementation of input validation and sanitisation measures, allowing for customisation and fine-tuning based on specific application requirements.

4.2.3.2. Weaknesses. Reliance on developer implementation: The effectiveness of input validation and sanitisation measures depends heavily on developers' adherence to best practices and thorough implementation, leaving room for oversight and human error.

Potential bypass techniques: Sophisticated attackers may employ evasion techniques, such as encoding or obfuscation, to bypass input validation and sanitisation checks, undermining their effectiveness.

4.3. Case Studies and Benchmarking

(Tang et al., 2020) Evaluate the effectiveness of multilayered perceptrons and LSTM models for SQLI detection. The environment utilised Ubuntu 16.04 and Pytorch, powered by a Dell PowerEdge server with an NVIDIA Tesla GPU.

They have achieved over 98% accuracy using the multilayer perceptron (MLP) model with three hidden layers, surpassing both one and two-layered models.

On the contrary, detection time was better for one-layered MLP, which proved practical for real-time applications. LSTM models achieved over 97% accuracy, which was subpar compared to MLP models. While there's a performance gap between MLP and LSTM, it has distinct benefits, such as learning the association of characters to differentiate SQL statements from normal statements.

In their investigation, Li et al. (2019) present compelling insights into the effectiveness of their proposed approach for identifying SQL injection attacks. Their study encompassed six datasets, amalgamating samples from vulnerability submission platforms and SQLMap runs. The positive samples, indicative of SQL injection instances, were obtained from Exploit-DB, WooYun, and SQLMap.

The experiments were carried out within the Ubuntu 14.04 LTS environment, utilising Keras 2.1.2 and Python 3.5.4. Their research extensively explored the impact of different feature vectors, revealing that Word2Vec-based vectors achieved an impressive accuracy rate of 93.47% and an *F*1-score of 92.99%, surpassing the performance of Bag-of-Words (BoW). Moreover, their proposed sample expansion method effectively mitigated overfitting concerns, resulting in significant enhancements across all parameters.

To offer a comprehensive perspective, the study compared their proposed method with traditional ML techniques such as SVM, *k*-nearest neighbours (KNN), decision tree (DT), Naive Bayes (NB), random forest (RF), as well as common deep neural networks including convolutional neural network (CNN), recurrent neural network (RNN), and MLP. The findings indicated that the LSTM-based method outperformed both conventional ML methods and common deep neural networks. Particularly, it exhibited a superior *F*1-score compared to RNN and CNN, underscoring its effectiveness in detecting SQL injection attacks.

Conduct an experimental review to evaluate the performance of three classifiers: SVM, KNN, and RF (Irungu et al., 2023). The evaluation encompassed benchmark metrics, with detailed mathematical expressions provided for precision, *F*1 score, and recall. Precision, indicating the accuracy and precision of results, was defined as the threshold of true positives from the predicted positives, as derived from Equation 3. The *F*1 score, aiming for a balance between recall and precision, was expressed as a function of both, as given by Equation 4. Recall, representing the sensitivity of actual positives compared to total observations, was calculated using Equation 5.

The simulation results revealed that the SVM classifier achieved the highest accuracy, nearing 99%, followed by RF at 97.53%, and KNN at 96.3% for anomaly injections. Despite KNN demonstrating the lowest precision among the three classifiers, it still exhibited a substantial precision of 96%. These findings underscore the effectiveness of SVM, RF, and KNN in detecting anomalies, with each classifier offering high accuracy and confidence in its predictions.

Joshi Padma et al. (2022) show that the simulation results from traditional models utilising 1,530 records for training and 510 for testing, an accuracy of 82.94% was achieved, with an error rate of 17.04%. The confusion matrix and subsequent metrics revealed the model's performance across different classes. In contrast, the proposed model, trained and tested on the same dataset, demonstrated an improved accuracy of 90.59%, with a reduced error rate of 9.41%. The comparative analysis showcased the superiority of the proposed model across various metrics. The LSTM-based method demonstrated potential for detecting web threats such as SQL injection in addition to XSS, highlighting its adaptability and scalability in threat identification.

Conduct experiments with models like improved TextCNN, LSTM, and ATTENTION mechanisms (Sun et al., 2023). They then demonstrated that these models outperformed traditional ML models like SVM, DT, NB, KNN, and RF. The deep learning model's superiority was attributed to its ability to automatically learn and extract features, reducing the reliance on manual feature engineering. Furthermore, a comparison with common deep neural networks, including RNN, CNN, and TRANSFORMER, showed that the proposed method achieved better results. The combination of TextCNN for local features and LSTM with ATTENTION for sequence features proved effective in handling SQL injection detection. The confusion matrix analysis across different datasets revealed that the proposed method achieved low false negative and false positive rates, showcasing its effectiveness in detecting SQL injection attacks. In conclusion, the deep learning-based approach presented in this study, incorporating an improved TextCNN, LSTM, and ATTENTION mechanisms, demonstrated superior performance in SQL injection attack detection compared to classical ML methods and common deep neural networks.

Employee three injection parameters, including user input fields, cookies, and server variables, to assess vulnerabilities in web applications (Demilie & Deriba, 2022). These vulnerabilities could be exploited by attackers to manipulate cookies and submit malicious input, potentially leading to SQL injection (SQLI) vulnerabilities.

To prevent such attacks, the researchers trained and evaluated various ML models, including traditional techniques like NB, RF, SVM, DT, as well as ANN and a hybrid approach combining ANN and SVM. The hybrid approach exhibited superior performance across accuracy, precision, recall, and *F*1-score metrics for both the training and test datasets. Nonetheless, this enhanced performance was accompanied by extended durations for both the training and testing phases.

The findings emphasise the importance of considering dataset characteristics and the trade-off between accuracy and computational efficiency when implementing SQLI detection and prevention systems. In Conclusion, the study suggests that future research could further enhance system performance by leveraging hybrid techniques on large-scale datasets.

5. Conclusion

This chapter provides a comprehensive overview of SQL injection attacks and their detection methods within web-based applications. Traditional detection techniques, such as signature-based methods and input validation, offer foundational approaches but are limited in adaptability and prone to false positives.

In contrast, ML methods, including feature-based models, anomaly detection, ensemble methods, and deep learning techniques, show promise in detecting subtle attack patterns and adapting to new threats. Experimental evaluations highlight the efficacy of ML models like MLP, LSTM, and ensemble methods in achieving high accuracy rates for SQL injection detection. The comparative analysis underscores trade-offs between accuracy, computational efficiency, and real-world applicability across different detection methods. Overall, this chapter contributes valuable insights for developing robust detection mechanisms to safeguard web applications against SQL injection attacks, emphasising the importance of continued research in enhancing model robustness, scalability, and efficiency to mitigate evolving cyber threats.

References

Bhatia, S., & Sharma, R. (2018). A review on SQL injection attack detection using machine learning algorithms. *International Journal of Computer Applications*, *180*(12), 22–27.

Brown, A., & Wilson, M. (2019). Syntax analysis techniques for SQL injection attack detection. *International Journal of Cybersecurity Research*, *15*(3), 245–260.

Choi, Y., & Kim, H. (2020). Impact assessment of SQL injection attacks: An international perspective. *International Journal of Cybersecurity and Privacy*, *15*(1), 112–130.

Demilie, W. B., & Deriba, F. G. (2022). Detection and prevention of SQLI attacks and developing compressive framework using machine learning and hybrid techniques. *Journal of Big Data*, *9*(124). https://doi.org/10.1186/s40537-02200678-0

Garcia, R., & Martinez, E. (2018). Input validation and sanitization techniques for SQL injection prevention. *Journal of Information Security*, *20*(1), 32–45.

Garcia, A., & Martinez, E. (2019). Exploring common techniques used in SQL injection attacks: An international perspective. *Journal of Information Security*, *25*(2), 78–95.

Garg, K., & Jain, D. (2018). SQL injection attack detection using machine learning techniques: A survey. *International Journal of Computer Applications*, *182*(40), 8–14.

Gupta, A., & Kumar, V. (2018). Machine learning based SQL injection attack detection in web applications. *International Journal of Advanced Research in Computer Science*, *9*(3), 189–193.

Irungu, J., Graham, S., Girma, A., & Kacem, T. (2023). Artificial intelligence techniques for SQL injection attack detection. In *Proceedings of the 2023 8th international conference on intelligent information technology (ICIIT '23)* (pp. 38–45). Association for Computing Machinery. https://doi.org/10.1145/3591569.3591576

Joshi Padma, N., Ravishankar, N., Raju, M. B., & Ravi, N. C. (2022). Surgical striking SQL injection attacks using LSTM. *Indian Journal of Computer Science and Engineering*, *13*(1), 208–220. https://doi.org/10.21817/indjcse/2022/v13i1/221301182

Kim, S., & Lee, J. (2020). Ensemble methods for SQL injection detection: A comprehensive review. *Journal of Machine Learning Research*, *25*(1), 56–72.

Lee, K., & Park, H. (2018). Feature-based models for SQL injection detection: A comparative study. *IEEE Transactions on Cybersecurity*, *5*(4), 320–335.

Li, X., & Wang, Z. (2021). Deep learning techniques for SQL injection detection: Challenges and opportunities. *Journal of Artificial Intelligence Research*, *40*(2), 210–225.

Smith, J., & Johnson, L. (2017a). Understanding SQL injection attacks: A comprehensive review. *International Journal of Cybersecurity*, *12*(3), 45–60.

Smith, J., & Johnson, L. (2017b). Signature-based detection techniques for SQL injection attacks. *Journal of Cybersecurity Engineering*, *8*(2), 112–125.

Sun, H., Yuejin, D., & Qi, L. (2023). Deep learning-based detection technology for SQL injection research and implementation. *Applied Sciences*, *13*(16), 9466. https://doi.org/10.3390/app13169466

Tang, P., Qiu, W., Huang, Z., Lian, H., & Liu, G. (2020). Detection of SQL injection based on artificial neural network. *Knowledge-Based Systems*, *190*, 105528. https://doi.org/10.1016/j.knosys.2020.105528

Wang, Y., & Zhang, L. (2019). Anomaly detection approaches for SQL injection detection: Challenges and opportunities. *ACM Transactions on Information and System Security*, *12*(3), 180–195.

Chapter 13

Role of Artificial Intelligence in Sustainable Environment Practices

Parijata Majumdar

Indian Institute of Information Technology, Agartala, India

Abstract

With its innovative solutions to some of the biggest environmental problems, artificial intelligence (AI) has become a disruptive force in a number of industries. Through increased resource efficiency, better climate change mitigation techniques, smarter waste management, and the promotion of sustainable practices across multiple industries, this chapter examines how AI can promote environmental sustainability. We go at real-life applications, possible obstacles, and future paths for using AI to make the world a greener place.

Keywords: Artificial intelligence; sustainability; climate change mitigation; intelligent waste management; sustainable practices

1. Introduction

The tremendous breakthroughs in AI have permitted its application in solving difficult environmental problems. AI-powered solutions aid in the efficient monitoring, analysis, and mitigation of environmental challenges in a variety of fields, including precision agriculture and climate modeling. AI can help with sustainability projects around the world by utilizing machine learning, deep learning, and data analytics. AI is essential to promoting environmentally friendly activities (Goralski & Tan, 2020). It helps governments and businesses to minimize waste, cut carbon emissions, and maximize the use of resources. While AI-powered monitoring systems assist in detecting pollution levels and enforcing environmental

Harnessing the Potential of Artificial Intelligence to Promote Environmental Sustainability, 213–216

Published under exclusive licence by Emerald Publishing Limited
doi:10.1108/978-1-83662-996-220251013

standards, AI-driven automation improves energy efficiency in smart grids. Precision farming in agriculture is made possible by AI-driven insights, which maximize productivity while reducing environmental damage.

Additionally, AI's predictive powers help to foresee natural calamities and lessen their effects, making the Earth more resilient and sustainable. Incorporating AI into environmental policies not only aids conservation initiatives but also advances the shift to a circular economy, which efficiently reuses and recycles resources (Kar et al., 2022).

The layout of this book chapter is as follows: The importance of AI in mitigating climate change is covered in Section 2. The importance of AI in resource conservation, including water management, biodiversity preservation, and sustainable agriculture, is covered in Section 3. The role of AI in waste management is covered in Section 4, along with initiatives related to the circular economy, predictive waste reduction, and AI-driven garbage sorting. Section 5 explains the challenges and ethical considerations, which include data accuracy, energy use, and regulatory difficulties. Future prospects are covered in Section 6, which also highlights new developments in AI for sustainability. The job is concluded in Section 7.

2. AI in Climate Change Mitigation

Through a variety of applications, AI is essential to comprehending and addressing climate change. AI-driven climate models help policymakers make well-informed decisions by predicting climate patterns and greatly increasing the accuracy of weather forecasts (Kaack et al., 2022). AI-powered smart grids lower carbon footprints and integrate renewable energy sources to improve energy efficiency. AI also aids in the optimization of carbon capture methods, increasing their scalability and cost-effectiveness, which supports carbon sequestration initiatives.

3. AI in Resource Conservation

AI uses a variety of creative methods to help conserve resources. By tracking water usage, identifying leaks, and improving irrigation in agriculture, AI-driven sensors and Internet of Things devices are utilized for water management (Yousaf, 2024). AI-based remote sensing and picture identification technologies aid in the tracking of wildlife populations, the monitoring of deforestation, and the prevention of illicit poaching in biodiversity conservation. Additionally, AI improves sustainable agriculture by enabling precision farming using predictive analytics, which maximizes crop yields while using less water, fertilizer, and pesticide.

4. AI in Waste Management

By bringing effective methods for garbage reduction, recycling, and sorting, AI has completely transformed waste management. Through intelligent garbage sorting systems, robotics driven by AI and machine learning algorithms enhance the processes of waste segregation and recycling (Olawade et al., 2024). AI-powered predictive analytics can identify patterns in trash production, allowing for proactive waste management techniques. Additionally, by encouraging reusability, lowering overall waste creation, and assisting in the design of sustainable products, AI promotes circular economy projects (Ihsanullah et al., 2022).

5. Challenges and Ethical Considerations

Notwithstanding its potential, there are a number of obstacles to integrating AI with environmental sustainability. Since AI models rely on large datasets that are occasionally biased or incomplete, data availability and accuracy present a significant barrier. The energy usage of AI systems is another issue because these technologies demand a lot of processing power and may have their own negative effects on the environment. To prevent abuse and provide equitable access, ethical and regulatory issues must also be addressed, making sure that the application of AI complies with legal and ethical standards (Nishant et al., 2020).

6. Future Prospects

Increased investment in green AI technology, policy-driven efforts, and interdisciplinary collaboration are key to the future of AI in environmental sustainability. It is anticipated that innovations like AI-powered smart cities, AI-driven carbon trading platforms, and AI-enhanced renewable energy systems would completely transform sustainability initiatives (Nishant et al., 2000). Additionally, AI will be crucial in enforcing regulations, monitoring environmental policies, and creating predictive models to reduce ecological risks. The upcoming decades will see AI-driven solutions that successfully address environmental issues while fostering long-term ecological balance, thanks to developments in AI and a coordinated worldwide effort (Al-Raeei, 2025).

7. Conclusion

AI has enormous potential to solve environmental issues and advance global sustainability initiatives. Businesses and governments may embrace more sustainable practices by utilizing AI's powers in data analysis, automation, and prediction. To maintain a balance between ecological preservation and technological progress, it is imperative to handle the related difficulties. By implementing AI responsibly, humanity can make great progress toward a sustainable future.

However, addressing a number of obstacles, including data reliability, energy usage, and ethical considerations, is necessary to fully realize AI's potential in environmental sustainability. It is essential to apply AI technologies responsibly in order to minimize unforeseen negative effects and provide fair access to technological developments. In the future, advancing AI-driven sustainability programs will require cooperation from researchers, legislators, businesses, and environmentalists. In order to create an ecosystem where technology and sustainability coexist, AI must be incorporated with ecologically friendly laws and procedures. AI has the potential to reduce environmental risks and open the door to a more resilient and sustainable future for future generations if it is used wisely. We can guarantee a better planet in the future by making investments in AI-driven sustainability solutions now.

References

Al-Raeei, M. (2025). The smart future for sustainable development: Artificial intelligence solutions for sustainable urbanization. *Sustainable Development*, *33*(1), 508–517.

Goralski, M. A., & Tan, T. K. (2020). Artificial intelligence and sustainable development. *The International Journal of Management Education*, *18*(1), 100330.

Ihsanullah, I., Alam, G., Jamal, A., & Shaik, F. (2022). Recent advances in applications of artificial intelligence in solid waste management: A review. *Chemosphere*, *309*, 136631.

Kaack, L. H., Donti, P. L., Strubell, E., Kamiya, G., Creutzig, F., & Rolnick, D. (2022). Aligning artificial intelligence with climate change mitigation. *Nature Climate Change*, *12*(6), 518–527.

Kar, A. K., Choudhary, S. K., & Singh, V. K. (2022). How can artificial intelligence impact sustainability: A systematic literature review. *Journal of Cleaner Production*, *376*, 134120.

Nishant, R., Kennedy, M., & Corbett, J. (2020). Artificial intelligence for sustainability: Challenges, opportunities, and a research agenda. *International Journal of Information Management*, *53*, 102104.

Olawade, D. B., Fapohunda, O., Wada, O. Z., Usman, S. O., Ige, A. O., Ajisafe, O., & Oladapo, B. I. (2024). Smart waste management: A paradigm shift enabled by artificial intelligence. *Waste Management Bulletin*, *2*(2), 244–263.

Yousaf, H. (2024). AI for environmental sustainability: Applications in resource management and conservation. *Artificial Intelligence Multidisciplinary Journal of Systems and Applications*, *1*(2), 13–26.

Index

Printed and bound by CPI Group (UK) Ltd, Croydon, CR0 4YY

13/09/2026

14961064-0002